HYBRID WARRIORS

ANNA ARUTUNYAN

Hybrid Warriors

*Proxies, Freelancers and
Moscow's Struggle for Ukraine*

HURST & COMPANY, LONDON

First published in the United Kingdom in 2022 by
C. Hurst & Co. (Publishers) Ltd.,
New Wing, Somerset House, Strand, London, WC2R 1LA
© Anna Arutunyan, 2022
All rights reserved.

Printed in Great Britain by Bell and Bain Ltd, Glasgow

The right of Anna Arutunyan to be identified as the author of this publication is asserted by her in accordance with the Copyright, Designs and Patents Act, 1988.

A Cataloguing-in-Publication data record for this book is available from the British Library.

ISBN: 9781787387959

This book is printed using paper from registered sustainable and managed sources.

www.hurstpublishers.com

To Mark, for all of his advice and support,
and because all wars eventually end.

CONTENTS

ACKNOWLEDGEMENTS

A number of people without whom this book would not have been possible have my eternal gratitude, and there are a great many more whom I cannot name. I am indebted to Sophia Pugsley, Mark Galeotti, Katharine Quinn-Judge, Mikhail Vizel, Matthew Rojansky, Michael Kofman, Oleg Kashin, Jonathan Brunson, Magdalena Grono, Will Pryor, Samuel Charap, Natalia Antonova, Alex Gabuev, Konstantin Krylov and Michael Suttles, just to name very few; and to Michael Dwyer and the team at Hurst for taking on this book and making it happen so quickly. My thanks go also to Mayak Intelligence, to the Wilson Center and the Kennan Institute, for the support they offered through my global fellowship there. And finally to my daughter Mary Vizel, for her precocious comments and observations, and for putting up with all this in general.

FOREWORD

At about 7 a.m. on 24 February 2022, shortly after the first Russian missiles began bombarding Kyiv and Kharkiv, I was woken by a telephone call from my panicked daughter, asking me what was happening. I didn't need to check my news feed to understand what she was referring to. I realized that what I had been dreading for eight years had come to pass: the culminating escalation of a conflict I had painstakingly investigated—and, yes, had had the hubris to hope that I could, through my contributions to policy, play some miniscule role in preventing. I also knew that, although we had been planning to move abroad that summer anyway, for personal reasons, we would now have to leave Moscow right away, to say goodbye to our home, our family and friends, not knowing when, if ever, we would see them again. I didn't look at the news pictures, because I knew exactly what I would see, and I knew exactly how I would feel: the same way as I felt when I watched an airplane slam into the World Trade Center from a few dozen blocks away, except magnified, made worse by years of threats, fears and expectations of exactly this. On some perverse level I even wished I was in Kyiv, and not Moscow. When they came out of their bomb shelters, they could run. I could emigrate, but I could never escape the knowledge of what people had done in the name of my country—a country that I love and which I will never disavow; the knowledge of what my country would become as a result.

I understood, too, that the book I was about to finish, which I had been writing for about a year and a half—but really, ever since I'd hopped on a plane to Simferopol in March 2014—would rub many people the wrong way. After Russian missiles leveled Ukrainian cities, after the atrocities of retreating Russian troops in Bucha, some might wonder if now is really the time for an excursion into the minds and souls of those first Russian militants who went to fight in Ukraine eight years ago, of the various businessmen and officials who encouraged them to go there, and of Vladimir Putin himself. Such an excursion, after all, would reveal things that won't make looking at this current war any easier. Rather than the usual small cast of famous monsters, mine was the story of a host of often-unknown human beings, driven by their own interests, feelings and fears, who—through a series of monstrous mistakes—had together set in motion a series of increasingly monstrous events.

Wouldn't it be easier to simply get answers to our most pressing questions: what is Vladimir Putin's plan with this full-scale invasion? How can we stop him and punish him?

I am afraid that readers looking for answers to these questions will be disappointed. I feel for them, truly: I wish I had those answers myself, and I wish that I could readily believe those who say they do. It would, at the least, offer me some hope of a solution at hand, an indication that this will all end soon.

Instead, I'm afraid that this book describes what all too often drives history: not a clear plan, but a kaleidoscope of agencies and actions; the interplay of millions of actors, agendas and coincidences. Unusually for a so-called authoritarian strongman, Putin's reign is marked less by grand strategy than by his propensity to avoid decisive action, to deflect responsibility for anything bad in his country; to let corrupt underlings, regional bosses and even non-state actors take the lead and the blame. To survive as long as he has at Russia's helm, Putin has hidden behind the old Russian trope of good tsar/bad boyar: the notion that he is a wise and benevolent ruler, and the aristocrats around him are to blame for whatever goes wrong. Thus, he has emerged seemingly unblemished from a whole assortment of problems simply because he refused to make a decisive choice. But refusal to choose is also a choice. Putin himself may have not ordered the murder of journalists and dissidents—but his decision not to bring those who did to justice has ensured that such murders have become acceptable. Putin himself almost certainly disapproved of the practice of electrocuting the genitals of homosexuals in Chechnya—but did nothing to stop the Kadyrov regime's henchmen from doing so. And, finally, as this book explores, although Putin felt too timid to launch a military operation on mainland Ukraine in spring 2014, he also didn't have the courage to stop Igor Girkin and many like him from taking matters into their own hands.

This indecision—Putin's penchant for deftly hiding behind the curtain of dark powers, while refusing to wield them outright—has played an interesting trick both on himself and on the country as a whole. For over twenty years, it created the illusion that, however corrupt his regime, however repressive, there was always someone more decisive, more aggressive and more repressive lurking around the corner, who would take Putin's place and make things much worse if he stepped down or even showed the slightest weakness. Perhaps this was no illusion; perhaps it was even true. But, in a self-fulfilling prophecy, sticking with a weak autocrat lest a stronger one came along has only hastened what everyone feared. In the end, Putin himself has become subsumed by the worst paranoias of his most hawkish allies and supporters: the spooks; the colonels; the disenfranchised would-be strongmen of his generation who yearn for a simpler, Soviet past. As the joke goes in Moscow, Russia refused to annex the Donetsk People's Republic—that neo-Soviet state-let, albeit poorer and more corrupt than its progenitor—so the DPR has annexed Russia.

But then, the reader looking for a quick solution, or easy blame, might ask: is this whole crisis not so much about Putin, but about Russia as a whole and its insatiable imperialist ambitions? And if so, maybe it is true that, as I keep hearing, not just from Ukrainians (understandably) and their Western supporters, but also from some Russians (especially wealthier émigrés), that Russia needs to be humiliated, needs to learn its lesson, so that it can become like Germany after 1945?

Well, no. I personally try to avoid using historical analogies as remedies, but the problem with this particular strand of wishful thinking (aside from its inherent Russophobia, masquerading as well-meaning policy advice) is that it's the wrong analogy. Post-Soviet Russia, if one really wants to draw those parallels, is more like Germany post-1918: permeated by a sense of defeat, loss, and the aggressive sense of grievance that inevitably accompanies the demise of power. Russians were already humiliated, by the breakup of the Soviet Union—the revanchism we are seeing today is but a delayed reaction to that humiliation.

Because what is key here is that aggressive revanchists, like those who feature in this book, exist everywhere, and are particularly symptomatic of waning empires: think of the American right-wing zealots who hijacked the GOP and ushered Donald Trump into the White House, or the proponents of Brexit and their hopes for a greater, more British Britain, free of Europe's technocratic yoke. Their deeply ingrained sense of grievance is the problem—it is the malaise which can metastasize into hostile and destructive ambitions.

But in the case of Russia's actions in Ukraine, there was no nationwide referendum to launch an invasion; no democratic election to vote a colonel like Igor Girkin into power. Instead, there was a weary autocrat grasping for support. After years of trying to find a value system, a national identity to unify a country and legitimize his regime, he finally opted for the laziest and most toxic ideal: the revanchism of the humiliated. Rather than invading Eastern Ukraine himself in 2014, when he would arguably have succeeded in achieving many of his objectives, Putin sat back for eight years and looked on as unprofessional irregulars on the one hand and an assortment of military and intelligence officers on the other played war in his name, driven more by their own beliefs than by any coherent set of orders from the Kremlin. But here is the difference between 2014 and 2022: however wrong or misguided their beliefs, they were at least genuine. Perversely, many of these freelancers of what came to be known as the Russian Spring proved at least the possibility of genuine national interests. The Kremlin, on the other hand, has acted on the assumptions of a stereotypical ad executive: that beliefs and values are for sale, that social movements can be manipulated and controlled to get what you want and that, ultimately, people have no agency of their own. This may yet be the regime's undoing, because it breeds, in part, the very paranoia to which Putin himself has now succumbed. If everything is for sale, then no one can be trusted, and the world is populated only by traitors and potential traitors.

Ultimately, no one quite understands what pushed Putin over the edge on the night of 23 February 2022—which was, incidentally, Defenders of the Fatherland Day. We don't know what made him take the very course of action that he had avoided for years, rightly believing it would be self-destructive. I have a deep distrust of those who, never having spent a moment in a room with Putin, purport to know for certain what he wants, or what he will and will not do, as has come into vogue in policy analysis since 2014, and even more so since February 2022. Incidentally, as a journalist, I myself have spent more hours in a room with him than I care to remember, and have tried to speak with him on a couple of brief occasions; but even that does not give me the ability to predict his will. Nothing does.

Nevertheless, this book traces the combination of strategic impulses and toxic emotions among the actors involved—right up to Putin himself—that brought us to where we are today. It does not purport to be exhaustive: the focus is largely on the Russian and pro-Russian actors in the conflict with Ukraine, and on why they did what they did. Moreover, Russian policymakers themselves have not always understood what was happening, and have been confounded by many of Putin's decisions. Over the course of eight years writing about this conflict, both as a journalist and as an analyst advising policymakers in the West, I can't pretend to have gathered all the interviews I would have wanted: the truly revealing, boozy sit-downs with Igor Girkin, Vladislav Surkov, Konstantin Malofeyev, or the actual decision-makers in the Kremlin. I have instead talked to those with various degrees of proximity to these people, but more so to multitudes of those in Russia and Ukraine who have been swept up in these events, as actors, onlookers, or oftentimes both. Of the hundreds of people to whom I have spoken during my research for this book, an overwhelming majority will remain anonymous, under different names or on deep background—this is both for their safety and mine. Whatever their positions and views, regardless of what they did or did not do, I am indebted to them for trusting me enough to talk to me. It was never my intention to find a smoking gun, or uncover some kind of secret key to this conflict; nor to build a case for either the indictment or the absolution of any particular person or party. I even—some time between finishing the manuscript in April 2022 and writing this foreword in June—gave up on my futile attempts to come up with some sort of possible solution to this mess. The point of this book was simply that: to convey the kaleidoscope of agency that is any war, but this war in particular.

In our increasingly eager quest for justice, we often lose patience for something without which justice is mere revenge: figuring out why things happen, and why people do what they do. That, I hope, is what readers will find in this book. None of this is to excuse what the Kremlin is doing in Ukraine, but the sense of disenfranchisement experienced by Russians in the former Soviet Empire is absolutely real. The border disputes that arose on the periphery of the USSR over the last thirty years prove just how dangerous it can be to toy with nationalist grievances. Annexing territories and starting ill-planned wars only exacerbates this disenfranchisement. Truly addressing these problems, and honestly identifying Russia's national interests, will take a kind of forward-looking leadership that the country does not yet have. However, this is sure to develop within a younger generation that, while currently muzzled, is watching in horror, yet learning from the mistakes of this dying regime.

London, June 2022

PART ONE

HOW A BUNCH OF GUYS
STARTED A WAR ...

1

THE ENTHUSIASTS

"They had no political ideas. They just wanted to defend their land. Just like that. Pick up a Kalashnikov, and defend their land."
"But from whom?"
"From the enemy."

Wife of pro-Russian Ukrainian insurgent, Kyiv, 2019

I

Dima and Sasha[1] never met. Not on the front lines in Slovyansk, where both fought, not in Donetsk, where each was transferred after being wounded, and most certainly not in Moscow, where one might expect their orders to fight on the same side of a proxy war Russia started in Ukraine to have originated, but for inexplicable reasons never did. But for now, this is the story of two small-time rebel fighters and their disillusionment.

They had never met, yet they had almost everything in common. The same beliefs, though neither was especially into political activism; the same background—their fathers served in the same Soviet military; both had spent childhoods in Ukraine;

probably the same ethnicity; and certainly the same language—Russian. In 2014, they fought under the same commander—the former Russian Federal Security Service (FSB) officer and war reenactor turned separatist warlord, a man who went by the name Igor Strelkov, and who in March led an initial unit of fifty-two volunteers westward across the Ukrainian border from Rostov.

But they had one difference. Dima was a Ukrainian citizen. Sasha was a Russian. How did both wind up fighting in the same war, on the same side, acting on orders that each interpreted the same way, but that in reality were never issued?

"I'm a Russian nationalist," said Sasha, describing his decision to pick up a Kalashnikov and fight for Strelkov in May 2014. "I lived in Ukraine for a long time, went to school in Kyiv. It was an obvious decision for me. For fifteen years, I knew that it was a matter of time before this war happened. And," he added in unexpected contempt, "I didn't expect any decisive action from Comrade Putin."

Although they had never met, never spoken, Dima's rationalizations were virtually identical. "I always knew there would be a war," he told me. "I mean, also my father kept telling me there would be a war. Between Russians and the so-called Ukrainians who didn't want to become Russian."

For both of them, though each admitted watching Russian television, none of this had anything to do with Comrade Putin. They both held a very low opinion of him and felt deeply that they had to take matters into their own hands. For both of them, judging by the way they spoke, it was a matter of necessity and morality, except that it was hard to discern a rational strategy in their vision. Somewhere along the line, it seemed that their grievances fused with their fears. They came to feel that they, Russians, were being told they were somehow inferior, that they had no place in the new Ukrainian nation. It could not occur to them, of course, that those very Ukrainian nationalists whom they decried themselves felt the same about Russia and Russians: each saw the other as a resurgent aggressor, just waiting for its chance to pounce.

"When the Soviet Union disappeared from the face of the earth, I didn't really accept the Ukrainian regime," Dima told me. "It was wrong somehow. We were being told that we are Ukrainians and that everything Soviet was bad."

He didn't understand that. Born in Druzhkivka, a city in the north of the Donbas region, Dima was a tween when the Soviet Union collapsed. His father was Ukrainian and his mother Russian, but it wasn't that which was confusing. As a teenager in the 1990s, growing up in a Ukraine riddled, like Russia, with corruption and crime, he felt he was being fed a myth about a new independent nation, a myth that only fueled contradictions about his identity that were coming to the fore. Like many would, he chose instead to cling to the old, Soviet myth.

Not that it helped him much. "When I turned eighteen, I faced a choice: go study or join the army. I was making money by then, but I couldn't afford college. So I made money to pay off a bribe and not get drafted into the Ukrainian army." He dodged the Ukrainian draft twice and in 2008 even tried, unsuccessfully, to enlist in the Russian army.

Dima finally managed to get a degree in light engineering, but his work was hollow and monotonous. In the spring of 2014, when he saw the first pro-Russian separatist protests spread through Eastern Ukrainian cities, he was working at a private security company, guarding a glass waste quarry about 30 km from Slovyansk. "I was dirt poor, overworked and bored. And while I was working, I was watching what was going on. The protests. I listened to Radio Russia at work. And yeah, some of it was propaganda, but it was clear it wouldn't end well."

When armed separatists seized government buildings in Donetsk, Luhansk and Kharkiv on 7 April to proclaim three independent people's republics, Dima had already joined the *opolcheniye*—self-organized fighters and thugs that called themselves the people's militia. Russian propaganda or not, the word was straight out of Soviet mythology. But it wasn't just connotations of the anti-Nazi partisan resistance during World War II that militants like Dima found so appealing. It was also the word's older roots. In 1612, during the Times of Troubles, a prince and a merchant amassed a force to chase Polish occupiers out of Moscow in what became known as *narodnoye opolcheniye*—people's militia. The anniversary has been celebrated in Russia as Unity Day since 2005, when nationalist groups would use the occasion to hold their yearly Russian March demonstration.

For Sasha, the pull to Donbas materialized as a similar mix of boredom and ideological longing, with an added twist. "On some level, I just wanted to run around with a Kalashnikov."

A down-shifter who liked to travel, in the spring of 2014 Sasha was working at a video arcade on the African continent, where he was living at the time—he was always an adventurer, and Donbas was no exception. From watching people running around shooting things on video game screens, he decided to go for the real thing. But the real inspiration came from a rising social media celebrity: Igor Strelkov, a man who, after Russia's annexation of Crimea, began all but crowdfunding a proposed intervention into Donbas.

"He was calling on people to join the *opolcheniye*." By late April, Strelkov was making YouTube videos calling on volunteers to join the ranks, saying they needed help because Moscow wasn't going to send any troops. Sasha wasn't surprised; he'd never harbored any illusions about Putin's decisiveness, he said. But Strelkov's videos were something else: "They inspired me to do it," he said.

Sasha said that he didn't really think about why he wanted to go to Donbas. "I just decided to go, picked up my things, and went." In May 2014, fearing the Russian as much as the Ukrainian authorities, he traveled furtively from Moscow to Rostov in southern Russia and then to a border town where a friend of a friend had given him contacts for a group that was about to volunteer to fight in Donbas. He joined a group of four, and then a likeminded associate helped them get across the border. In the forests and rivers, they were dodging Russian—not Ukrainian—border patrols, and at one point nearly got arrested by the Russian police. It took a phone call to a sympathetic local official in Rostov, who then called the police department, for the reluctant officers to let them go. Once they got to Luhansk, Sasha joined a unit of about ten men, eight of whom were native Ukrainians.

Hooking up with weapons and gear was another story—a sympathetic friend had tipped him off about a store in a border town that would sell him some kit, but as for guns and ammo, there were none to be found until he joined his unit in Luhansk, and even that was a disappointment.

Dima was disappointed too. "When I joined Strelkov's forces, I saw really old, worn-out weapons. We started throwing armored thrusts at [the Ukrainians], with BMPs, MT-LBs, MANPADS, PTURs ..." he said, citing the 1960s vintage infantry fighting vehicles, even older MT-LB personnel carriers and the primitive first-generation Malyutka anti-tank missiles, which were the best they had available in those early days. "I mean they were old and broken but all we had. Our liaison officers would reach out to Ukrainian forces and arrange to buy weapons off of them. These liaisons didn't want to fight, but they wanted to help. They were the first humanitarians. They would bring in rocket launchers in Zhigulis," he said sadly, referring to the old Soviet car model.

Sasha, a Russian, harbored few illusions about Putin's regime and its ability to act decisively in what Sasha believed were Russia's national interests. But he also seemed more at ease with the other motivation he had for joining—the sheer adventure of it. For Dima, on the other hand, the state of affairs in April deeply disillusioned him: men were dying for promises no one intended to keep.

"In April, we were holding our positions," he told me. "And we were being told, you hold your positions, and the Russian reinforcements will come soon. Up until 26 April they kept hammering this idea—that there would be a major Russian contingent. Those same little green men [that arrived in Crimea]."

But they were not coming. Not then, anyway.

II

This was eight years before Russian air raids leveled parts of Kharkiv to rubble during the 2022 invasion, killing Russians and Ukrainians alike. Eight years before a demoralized and confused Russian army retreated from Kyiv, leaving streets strewn with executed civilian bodies, their hands tied behind their backs. Then, the streets of Donetsk were quiet: city workers were planting flowers by the curbs of freshly swept sidewalks, couples strolled in parks with their baby carriages, cafés bustled. But just a few blocks away from these spring cityscapes was a warzone in miniature: a government building barricaded with barbed wires, boards, trash and tires, as armed men ran to and fro with a sense of their own importance and flyers warning of Ukrainian Nazis and saboteurs churned out of the photocopier.

It was 9 May 2014, and by then the city was in the grip of an assortment of self-mobilized separatist militias, Russian volunteers and roaming gangs armed with wooden bats, metal rods and whatever else they could lay their hands on. "We are protecting law and order," one of these men, wearing a balaclava and speaking with a local accent, told me. "We are protecting the city from fascists." When I asked a police officer patrolling the streets about the masked gangs patrolling alongside them, he simply said, "We don't coordinate with them, but they're not giving us any trouble." A few weeks earlier, these militias had raided and seized the seat of the regional government, an 11-story building in the middle of the city, and declared the Donetsk People's Republic (DPR). There were still local officials and law enforcement who were loyal to Kyiv, but even their loyalties were confused and confusing: police had ceded de facto control of the city to these roaming gangs that had twice the fervor and none of the discipline of the militias I had seen earlier in Sevastopol, Crimea.

What was their point, aside from the tangle of grievances, myths and misplaced anger that had driven Sasha and Dima to pick up a Kalashnikov? As men drank coffee at a sidewalk café and spoke of a Russian protectorate, an armored personnel carrier (APC) drove up triumphantly into a green, sunlit city square in central Donetsk, while passersby took selfies alongside the curiosity. From the top of it emerged a boy, no more than twenty, dressed in fatigues with an orange and black ribbon pinned to his chest, and a knife strapped to his calf. His name was Radik, and he said he'd taken the APC from an abandoned arms depot on the outskirts of the city. "We will show Putin that the people here stand with Russia. And he will send help, and it will be just like Crimea."

* * *

The prevailing view of Russia's war in Ukraine over the last eight years, later cemented by Moscow's full-scale invasion in February 2022, was that the Kremlin has been behind everything that happened from the very beginning, deploying special agents, political activists and mercenaries to Ukraine starting in the spring of 2014 to foment a pro-Russian insurgency and establish some kind of control over the country. In a general sense, this is largely accurate. However, it misses an important and widely contested dimension: the extent to which local Ukrainian separatists and the Russian non-state fighters and activists who initially came to fight alongside them shaped the insurgency and the war it sparked. Most of these people, as this book will demonstrate, were driven not by Kremlin orders but by genuine sentiment and their own ambitions.

This created two serious problems, largely intertwined. The objectives of the separatist movement in Donbas very quickly came to be at odds with the Kremlin's. As a result, the Donetsk and Lugansk People's Republics, as they declared themselves, proved highly ineffective proxies for Moscow, which realized, over the course of 2014 and 2015, that its control over them was limited. So it sought to impose direct control over the separatist movements in 2015 and 2016, setting up a complex architecture to manage the statelets while taking great pains to ensure plausible deniability. In the process, its increasingly complex relationship with these proxies actually made it harder for Moscow to accomplish its own objectives, severely limiting its options in its relations with Ukraine and the West more generally. By the winter of 2022, Putin had backed himself into a corner.

This dimension, of the agency of Ukrainian separatists and their non-state Russian backers, has been difficult to investigate and even acknowledge. The main reason is that it was central to the deception that the Kremlin used from the start of the war up until its 2022 invasion: that this was purely a civil conflict within Ukraine, one to which Russia was not a party, and that if Russians took part in it, all of them did so in a purely voluntary capacity. Because Moscow applied the same deception during its annexation of Crimea in February and March 2014 and then, when that operation proved successful, admitted that the polite "little green men" that had seized the peninsula were, in fact, Russian soldiers, it was reasonable to assume that most of the militants who seized government buildings in Donbas in March and April 2014 were also in fact Kremlin agents and Russian special forces. It did not help matters that by mid-April, thousands of Russian volunteers, led by former FSB officer Igor Girkin (aka Strelkov), flocked to their cause and, indeed, had the backing of the Russian FSB and several members of the Presidential Administration in doing so.

As a result, fighting and resisting Russian aggression in Ukraine also became about fighting its deception—even the parts of that deception that were ostensibly true. Russian information warfare had to be countered with Ukrainian information warfare, which sometimes merely contradicted the Kremlin narrative wholesale, denying important details and sometimes incorrectly ascribing the Kremlin's intent. This is entirely understandable in the context of fighting the aggression of a more formidable adversary. However, at times this approach has perversely helped the Kremlin in its own efforts to blur the line between fact and fiction. Automatically assuming that everything the Kremlin has said about the conflict is nothing but a lie, and equally presuming that there is not even an occasional and partial truth in its statements, has made it difficult, if not impossible, to understand, predict and thus effectively deter the Kremlin.

Thus, the new Ukrainian government, disoriented by Moscow's annexation of Crimea, cannot be faulted for initially assuming all of these "terrorists," as Kyiv often referred to them, were nothing but Russian agents and launching an anti-terrorist operation in Donbas. But while the operation arguably made the Kremlin more reluctant to overtly back the nascent separatist movement, it also had the unintended effect of galvanizing the separatists, their Russian non-state backers and their individual patrons in the Russian government. They, in turn, used this to persuade an initially reluctant Kremlin to begin arming the militias and providing them with funds, materiel and moral support. This was to lead inexorably to Russia's limited, denied military invasion in the second half of 2014, as the Kremlin felt it was already too committed to back down. A conflict the Kremlin had not really chosen to start had become one it felt it could not allow to end, other than with a victory. Over the next eight years, Putin, a man who has a track record of making decisions at the last moment in order to leave himself as many options as possible, ended up leaving himself only one: to take full ownership of the Russian nationalist and Ukrainian separatist insurgency he had half-heartedly inspired. As a result, he utterly lost his quest to keep Ukraine in Russia's sphere of influence. He had driven the largest country in the world into the dead end of becoming a pariah state.

Russia's war in Ukraine can be separated into three stages—hybrid (2014), proxy (2015–21) and full-scale military (2021–2). The hybrid war stage began in February 2014 with Moscow's use of state and non-state actors to seize Crimea and continued through 2014 in Donbas, driven predominantly by non-state actors. As it looked likely that Kyiv would be able to reimpose its control over the contested regions in the second half of 2014, Moscow covertly deployed troops to prevent that, and also to start to enforce direct control over the militias. Although the Kremlin sought to rein in the militias in 2015, the conflict took on all the features of a proxy war, with the caveat that Moscow and its non-state proxies seemed to be pursuing different agendas. In that sense, *hybridity*, or the extent to which non-state or *hybrid* actors shaped the Kremlin's actions, remained the defining feature of the conflict up until Moscow's full-scale military invasion in the winter of 2021–2.

Hybrid war has become a catchphrase in describing Russian activities since 2014, and on some level, it remains a convenient term to describe a complex war involving a plethora of non-state actors and non-kinetic components. But as a concept used to understand the Kremlin's strategy and what it has actually been doing, it is deeply problematic. The main misunderstanding is that hybrid war represents a novel, and specifically Russian, way of warfare. It is not, in fact, uniquely Russian, as many scholars have argued: it is, instead, more of a product of American military thought to which Russian military strategists felt they needed to respond.[2] Nor, as Mark Galeotti has argued, is it new in the sense that, since the dawn of civilization, states have deployed any instruments at their disposal, from disinformation to political destabilization and a host of other non-kinetic means, to coerce their adversaries. Furthermore, the use of non-kinetic means in a conflict can precede, but does not necessarily predict, direct military intervention.[3] As this book demonstrates, the Kremlin shifted its strategy and objectives in Ukraine multiple times from the frigid, soggy night in April when Russian volunteer militants hiked across the border from Rostov region into Donbas, to the snowy morning in February when Russian missiles descended on the outskirts of Kyiv. The Kremlin's invasion—contrary to many of the emotional predictions coming from the West—was never a foregone conclusion, not even when Washington declared it "imminent." It was, in many ways, the product of a Kremlin fumbling in the dark, staggering to respond to a multitude of real and perceived threats and opportunities, and proving itself largely incapable of distinguishing one from the other.

And yet, precisely because the Kremlin was responding to—and itself utterly misunderstanding—what it believed to be a Western hybrid war, one that it felt it did not have the capabilities to resist, it relied on non-linear means and non-state actors to a highly unusual degree, allowing the methods and the non-state participants to shape its policy. This book explores many of the circumstances of why that was the case and how the Russian nationalists that the Kremlin unleashed upon Ukraine ultimately ended up consuming Putin and his agenda—or, to be more precise, how Putin allowed himself to be led and ultimately consumed. As Timothy Frye has argued in *Weak Strongman*, the key paradox of Putin's Kremlin is the limitation of his power.[4] Putin's reliance on and mismanagement of businessmen, regional bosses and grassroots initiatives in what is otherwise an authoritarian regime—in other words, a bottom-up vertical—is an aspect of his regime that I explored in *The Putin Mystique*, and it has become the defining—and most confounding—feature of his war on Ukraine. This book traces the evolution of this war from the perspectives and motivations of its participants, from the bottom to the very apex in the Kremlin.

III

Eight years before the residents of the coastal Donbas town of Mariupol—most of them Russian-speakers—fought ferociously against the full force of the invading Russian military, before Moscow's missiles bombed a maternity ward and then lied about it, and before Russian aviation had leveled whole sectors of the city to the ground, many of the locals of the same city had successfully fought off the troops of the Ukrainian National Guard.

By the time I arrived in Mariupol from Donetsk on 9 May 2014, the fighting had already stopped, and the war of narratives began. In the central square, a couple of tires were still on fire, billowing thick black smoke. A lonesome APC stood abandoned, pocked by burnt patches, lending an otherwise peaceful-looking town a surreal air. Who were the belligerents? What sparked the combat? Who called the shots?

Official accounts by Kyiv's interim government, which had recently launched its "Anti-Terrorist Operation" against pro-Russian separatists in the East, said that a mob of armed pro-Russian protesters had attacked the police building. Kyiv deployed the National Guard to disperse the protesters and reclaim the police station. Twenty-one people—all but one of them on the pro-Russian side—were killed.[5]

But around the perimeter of the burnt-out hull of the city police station lay bodies; corpses of police officers dressed in blue, their faces gray, hastily and only partially covered by tarp. Whose casualties were they? The still-smoldering police department suggested that disproportionate use of force had been used to destroy a government building that the National Guard only feared would be seized by separatist insurgents. The moment I and a photographer got out of the car, we were surrounded by a group of local women, screaming and crying at us to "tell the truth"—as if they were already expecting to be misrepresented to fit the political narrative of their enemies. The National Guard had sent tanks to disperse a peaceful Victory Day demonstration of Russian-speakers, they said.

"The demonstrators begged the police to give them weapons," a local protester told me at the scene, gesturing at the bodies, "but the police refused. And so we have what we have. And they got shot at too." Even after the fighting had ended, the same argument was still going on outside the police station: a tired police officer was sympathetically nodding to a group of locals who begged him to give them weapons if the police couldn't protect them from the National Guard. But in the end, he would only shrug and sigh—there was nothing to be done.

According to the version of events recounted to me by several protesters, Ukrainian Interior Troops attacked the local police station because it refused to put down the demonstration and fight back against a group of pro-Russian protesters, some of whom were armed. Locals said that the police were branded "terrorist sympathizers" by Kyiv and shot at. This explained the police corpses on the ground, the burnt-out shell of the police building, and it explained the enraged local women who supported the Russian insurgents. The stories of these locals, however, proved too complex for the overarching contingency of the new government in Kyiv. It was convinced that it was facing a full-blown Russian invasion fought with local "puppets" and "terrorists." The locals felt silenced, further exacerbating divisions and, for many of them at the time, making the separatist cause more appealing.

The Victory Day battle, despite the casualties on the pro-Russian side, was a defeat for the government forces. They had left the city shortly before I arrived, losing an APC in the process (and probably some weapons—explaining, as will be detailed later, where separatists got their arms before Moscow upped its reinforcements later in the summer). Their defeat wasn't because they had been overpowered by Russian prowess. It was about blurred lines of loyalty on the ground; hard choices made by police officers about whether to shoot at Ukrainian citizens who refused to recognize the new government in Kyiv, or whether to risk being shot at by the new government in Kyiv. Those choices were not uniform: in some cases, the violence of the Interior Troops was a deal-changer, tipping some officers to side with pro-Russian insurgents where otherwise they wouldn't have. What many locals saw unfolding before their eyes that day fused with the propaganda they were seeing on Russian television and made it easier to believe Kremlin spin about a violent, fascist junta.

Ultimately, though, pro-Russian support in Mariupol turned out to be weak and unsustainable. A month later, helped by local steelworkers, Ukrainian forces took the city back from separatist control.

But that early battle, and the Rashomon-like multiple interpretations from the locals and the officials in Kyiv, revealed that in those days at least, the pro-Russian movement had its own agency. Each of its members were making their own choices, fueled by their grievances and the political and economic contingencies on the ground.

* * *

Relations between Russia and Ukraine had been tense since 2004, when Moscow failed to sway the presidential election towards its preferred candidate, Viktor Yanukovych. The former Donetsk oblast governor had initially won the runoff against the pro-Western Viktor Yushchenko, but given that Yushchenko had survived being poisoned with a dioxin that left his face disfigured during the course of the election campaign, the result was widely contested. Popular protests erupted against Yanukovych amid allegations of voter fraud and intimidation. In what became known as the first Maidan Revolution, Ukraine's Supreme Court ordered a second runoff, which Yushchenko won. Yanukovych would go on to run for president and win the elections in 2010 in what international observers recognized as a free and fair contest, but the issue remained a sore point for Moscow, which came to see Yushchenko's victory as the result of Western meddling, even though the Kremlin was generally considered to be behind Yushchenko's poisoning in the first place.

"They didn't learn their lesson in 2004," said a former Kremlin official of his colleagues at the time. "They kept overestimating pro-Russian sentiment in Ukraine and thinking that with the right political technologists they'd get what they want."[6]

In November 2013, the Kremlin pressured Yanukovych to abandon an Association Agreement with the European Union, sparking initially peaceful protests by pro-European students on Kyiv's central Maidan Square. The agreement would have facilitated free trade with the EU and paved the way for eventual membership, but it risked dividing Ukraine. Donbas—Yanukovych's constituency—and Crimea had robust trade with their eastern neighbor, close ties with Russians across the border and would have a free trade agreement if Ukraine joined Putin's own customs union, the Eurasian Economic Union. However, the Association Agreement in effect ruled that out, and Brussels wasn't particularly keen on bringing Moscow into the talks.

Sidelined, Moscow resorted to economic pressure. Putin, insiders say, felt he had lost too much to Western interference and could not lose Ukraine as well.[7] Yanukovych caved to Moscow. But when protesters turned up on Maidan, he made the mistake of using force to suppress them. What began as peaceful student demonstrations over an economic agreement became about Ukraine's independence from Russia and its very identity. It became a Revolution of Dignity, as democratic, pro-Western protesters faced off against Yanukovych's Soviet-style oppression and corruption.

But it wasn't just about Ukraine's independence from Russia and Moscow's meddling, although this was the aspect that made the revolution so appealing internationally. Social, economic and cultural distinctions between the predominantly Russian-speaking, mining communities of Donbas and the European-leaning towns of Western Ukraine predated Euromaidan by decades, if not centuries. In some ways, Donbas, short for the Donets Basin, the coal-rich area in Eastern Ukraine and parts of Russia's Rostov region, became the cradle of a quintessential Soviet identity. Under the Russian empire, ethnic Russians constituted a large minority of residents of Donbas, but as the region industrialized in the late nineteenth century, the urban workforce was predominantly Russian. The Soviet government sought to create a society of Russians and Ukrainians under the common identity of industry, the Communist emblem of the Stakhanovite coal miner heroically overfulfilling the Five-Year Plan. The collapse of the Soviet Union hit the area particularly hard, draining both the economy and the population. When Yanukovych tried to revive the coal-producing economy in 2010, he was able to do so only at great cost both to Kyiv and the local population. Subsidies and coal production grew; local incomes did not. To bolster its power and ensure Donbas' livelihood, Yanukovych's Party of Regions relied on good relations with Moscow to maintain subsidies while also playing to populist local narratives in which Donbas was the cradle of industry.[8]

Economic tensions were exacerbated by cultural ones. Some in Kyiv, representatives of a society increasingly aware of a new, burgeoning Ukrainian identity separate from Russia's, were even then describing Eastern Ukrainians as backwards and intrinsically susceptible to Russian "brainwashing." "They are all Sovoks over there," a Ukrainian student told me in Kyiv in 2015, using the derogatory term for working-class beneficiaries of the Soviet system. "They can't help it." This rhetoric fueled fears on the part of many Russian-speaking Donbas locals who felt that the new interim government in Kyiv regarded them as "enemies" and made them think that representatives of the Kyiv government were "enemies" in turn. The economic and cultural tensions fused with the political: Moscow and Kyiv were engaged in an energy war, while Kyiv sought closer ties with the EU.

The Euromaidan, aside from a few sporadic protests, did not take in the East. Instead, after the revolution ultimately toppled Yanukovych in February, demonstrations erupted in Donbas against the new interim government, led by members of the Party of Regions. It wasn't that they supported Yanukovych—if anything, many of these demonstrators reviled him for his perceived betrayal.[9] It was rather that they felt alienated by Kyiv. Just like the Euromaidan protesters in Western Ukraine, some groups in the East started taking over buildings. In Kharkiv, MPs from across the Eastern regions held an anti-Maidan congress on 22 February opposing what they called an illegitimate government in Kyiv, attended by over 3,500 deputies.[10] Yanukovych and members of his party had even reportedly proposed secession, but given that he had lost his authority, such calls were not initially popular.[11] Moscow, eager to co-opt and further fuel the separatist movement, moved in with its political technologists.

The conflict that was unraveling in Eastern Ukraine in the early months of 2014 was thus as much civil as it was geopolitical; as much fueled by local divisions as it was by Moscow's meddling. If the conflict could not have happened without Moscow's involvement, as many scholars correctly insist, then the opposite is also true: it could not have happened without existing social divisions, without the agency of local people and their willingness to protest and, in some cases, to fight. What, exactly, were those divisions about? According to the Greek political scientist Stathis Kalyvas, who has studied the motivations of fighters in civil wars, it is only on the surface that civil conflicts are binary, or fought over one cleavage. The reality is more multifaceted, as fighters bring their own identities and issues into the cause.[12] In Ukraine in particular, there was no single identity cleavage—the question was never so simple as Russian or Ukrainian. Identity in Ukraine, according to scholar Anna Matveeva, is not fixed but is rather forged by the "pressure of circumstance." According to one survey she cites, one in ten Ukrainians identified as "Soviet" rather than Russian or Ukrainian.[13] Many of the pro-Russian supporters I interviewed in Donetsk in May 2014 said that it wasn't so much Russia that they wanted to join, unlike their mentors in Crimea. Instead, it was some version of the Soviet Union.[14] By April 2014, 27.4 percent of respondents in Luhansk oblast and 30.3 percent in Donetsk oblast favored secession and joining Russia; while not as overwhelming as in Crimea, this constituted a sizeable minority. Even more popular in Donbas was either decentralization or federalization, though.[15] In other words, most still wanted to be Ukrainian. However, the Revolution of Dignity, their increasing alienation from Kyiv and the pull from Moscow meant that many who had never had to choose between Russian and Ukrainian, between West and East, felt forced to take a side. The identities that many of them felt forced to choose, as they encountered roaming armed gangs belonging to any number of separatist or pro-Maidan groups, had a number of components: ethnicity, language, religion, culture and economy. All of these were triggered by the political rhetoric coming from the new, post-Maidan government in Kyiv on the one hand and from Moscow on the other, and, especially, by Russia's annexation of Crimea.

But these were overarching identity narratives, and they were layered onto the multitude of personal identities and accumulated grievances that many in the Donbas harbored. For Dima, his personal poverty in youth, his anger at not making it in the new environment and his refusal to serve in the Ukrainian armed forces all festered over the years, and when the time came, he, just like Sasha, had a whole buffet of identity cleavages to choose from to justify his grievances.

Prior to Russia's invasion in 2022, there were around 40,000 armed men in the militias of the unrecognized Donetsk and Lugansk People's Republics. They were a far cry from the early days of the conflict, when the Dimas and Sashas and Strelkovs fought and shed blood in the genuine belief that Moscow would back them in their fight for independence and perhaps "reunification" with Russia. But many of them originated in that initial grassroots movement. Over time, since May 2014, Moscow would replace their leaders with more manageable men and, in a break from the early days, would increase the number of officers of the Russian armed forces "unofficially" sent to command local units.

But that still left tens of thousands of fighters—idealists, enthusiasts, mercenaries, drifters, men and women with criminal pasts—who were not acting under orders from Moscow but were used because their choices and desires aligned, briefly, with a half-baked Kremlin plot. These were people who felt aggrieved because they believed they had been forgotten, maligned and misunderstood—pushed out to the margins of history.

The Kremlin was never really on the side of these self-proclaimed underdogs. It used them as fuel and fodder. But it could not have acted without them, without their grievances and without their alienation from the West.

2

THE LITTLE GREEN MEN

The soldier standing in front of me bore no insignia, no colors or flags on his specialized, modern body armor. His arms rested lazily on a Vintorez silenced sniper rifle, and only his eyes were smiling as I asked him question after question. Was he Russian? What was he doing there? All I, or anyone else, knew for sure was that he was one of about 100 soldiers who had surrounded the Ukrainian military base, about a half-hour drive from the capital of the Crimea, Simferopol.

At Perevalne, the military base housing Ukraine's 36th separate mechanized coastal infantry brigade, the sun-burnt beige slopes were showing tinges of green grass. The soldiers stood peacefully around the walls of the base. With hardly an incident since the start of the conflict, they had the appearance of zoo animals, curiosities that groups of journalists were trying, unsuccessfully, to chat up. And while they appeared to bask in the attention, their chief objective, aside from guarding the Ukrainian marines inside the base, was seemingly to avoid letting on who they were or what they were doing.

Soldiers like him, as well as an assortment of local self-defense forces, had fanned out over the peninsula ahead of a referendum on seceding from Ukraine and joining Russia. Moscow had insisted for weeks that it had no plans to invade, let alone annex, Crimea. According to the Kremlin, what the Western press had widely termed "little green men" were actually local self-defense militias who had voluntarily amassed to resist what they believed was an illegal fascist coup in Kyiv. Moreover, under its 1997 treaty with Ukraine on the conditions for stationing its Black Sea Fleet in Crimea, Russia could maintain up to 25,000 troops there, and technically whatever soldiers were present fell under that agreement.

But these conflicting narratives, blasted forth from Russian state media in the confusion of the protests and counter-protests following the collapse of Yanukovych's regime, masked what was already, for all intents and purposes, an invasion. When I arrived in Simferopol, days ahead of the 16 March referendum, I saw groups of well-armed soldiers and militias patrolling the street and guarding government buildings. Some were wearing a mix of plain and military gear, armed with a seemingly random mix of old and new Kalashnikovs and handguns, and speaking in a local, southern accent. Others were much better armed and equipped, and spoke not at all. So which were they? Local, self-mobilized militias, or soldiers of the Black Sea Fleet?

Such was the beauty of the deception.

Some of the scholarly writing on what happened in Crimea in 2014 portrays it as a largely conventional military operation, with Russian soldiers pretending to be local militia.[1] That, however, accounted for only half of the story.

Looking closer, not all the little green men were alike. Standing on guard around the perimeter of the military bases and strategic government objects were masked, armed soldiers whose kit could not have been randomly distributed or bought in weapons stores. There was another difference between the militiamen and the soldiers: the stone-faced silence of the latter.

The soldier at Perevalne, smiling under his mask, remained silent when I asked my questions. Until, that is, I pointed to the strange white bands he had on his wrists and asked what they were. I had exhausted all possible formulations that could get him to talk, and I thought, wrongly, that this would be an innocuous enough question. It wasn't, but the soldier finally spoke up: "That's so that I can be spotted from outer space."

He was, of course, ridiculing my question, because those bands inadvertently revealed a great deal. Traditionally, white armbands were used by Russian soldiers to distinguish themselves from enemy combatants dressed in similar uniforms—as was the case with the Ukrainian marines that they were guarding. Eight years later, observers would notice ominous symbols—Zs, triangles and squares—painted on Russian tanks and equipment prepositioned on the border with Ukraine before their attack in February 2022. The markings—the Z would become a domestic symbol of the "special military operation" in the Kremlin's propaganda campaign—initially served the same purpose and underscored just how close the two militaries were.

At that moment, a militiaman in hunter's camo approached and ordered me to stop talking to the soldier. He asked to see my documents, and when I assured him that I was Russian, his demeanor became distinctly less threatening. What were they doing there, I asked, what was the sentiment around the base?

He livened up. "We're guarding against provocations," he said, and by his account, there were many. Just the other day, he got in a scuffle with pro-Maidan activists who tried to enter the base. "Look at this!" he said, pointing to a bruise on his wrist, brandishing it as a display of the activists' violence. "They're not peaceful at all!" The man was a local veteran, a volunteer, and he showed me the tent where his men were based, where they sat, in various stages of inebriation, around a table laden with half-eaten tin cans of fish, ramen, teacups and cigarette butts. They offered me tea.

Other militiamen patrolling the streets of Crimea were equally talkative, in sharp contrast to the better-armed soldiers stationed at Perevalne and guarding some of the other strategic objects. Outside the Sevastopol headquarters of the Ukrainian Naval Forces, about half a dozen soldiers in body armor and masks and armed with rifles guarded the entrance to ensure that Ukrainian soldiers still loyal to the Ukrainian government would not leave. In front of them, however, was a group of armed volunteers in plainclothes, and I asked one of them who the armed men were.

"Those are Russian troops. What, haven't you seen your own soldiers before?" he said with disarming candor. The troops were there, he said, just like the other militiaman at Perevalne, to prevent "provocations." According to another militiaman in Simferopol, the local "self-defense forces" made up of volunteers, police and military veterans and Cossacks coordinated their defense with officers of the Black Sea Fleet, who were on the peninsula legally.

It would occur to me much later that there was a very good reason why the militiamen were as talkative as the Russian soldiers were silent. Soldiers could not be trusted to lie, and thus were given orders to keep quiet. But the militiamen had to lie very little, if at all, in order to present the narrative behind the military operation. The amateurishly dressed "little green man," so eager to offer me tea and tell me about the "fascist" junta in Kyiv, reveling in his own victimhood, was genuinely there of his own, fervent volition and believed wholeheartedly in every word he said. He may have embellished the "provocation," but it was not entirely a fabrication. He was proud of what he was doing and had nothing to hide.

Just as there were Russian soldiers pretending to be volunteer militias, the reality was that there were also volunteer militias pretending to be Russian soldiers.

But why?

THE LITTLE GREEN MEN

I

Putin claims that the decision to annex Crimea was taken at 7 a.m. on 23 February 2014, but by all accounts, it was not unanimous and there was a great deal of uncertainty about how, and even whether, to implement it at all.

In fact, "reuniting" Crimea with Russia was no pet project of the Kremlin, at least not until then. Sergei Shoigu, the defense minister and widely popular former emergency minister, was reportedly opposed to a military operation. So were other key Kremlin officials, notably the powerful Kremlin aide Vladislav Surkov, who would nevertheless eventually go on to manage the separatist movements in Donbas. The Foreign Ministry was also not in favor, though by that point, the Kremlin hardly listened to what they had to say. Based on what could be gleaned from their public statements, the truth was that even those who were opposed to the operation certainly *saw* Crimea as part of Russia, but felt that wresting it from Ukraine was too costly.

Indeed, the role of so many volunteers and self-mobilized militias in Crimea was symptomatic of the Kremlin's improvisation as it began annexing the peninsula. The operation was a hybrid one: the formal command and control structures collaborated with the informal local initiative; the state actors worked alongside non-state actors. In a way, the Crimea operation owed its success to the same system of dual power from which Putin's Kremlin has derived its stability for over two decades. On the one hand, there is the formal, institutional vector, where decisions are made by those with the legal mandate to do so and passed down to those authorized to implement them. But the Kremlin, aware of the weakness of institutional rule at home and its vulnerability on the world stage, must rely in equal measure on the informal vector, where businessmen, politicians and freelancers in all walks of life curry Kremlin favor.

In Crimea, the illusion of the premeditated efficiency of the operation to secure the peninsula and then to annex it lay in the seamless interplay between the two approaches. The Kremlin could have simply taken the peninsula through a conventional military operation alone; but in purely numerical terms the forces it could afford to deploy there were outnumbered, and an overt campaign might have pushed the local Ukrainian garrisons into fighting back, to mention nothing of the international backlash. In short, it couldn't have carried out the seizure with so little bloodshed for its own forces without relying on volunteers and non-state actors.

But its swiftness and efficiency also belied a degree of improvisation and indecision to which neither Putin nor the key actors involved in the decision-making would ever admit. On 22 February 2014, Putin gathered the most powerful men of his government in a situation room at his residence in Novo-Ogaryovo. All night, they debated what to do and how to do it, and by the morning of 23 February had reached a decision. There were four key men there. Security Council secretary Nikolai Patrushev, Defense Minister Sergei Shoigu, Chief of Staff Sergei Ivanov, and Vladimir Putin himself.

They were to set in motion a set of events that the Kremlin had up until that point refused to consider, despite decades of persistent calls from various sectors of the Russian political elite.

* * *

Indeed, the pull of Crimean "reunification" had always been stronger at the bottom than it was at the top, rendering the Kremlin, in many ways, an outlier of Russian public and political opinion. Given the Western fascination with the "liberal" or pro-Western opposition in Russia, which took little interest in these issues, relatively little has been written about grassroots nationalist dissent in English. And while there is a good deal of literature on the problem of ethno-nationalism in Russia, much of this has focused on the Kremlin's collaboration with it. The opposition of most nationalist groups to the Kremlin, and the Kremlin's efforts to suppress these groups, has not been anywhere near as widely addressed. For nearly a quarter of a century of talk, activism and lobbying, these various nationalists have been making futile efforts to fix what they believe to be a fatal error in a historical equation. And, for nearly a quarter of a century, the sheer complexity of it, the tangled balance of interests that kept a precarious peace, had forced the Kremlin to brush this issue under the rug.

Historically, the signing of the Belovezha Accords in December 1991 signified the annulment of the Union of Soviet Socialist Republics. But then, and since then, what made this historic event so controversial was not about the way communism was supposedly replaced by democracy. Rather, it was about a societal problem of nearly civilizational proportions: what to do with the millions of ethnic Russians and Russian-speakers who wound up as foreigners in newly sovereign states? And it wasn't just a Russian problem. As borders of new states were erected and redrawn, whole swaths of ethnic groups found themselves cut loose in de facto foreign, at times hostile environments. The irony of "Russia" seceding from the Soviet Union as an example for other republics to follow raised another interesting question for *autonomous* republics within newly sovereign countries: if sovereignty from the USSR was possible for Georgia and Kazakhstan, was it also possible for Chechnya and Tatarstan to secede from Russia? What about the Armenian enclave of Nagorno-Karabakh in Azerbaijan, with whom the Armenians shared neither a language nor a religion, only a blood vendetta going back to the Armenian genocide by Turks in 1915? What about the Ossetian and Abkhazian enclaves in Georgia, with which these people shared neither a language nor a culture? The ethnic Russian majority in Northern Kazakhstan? "Grab as much sovereignty as you can swallow," said Boris Yeltsin in 1990 as he advocated for the end of the USSR, before bombing Chechen capital Grozny into submission for declaring independence five years later.[2]

In the economic chaos and misery that accompanied the collapse of the Soviet Union, the new government hadn't the resources to address, let alone resolve all these contradictions. Who got sovereignty or merely autonomy? What responsibility did the Russian Federation as a successor state to the Soviet Union have to citizens abroad, who had effectively been cut loose? Some autonomous republics within Russia—like Tatarstan—were peacefully granted autonomy within the new federation, while bloody wars were fought over statelets abroad, whose sovereignty neither Russia nor the rest of the world recognized, such as South Ossetia, Abkhazia and Transnistria. Today, there are those who argue that the Soviets were merely the heirs of an older imperialism, that Russians have been the oppressors of minorities for centuries, and so their concerns are not real and should not be addressed. This, however, contradicts the very logic of history and the root cause of most wars: the oppressors become the oppressed when tides change, but sons and daughters are not the same people as their parents and usually refuse to accept a punishment that is directed at people long dead.

Yeltsin's Kremlin and then Putin's left these contradictions unaddressed, sometimes fueling the fire when it suited their political needs, sometimes brutally quashing independence movements within. The unfinished business of Soviet dissolution became the purview of nationalist and communist revanchists who used it to buttress their other ideological grievances and agendas, without actually dealing with the problem. When, in October 1993, Yeltsin shelled the Congress of People's Deputies of the Russian Federation out of existence, he also deprived a lot of these revanchists of their only institutional outlet, cutting off any possibility of a democratic debate that, however ugly at the beginning, could have produced more moderate, peaceful and civilized solutions.

Possibly the most salient—and overlooked—problem emerging from the calamity of disintegration was Crimea. A part of Russia ever since Catherine the Great annexed it in 1783, it went on to become an autonomous republic within the Russian Soviet Federated Republic, until Nikita Khrushchev, in a particularly magnanimous gesture, gifted Crimea to the Ukrainian Soviet Federated Republic in 1954. Given that, like nesting dolls, all these entities were part of the Soviet Union, the administration of an internal region within a different internal republic but part of the same sovereign union would hardly differ. The gesture, in other words, was geopolitically meaningless—until Russia and Ukraine became separate states. Russians also never fail to observe that Khrushchev himself was a Ukrainian.

In 1991, disputes about the status of Crimea became a problem both for Kyiv, which worried that Russian revanchist imperialist ambitions would use it to wrest back the peninsula, and for Moscow, which at the time was oriented towards integration with the West and feared the revanchist imperialist label. But it was mainly a problem for the Russian-speaking communities of Crimea itself. With ethnic Russian-speakers making up an overwhelming majority of the peninsula, from the start many of them felt increasingly alienated by Ukraine and ignored by Russia.

In January 1991, with the cohesion of the Soviet Union hanging by a thread, Crimea, at the time an oblast, or region of Ukraine within the USSR, held a referendum on re-establishing the Crimean Autonomous Soviet Socialist Republic within a new Union Treaty proposed by Soviet leader Mikhail Gorbachev. The Union Treaty would have given Crimea sovereignty on par with Ukraine within the union. Ninety-three percent voted in favor.

Three months later, a referendum on preserving the USSR as a union of *sovereign*, rather than *socialist* federated republics, was held among all Soviet entities, barring a few republics that boycotted it. An overwhelming majority voted in favor of preserving the union, but the hardliner KGB coup in August of that year rendered it moot. By the end of the year, the Belovezha Accords, signed by Yeltsin and the leaders of Ukraine and Belarus without being put to a vote, would formally dissolve the Soviet Union. The accords would unilaterally fix the borders of the newly emerged post-Soviet republics while writing off the aspirations of sovereignty for several ethnic constituencies, creating fertile ground for a whole slew of national and ethnic conflicts. Crimea wouldn't yet get embroiled in bloody wars of independence like those that erupted in the Autonomous Republic of South Ossetia or the Autonomous Region of Nagorno-Karabakh. Still, a significant portion of Crimea's constituents were not content with being forced to remain an autonomous republic *within* Ukraine and subordinate to the Ukrainian constitution: a 1996 Gallup poll, for instance, showed that 59 percent of ethnic Russians and, what was even more noteworthy, a sizeable minority—41 percent—of ethnic Ukrainians in Crimea, favored joining Russia.[3]

Aspirations towards full autonomy from Ukraine and towards unification with Russia persisted. During parliamentary elections held there in 1994, the pro-Russian Republican Party of Crimea formed a bloc and won control of the Crimean Supreme Soviet. A longtime advocate of autonomy and unification with Russia, the nationalist Yuri Meshkov was elected president of Crimea. That spring, he held a plebiscite, seeking to introduce a constitution that would, in effect, supersede Ukraine's and establish sovereignty. Fearing separatism, Ukraine's parliament overruled the Crimean Supreme Soviet and voted both the Crimean constitution and the post of Crimean president out of existence. Meshkov, having failed to navigate the legal impasse or secure

Yeltsin's backing, was forced to flee Crimea.[4] Only the name—Autonomous Republic of Crimea—remained, but hardly any autonomy came with it.

For the Republican Party of Crimea and the other pro-Russian movements on the peninsula, the failure to secure autonomy on their own terms was the result not only of the weakness of their own civil society and their inability to advocate effectively for their interest in Kyiv but because, as many of them felt, the cards were stacked against them from the start. In Ukraine in those years, Russian interests in Crimea were equated by many Western advisors and journalists with Soviet revanchism and thus not taken seriously by Kyiv. Many Russians felt that the interests of Crimean Tatars—a small ethnic minority that had been brutally deported during the Soviet period and had only recently returned—were much better represented in the national and international agenda. But more importantly, the parties and movements speaking for Russian interests in Crimea felt powerless against the tide because they lacked any support from Moscow.[5]

But what was Russia going to do? It wasn't as if Ukraine was prepared to return the peninsula or grant it autonomy. Nor, under the terms of the 1994 Budapest Memorandum—in which Ukraine agreed to give up its share of Soviet nuclear missiles in return for guarantees of its sovereignty—was it required to. Yeltsin, faced with his own separatist revolt in Chechnya, and struggling to broker peace in two other bloody ethnic conflicts on Russia's periphery, was in no position to fight for Crimea. The separatist movements that had simmered since 1991 simply weren't a top priority for a Kremlin that was loath to get into any new conflict, especially an armed one. In 1997, in a bid to put this talk to rest, Yeltsin's government and the government of Leonid Kuchma signed a Treaty on Friendship, Cooperation and Partnership, affirming the inviolability of existing borders.

But the talk never went away. The fringe issue of the rights of Russians abroad generally, and in Ukraine in particular, became a choice agenda for a whole assortment of parties on the left, the right and even in the center—so much so that these ideas ceased being "fringe." It was clear how far this had become a mainstream view when Moscow Mayor Yuri Luzhkov made several public statements in 2008 calling for Crimea to be returned to Russia.[6] Meanwhile, ethno-nationalism and retrograde imperialist chauvinism were already on the Kremlin's radar as potent sociopolitical ills. The late Eduard Limonov of the National Bolshevik Party—a volunteer veteran of the Balkans, whose followers actively went on to fight in Donbas—was arrested in 2001 for plotting an armed insurrection in Northern Kazakhstan.[7] The charges were likely fabricated or at least exaggerated—Limonov's followers just didn't have that kind of muscle—but the talk was real. However, in part because the talk was symptomatic of a genuine problem that no one knew how to fix, the Kremlin pretended it existed only in the inflamed imaginations of the outcasts of history.

These weren't just ethno-nationalists or Stalinists, the kind that appeared regularly on the pages of the Communist-nationalist *Zavtra* tabloid or Limonov's pamphlets. In the early 2000s, after Putin's rise to power, a movement of so-called "new conservatives" emerged in Russia, consisting of young, cosmopolitan intellectuals who rejected the leftist strands of Russian thought but also distanced themselves from the pro-Western liberal movement. Some of them flirted with nationalism. They debated in newspaper columns and drank themselves silly in the old apartments of the Moscow intelligentsia or in ethnic South Caucasian restaurants where they plotted, half in jest, the policies they would implement "once we come to power."[8] It was at one of these meetings that one of the most interesting ideologues of the Russian nationalist movement, Konstantin Krylov, described how he saw the problem and why it would take Russian national-ism to resolve it: "Imagine the Soviet Union as a communal apartment," he told me. "When it was privatized, ethnic repub-lics got the rooms, while the Russians got the corridor, the kitchen and the toilet."[9]

While not necessarily self-styled nationalists like Krylov, a whole assortment of people in power harbored similar views and vocally disagreed with both Yeltsin and Putin on how to address these issues, even as they worked within the system of power to address them themselves.

The question of Russian-speakers abroad, and of putting Russians first at home, became a domestic issue with imperialist overtones. However much Kremlin officials and the Russian security and military community espoused these views, they were not official policy, simply because the Kremlin felt there was little it was willing or able to do to pursue it as part of its foreign policy. It was still wary of nationalism.

A pivotal change in the Kremlin's thinking took place in 2008. That year, Kosovo declared independence from Russian ally Serbia and was immediately recognized by a majority of NATO countries. Crimean pro-Russian movements thought this deeply unfair and took the precedent as a call to action to lobby for more support from Moscow.

So, too, did many in Russia. That spring, in the wake of the recognition of Kosovo, Moscow Mayor Luzhkov got himself declared persona non grata by Ukraine for insisting that Sevastopol was a Russian city. Joining a chorus of other politi-cians, he continued to call for the return of the peninsula. Yet despite the noise, observers saw it as just another personal opin-ion—albeit a very popular one—that shouldn't be seen as reflect-ing the will of the Kremlin.[10] The government still distanced itself from Crimean separatism.

Indeed, despite mounting fears, there was nothing in 2008 to indicate that the Kremlin was seriously considering such a risky move. In August, Moscow fought a short, sharp war with Georgia, ostensibly to secure the independence of South Ossetia and Abkhazia, and some more radical nationalist groups hoped this presaged a new policy of standing up to what they saw as NATO-backed countries. They hoped that Russia would likewise stand up to Ukraine in support of Crimea's independence and take it under its wing.[11]

It was not to be. Indeed, later that year, Deputy Prime Minister Sergei Ivanov even commented on how Moscow was prepared to move its Black Sea Fleet out of Sevastopol if Ukraine refused to extend a treaty allowing Russia to use its port there. "I love Crimea, I have relatives there, but it's Ukraine's problem, not Russia's."[12]

This dynamic continued—growing popular and political fervor from below, stifled by the Kremlin's cold indifference from above. It took a seismic geopolitical event—the ouster of Viktor Yanukovych in what the Kremlin saw as a Western-engineered coup and plans by the new Ukrainian government to join NATO—to trigger the Kremlin to take up the issue of Crimea. But for its own reasons, and on its own terms.

II

We can never know for certain which gears spinning in Putin's head turned his focus on Ukraine and made him act decisively to seize Crimea, but from his own words and from the events leading up to that moment, it is not hard to deduce what was likely going through his mind. As he looked at the events of Kyiv's Maidan unfolding on the television screen of his situation room in Novo-Ogaryovo during the sleepless night of 21–22 February 2014, only one thing seemed clear.

Russia was not safe.

In September 2008, shortly after Russian troops invaded neighboring Georgia to recognize and assert the independence of

South Ossetia and Abkhazia, after seventeen years of declining to do so, Putin started to consider his legacy. "Tell me," he asked Alexei Venediktov, a well-connected opposition journalist, after watching him drink a whole bottle of wine. "You're a historian. What are the history books going to say about me?"

At a loss, Venediktov mumbled something about the reunification of the Orthodox Church the previous year. "That's it?" Putin asked.

"Well, history books aren't going to write that Russia got up from its knees."

Venediktov remembered that incident because six years later, after the annexation of Crimea, Putin asked him again, this time rhetorically: "Now what are they going to write about me?"[13]

But back in 2008, even Crimea itself didn't seem to be on his mind. Days after Russia's recognition of Georgia's breakaway statelets in August, a German journalist pointedly asked him about Crimea. Given the precedent Russia seemed to have set with its actions that month, and given the precedent of Kosovo's recognition earlier that year, Crimea seemed to be the next logical step in the minds of both Russian proponents and foreign observers.

But Putin demurred; once again he moved to shut down the domestic chatter about Crimea. "Crimea is not a contentious territory," he said:

> Russia has long ago recognized the borders of today's Ukraine ... The idea that Russia would have such aims, I consider a provocation. There are complicated processes going on in Crimea. There are problems regarding Crimean Tatars, the Ukrainian population, the Russian population, the Slavic population more generally. But that is an internal political issue of Ukraine itself.[14]

In fact, Putin would continue to demur and deny right up until *after* the Crimean referendum of 16 March 2014.

And yet, already in 2008, Russia's decisive move into Georgia reflected Putin's growing sense that something was not right with the world. As he had said in a keynote speech in Munich in February 2007, in his view the United States was essentially trying to impose its hegemony on the world, justifying its "political expediency" with hypocrisy and double standards.

"No one feels safe!" he complained. "I want to emphasize this—no one feels safe! Because no one can feel that international law is like a stone wall that will protect them."[15]

In the meantime, back home, seismic shifts were taking place in Putin's trajectory as leader and, by extension, in the Russian political establishment as a whole. In 2008, Putin, in a controversial move, decided to adhere to the term limits of his presidency and not seek to change the constitution to allow him to stay in office, despite public requests and a general expectation that he would. Instead, he nominated the relatively liberal reformer Dmitry Medvedev as handpicked successor, and Putin stepped aside into the role of prime minister. This allowed him to retain a great deal of power at home in case Medvedev's liberalization went awry—not least as the security agencies still considered him the boss—but it also limited his freedom of maneuver internationally. Perhaps for this reason, to feel safer, or in a bid to make the world a safer place, he had Medvedev appoint the longtime FSB chief Nikolai Patrushev to the chairmanship of the Security Council.

With the Security Council up until then largely an advisory body, it was immediately understood that Patrushev would make the council matter. A longtime KGB man himself, Patrushev had served as Putin's deputy when he briefly headed the FSB in 1999. Patrushev was a man who saw the world through the prism of risk, threat and security, and he was a man Putin felt he could trust. With Medvedev president, and formally in control of the FSB and the Defense and Interior Ministries, Putin may well have needed another powerful institution he could rely on more informally, so much so that the Security Council's remit expanded beyond domestic affairs into the world stage. When the Georgian war broke out in August 2008, it was Patrushev and his council "making decisions" on the conflict[16]—even when its formal role was still advisory.

There was a lot of speculation that Medvedev was merely Putin's puppet, a weak but trusted placeholder in the Kremlin so that Putin could take advantage of a constitutional loophole and return to the presidency in 2012. And yet, those four years saw a great deal of competition not just between political classes and within the ruling United Russia party, but between Putin and Medvedev himself. By 2011, there was a robust camp within the political establishment, including United Russia, that supported Medvedev's reforms and his attempt at a "re-start" with the United States and wanted him to run for re-election. Likewise, there was a growing camp that rejected all these liberal leanings and mistrusted any possibility of reconciliation with the West. Among them were Patrushev and those who thought like him—that in a dangerous world, the West could never be trusted, and that by liberalizing, Russia was only making itself weak for when "political expediency" prompted the West to attack. And while Putin and Medvedev maintained the pretense of an amicable co-dominion, tensions were bubbling underneath, evident in the increasing arguments between their two respective camps.

As he ruminated over whether to return to the presidency in 2012 or step back and allow a successor to rule Russia, Putin seemed caught by the country's two-headed eagle. Whereas in the emblem, one head looks to the west and the other to the east, in this case both eagles were looking at Putin, stuck in the middle. One yammered to him about the need to modernize and reform, while the other hissed about the West's betrayal.

Libya became the clearest point of contention. In the spring of 2011, anti-government protests known as the Arab Spring swept through Tunisia, Egypt, Syria and Libya. There, Muammar

Gaddafi, a longtime Soviet and Russian ally, called on his troops to suppress the protests, and civil war broke out. The United Nations and most NATO countries sided with the protesters, who had, as in many Arab states, initially demonstrated against corruption and abuse of power. In March, the UN passed Resolution 1973, establishing a no-fly zone over Libya and authorizing the use of military force against Gaddafi's troops in order to protect civilians. Russia abstained from the vote rather than using its power of veto; in Medvedev's words, this was not because Russia thought the resolution wrong, but because it would not take part in enforcing the no-fly zone.

Whether this was because Medvedev genuinely believed the resolution to be just and fair, or whether he was currying favor with the United States in wake of the "reset" the countries had announced two years earlier, his gesture had the clear appearance of the latter. This was especially because the United States appeared to be using Resolution 1973 as a cover to launch an air campaign that was actually intended to bring down Gaddafi. From the Kremlin's point of view, international law, in other words, was once again being bent in the name of American "political expediency." This inevitably rattled Russia's hardliner camp. Breaking a practice in which the two leaders never openly disagreed, Putin directly spoke out against the resolution, saying it resembled "medieval calls for crusades" and would "lead to a clash of civilizations."

As president, this put Medvedev on the spot. Somewhat passive-aggressively, he countered Putin's rebuke: "It is unacceptable to use expressions that in effect lead to the clash of civilizations. Such as 'crusades' and the like. That is unacceptable. Everyone must bear this in mind," he told journalists.[17]

But Medvedev could do nothing to prevent NATO from supporting Libya's opposition, even if he wanted to. That October, a wounded Gaddafi was dragged from a drainage pipe where he was hiding and killed.

The unusual disagreement between Putin and Medvedev did not lead to any open political debate, but it certainly heightened the tensions. The yammering and hissing of the two-headed eagle intensified. To be strong, Russia needed to modernize and liberalize, to join the Western community. But how can Russia be strong, if its own president had just been duped by a West that clearly wanted nothing but to undermine Russia? That summer, Putin decided which of the eagle's heads needed to shut up.

In September, to howling cheers and applause from party delegates, Putin and Medvedev stood together on the stage at the United Russia convention at Moscow's giant Luzhniki Stadium and said they had both agreed "years ago" that Putin would run for president again and Medvedev would step down. In hindsight, however, Kremlin insiders told me that Putin had considered the possibility of allowing Medvedev to run for re-election right up until that summer. He'd had many qualms, not least of them relating to domestic infighting and fears that Medvedev wasn't strong enough to manage the various clans that would vie for power in Putin's absence. But the final straw was the disagreement over Libya. The world was not safe enough to allow Medvedev to blithely focus on liberalization.

Indeed, Libya, the foreign intervention and Gaddafi's brutal death loomed large against the backdrop of that fall's events. The decision of the tandem dashed genuine hopes among the liberal camp and the growing cosmopolitan middle class that a real democratic process was coming into being. Following parliamentary elections that December, tens of thousands of demonstrators took to the streets, filling Moscow's Bolotnaya Square and protesting first against vote rigging in the elections, then against Putin himself. He was called a "thief" and a "false tsar," and even "a used condom." That his election—and his inauguration—was so besmirched by mass demonstrations reportedly infuriated Putin, who believed that he had fostered this urban middle class by providing them with stability and prosperity, and then they betrayed him.

But it wasn't just the middle-class's betrayal that weighed on Putin. He had become convinced that the 2011 protests were engineered by then Secretary of State Hillary Clinton. Speaking to the Organization of Security and Co-operation (OSCE) that December, Clinton said the United States had "serious concerns over the conduct" of the elections.[18] Putin had not spent enough time in the United States to fully understand that the greeting "how are you" has all but zero semantic value and that, most of the time, Americans don't care a whit about how your day actually went when they ask this. So too their expressions of "serious concern" usually amount to nothing. But Putin had the brutal fate of Gaddafi before his eyes, and because he feared American interference so much, he began to take every innocuous or token comment as evidence of serious intent. American spies were active in Russia, after all. What else could they have been doing?

This strain of thinking—that the United States was bent on destroying Russia—had, with the rise of Patrushev, increasingly made its way into the mainstream. A particularly bizarre example of this paranoid reasoning was the belief that former Secretary of State Madeleine Albright had claimed that Siberia should not belong to Russia. It started as an internet meme in 2005, but the following year, Major General Boris Ratnikov, a secret service officer, revealed that the Federal Protection Service had a special psychic division that "scanned" the subconscious of foreign statesmen, including Albright. "In her thoughts we discovered a pathological hatred of Slavic people" and a belief that it was the United States, not Russia, that should control Siberia.[19]

There is almost no doubt that Patrushev, and thus the man who was increasingly listening to him above all others, Putin, were aware of these esoteric revelations as the events of 2011–12 unfolded. Patrushev did not say as much then, but in 2015 he finally asserted:

> The United States wishes that we didn't exist at all ... Because we control a wealth of natural resources. But the Americans think we control them illegally ... You probably remember the words of former US State Secretary Madeleine Albright, who said that Russia owns neither the Far East nor Siberia.

It was with this intent, he said, that America was destabilizing Ukraine.[20]

What was on Albright's mind must have been on her successor's, too, they reasoned. During the Bolotnaya protests, Putin announced that Clinton had "set the tone for certain activists inside our country, sent a signal, and they heard the signal ... And with the support of the State Department, they began to act ... [Western governments] felt they had leverage inside our country."[21] Putin allowed the protests, up to a point, but then began a crackdown, launching a witch-hunt against the opposition that ensued for years. "They ruined my big day," an apocryphal quote attributed to Putin goes. "Now I'm going to ruin their lives."[22]

It was against this backdrop that Putin saw the first sniper shots being fired on Kyiv's Maidan in January 2014.

When pro-EU demonstrations had broken out there in November, initially against Yanukovych's decision not to sign an Association Agreement with the EU but more generally against his regime's corruption, Putin advised Yanukovych to suppress them. From Putin's vantage point, the plot to violently overthrow a democratically elected leader in order to install a Western puppet was already underway, just as in Libya, and political negotiations would not deter the Ukrainian opposition and their Western backers. The events on the ground only vindicated Putin's paranoias. By January, the protests had turned violent, with Yanukovych's Berkut riot police openly shooting at demonstrators, who retaliated with Molotov cocktails. Over 100 died, with the circumstances of the violence yet to be fully investigated. In a leaked audio recording, Assistant Secretary of State Victoria

Nuland was heard telling the US ambassador who should be in the next Ukrainian government, promoting the very people who would go on to head the new administration, and saying "fuck the EU," inadvertently playing into an increasingly widespread perception of an arrogant US administration calling the shots on EU security.[23] She was also filmed handing out sandwiches to protesters on Maidan, a trivial piece of political grandstanding that the Kremlin convinced itself demonstrated the degree to which this was an American project through and through.[24]

But the final blow for Putin was the betrayal of an agreement on settling the crisis that had been signed by Yanukovych and the opposition on 21 February. It required the government to restore the constitution of 2004, hold early presidential elections, and for both sides to refrain from the use of force. France, Germany and Poland stood as guarantors to the agreement. While Ukraine's parliament passed a law restoring the 2004 constitution and freeing prisoners, that very evening, radical groups began to attack and occupy government buildings. Yanukovych, against Putin's advice, fled the city. Once again, what Putin saw on the screens in his situation room seemed to confirm what he had feared all along: defying all laws and agreements, a violent mob, backed by the West, ousted a democratically elected leader simply because they didn't like him.

"Obama called me that evening to talk about how the agreement would be implemented," Putin would recall.[25] "Our American partners asked us to do everything to prevent Yanukovych from using force." But the same evening the agreement was signed, the opposition—using lethal force and, according to Putin, even burning people alive—seized the Presidential Administration. "At least they could have called," Putin lamented about his "American partners." "At least they could have said they tried. But not a word. On the contrary, they completely supported those who carried out a state coup. It was probably the first time [the United States] lied to us so blatantly."[26]

Putin felt he had been betrayed. It was finally time to stand up to his treacherous, two-faced "Western partners," to demonstrate that Russia wasn't going to roll over as its interests were trampled on, and to seize from Ukraine the peninsula that most Russians believed was theirs anyway, the peninsula that was also the historic and strategic home of Russia's Black Sea Fleet. Sitting next to him in the situation room was Patrushev, by then his most trusted advisor, who had known all along that this would happen. Patrushev had known, because it was his professional remit to know (even if it was the only thing he knew), that Russia was not safe.

III

What to do? Insiders say that a tactical contingency plan to seize Crimea had existed for years and all that was needed was to pull the folder off the shelf and dust it off.[27] This is no doubt true, but modern militaries are expected to have contingency plans for all kinds of potential scenarios whether or not they ever expect to activate them.

But those plans were about the seizure, not the annexation. That morning, all that the decision seemed to amount to, based on subsequent actions, was launching a special operation to seize control of Crimea. But judging by accounts of how decisions were subsequently made in Simferopol, Moscow didn't seem to have worked out a clear plan about what to do with the peninsula afterwards. See if tensions stabilized and then withdraw the troops? Make do with merely recognizing Crimea's autonomy and independence? Or move to do the one thing that an overwhelming majority in both Russia and Crimea wanted to do, but knew full well was nigh impossible?[28]

It was for this reason, perhaps, that the man who would be put in charge of the operation, Defense Minister Shoigu, was widely said to be opposed to using the military.[29]

Shoigu, unlike the ever vocal and opinionated Patrushev, hasn't voiced much of an opinion on the operation either way. In 2015, he asked a war correspondent to write a book about the annexation of Crimea, but the book itself, edited, advised on and redacted by government ministries, complete with nefarious secret plots hatched by US Ambassador Michael McFaul, predictably weaves a Kremlin-sanctioned story, with Shoigu heroically well aware of the obvious need to return Crimea even before Putin was.[30] The real Shoigu, however, is far more complex. In his own book, *About Yesterday*, he focuses on his formative experiences as a rescuer. In 1991, Shoigu formed the Rescue Corps and then built up the Emergencies Ministry from scratch. A man who for all intents and purposes seems made for the military was actually a civilian who single-handedly created a militarized ministry, which today has its fleets of helicopters and even "special forces" who parachute into the middle of forest fires to rescue civilians and train for a second Chernobyl-style nuclear disaster. The terse, efficient, Tuva-born constructer grew wildly popular: for two decades, it was Shoigu at the scene whenever things went wrong; while Putin was talking about "manual control," Shoigu was working hands-on, quietly implementing all the facets of rescue and relief operations from floods to earthquakes, air crashes to terror attacks. What Shoigu seemed best equipped for was not searching out enemies within and without. It was how to try and save a child from the rubble of a collapsed building and then inform the mother that it had died afterwards.[31]

As a man who was about getting things done as quietly, efficiently and painlessly as possible, he may have voiced his reservations, but when tasked to launch the operation, he mobilized to the task not just the full force of his ministry but all the connections that his popularity afforded him.

Even before the final decision was made, the Defense Ministry was reacting to the threats it saw emanating from Kyiv to Russia's

Black Sea Fleet on the Crimean Peninsula. On the night of 21–22 February, while Putin was reportedly still pondering whether to act, various marine and Spetsnaz units were transferred to Crimea and the Anapa airfield on the Russian mainland, which became a key logistic base of the invasion. Indeed, Crimea became the first mission of the newly created Special Operations Forces, the SSO, the most elite units of the Spetsnaz.

On 26 February, Crimean Tatars clashed with pro-Russian activists outside the Crimean Supreme Soviet building in Simferopol. That night, Shoigu deployed ten aircraft carrying paratroopers from the Pskov 76th Guards Division to Simferopol. Putin would justify the move as nominally legal, given that Russia could deploy up to 25,000 servicemen as part of the agreement whereby Crimea hosted the Black Sea Fleet. Even so, the paratroopers bore no insignia and came to be known as the "little green men"—covert soldiers of a deniable operation. Admittedly, their role was officially acknowledged later, when Shoigu formally awarded them the Order of Suvorov for their role in the operation to "return" Crimea.[32]

On 28 February, when the invasion began in earnest, up to fourteen Ilyushin-76 aircraft delivered an estimated 1,400 Spetsnaz to the Gvardeiskoye airfield near Simferopol. And while in sheer numbers alone, according to some analysts, the deployments were barely sufficient to tip the balance of forces in Russia's favor, the Russian Spetsnaz displayed a level of professionalism and efficiency that was not expected of the Russian armed forces. The element of surprise, their formal, though hardly plausible, deniability under the pretext of the Black Sea Fleet agreement, coupled with their unexpected sophistication, all contributed to the shock and awe that allowed Russia to swiftly annex the peninsula almost without any bloodshed. The Russians and Ukrainians even held an impromptu football match—which the Russians lost.[33]

But the success of the Crimea operation also hinged on its deft deployment of non-military instruments, of what in hindsight would come to be seen as political war.[34]

Russian generals didn't really see themselves as having tried this playbook before. For them, it was the West's new way of waging war, and given that the West had brought this political war to Russia's doorstep, they felt that Russia must quickly learn how to respond in kind. To understand their thinking, one need look no further than the writings of Russia's senior officer, Chief of General Staff Valery Gerasimov. A year before the events in Crimea, he wrote:

> The experience of military conflicts—including those connected with the so-called coloured revolutions in north Africa and the Middle East—confirm that a perfectly thriving state can, in a matter of months and even days, be transformed into an arena of fierce armed conflict, become a victim of foreign intervention, and sink into a web of chaos, humanitarian catastrophe, and civil war.

> The very "rules of war" have changed. The role of nonmilitary means of achieving political and strategic goals has grown, and, in many cases, they have exceeded the power of force of weapons in their effectiveness. The focus of applied methods of conflict has altered in the direction of the broad use of political, economic, informational, humanitarian, and other nonmilitary measures—applied in coordination with the protest potential of the population.[35]

What the Russian military saw taking place in Ukraine was precisely the West's deployment of non-military measures—like street protests—to take control of a territory. So that was what they were going to do in Crimea. Achieving the military objectives on the peninsula was going to be the easy part. Much harder—and Shoigu seemed to understand this—was to prevent and preempt the kinds of protests that had overtaken Kyiv and Western Ukraine. And the pro-Maidan civilian activists—civilian organizers, protesters, sympathizers—were clearly present in Crimea, even if they were in a minority.

The Kremlin—and hawks like Patrushev in particular—felt, in fact, that their political operations in Ukraine were clearly lagging far behind those of their Western adversaries. In part because they believed that they were playing catch up against the political war the West was already waging, they had been trying to increase their political influence in Ukraine for years. But according to the leader of the Crimean Communist Party, Leonid Grach, Patrushev was the "only one" who had been helping pro-Russian movements on the peninsula. "He was the only person in Moscow who wasn't just engaging in empty talk."[36]

When he had been head of the FSB, such political operations were indeed part of Patrushev's remit, and it appears that when he moved to the Security Council in 2008, he reshaped it in a way that would give him more power to do so. In December 2013, Patrushev had met with chairman of the Crimean parliament, Vladimir Konstantinov, who told him that the peninsula was ready to join Russia if Yanukovych was deposed.[37]

It was precisely the political component of the endeavor that proved so tricky, and, in hindsight, would reveal how undecided the Kremlin actually was about what to do with Crimea. And while the enthusiastic Patrushev may have been over-confident in thinking that Konstantinov's readiness to join Russia was enough, it was Shoigu who would be responsible for the tactical implementation of political warfare. But Russian soldiers and military officers alone weren't enough. Politics meant people well outside of the government's command: people with their own agendas and agencies, determined not by Kremlin orders but by the events on the ground—responses to threats real or imagined, or simply making do and adapting to chaos by grasping at the opportunities as they presented themselves.

3

THE HYBRID WARRIORS

The good guys here aren't that good, and the bad guys aren't that bad.

American photographer, on assignment in Donbas, May 2014

On the eve of the referendum, Crimea's coastal city of Sevastopol, the headquarters of Russia's Black Sea Fleet, was quiet. Russian soldiers in unmarked uniforms and self-defense militia made up mostly of locals patrolled the streets, while plainclothes snipers manned some of the rooftops—but they all did so silently, with an air of utter normalcy and order, as pedestrians stopped to take selfies with them. They were mobilized, from the top and from the bottom, to resist what they seem genuinely to have believed was the West's hybrid war against Russia.

On the outskirts stood a row of typical Soviet 5-story tenements. As was usually the case in Crimea, they were quite a bit more dilapidated than their Russian counterparts. Ivan,[1] a pro-Maidan activist, had invited us into his apartment for an interview. It was cluttered, every surface occupied by video equipment, flyers, documents, knickknacks and toys. But there was a lot of work to do, as Ivan was inspired to resist what he believed with equal conviction was Russia's hybrid war against Ukraine.

Ivan was young, in his early twenties, tall, thin, his face, with its short beard, hinting at a poet. He was articulate, literate, calm and sounded little like the fiery-eyed activist he was supposed to be. In Kyiv, where he was based, he had joined the Maidan movement early on, protesting against the corruption and lies of the Yanukovych regime. But when the Russian shadow invasion started sweeping Crimea, he came back home. He had friends in the military and was determined to help them fight back any way he could. Together with fellow activists, he smuggled packages of clothes, food, chocolate and, most importantly, streaming equipment into blockaded garrisons. As far as he was concerned, what was happening was a crime, and the best way to counter it was to expose it on video. Shortly after our interview, he was arrested by local Berkut police—the force that had been loyal to Yanukovych and ordered to disband by the new government in Kyiv for its initial role in violently suppressing the Maidan protests.

Ivan would be released shortly afterwards. During another, more brutal detention the following day, police tried, unsuccessfully, to beat out of him any possible connections to the Ukrainian ultranationalist Pravy Sektor movement that, according to Russian propaganda, was bent on starting a bloody race war in Crimea. They found no such affiliation: Ivan had nothing to hide. After being released a second time, though, he didn't test his luck again and went straight back to Kyiv to join his wife and children.

I had little sympathy for the lies that were being spun and promoted by Russian news agencies, including the one from which I had just days ago resigned.[2] Pro-Russian groups in Crimea, and their supporters in Moscow, were warning—claiming—that groups like Pravy Sektor, backed by the pro-Western interim government, were about to massacre Russians in Crimea. Many believed that without Russian military involvement,

Crimea and parts of Russian-speaking Eastern Ukraine would descend into Balkan-style bloodshed, and Kremlin-controlled news media eagerly amplified these fears. Most Western journalists were reporting on Moscow's disinformation as a tactic of the Kremlin's covert invasion, fortifying the growing image of Putin's Russia as a newly belligerent aggressor. But shouldn't the Russian-speakers who looked to Putin for protection and the local defense militias genuinely believing they had more to fear from Kyiv still have a voice, even if they were wrong? So I asked Ivan: what about the Russian majority of the peninsula that genuinely favored unification with Russia? Were these merely brainwashed Kremlin puppets who should be ignored?

He looked at me unemotionally. "The Russian-speaking occupiers in Crimea that don't like the new government will be killed," he said baldly. "And the rest can go back to Russia."

I

On 26 February, as the first Russian soldiers and local armed militias quietly began appearing across the peninsula, leaders and activists of the Crimean Tatar community broke an unspoken but longstanding rule of not protesting in the same place where pro-Russian communities were gathering. The understanding had been in place to avoid the possibility of clashes, given simmering tensions over which allegiance which group preferred—Russian or Ukrainian. But on that day, both groups assembled in front of Crimea's parliament in Simferopol. "We came to protect our government," one of the Tatar leaders, a former municipal head, said then. "According to our information, [parliament] was going to take separatist decisions—to call on Putin to accept Crimea into Russia and hold a referendum."[3]

The Tatars, who made up just over 14 percent of the Crimean population, harbored historic grievances that threatened to tip over into clashes with the Russians. Unlike the ethnic Russians or Ukrainians, they were indigenous to the peninsula, descendants of various nationalities over the centuries, including Khazars, Greeks and Circassians. What united them and set them apart from the Slavs who would, over the centuries, come to make up a majority, was a Turkic language and the Muslim faith. In the 1940s, Stalin had deported 200,000 Crimean Tatars to Siberia, half dying on the journey. Many returned when Ukraine became independent in 1991, and few looked to Moscow with much enthusiasm. Some looked for protection elsewhere, to those whom many Russians increasingly considered their enemy. The Americans, for example: "Our only hope is on the international community and [US President] Obama. Putin needs to be stopped," one Tatar protester, told me before the referendum.

There were genuine, mutual fears of massacre, of Maidan-like protests and counter-protests that could spiral into bloody ethnic clashes of the kind that had raged on Russia's periphery in the 1990s, that time sparing Crimea. Already in mainland Ukraine, even before the collapse of Yanukovych's government, the pro-Western Maidan movement was met with mass counter-protest rallies. A 15,000-strong rally in Donetsk as early as December 2013 had the organizational backing of Yanukovych's Party of Regions, with dozens of buses bringing in allegedly paid protesters, but the galvanization of these protests after Yanukovych's exile and the party's collapse suggested that a considerable portion of them were genuine. Nowhere, however, were they as critical and as tense as in Crimea, the home of the Russian Black Sea Fleet, where far more was at stake.

With something of a power vacuum in the capital, the local authorities in Simferopol were mindful of the opportunity to revive their pro-Russian agenda, but on the whole they were no less disoriented than their counterparts in Kyiv. Rustam Temirgaliev, then Crimea's deputy prime minister and a longtime proponent of closer ties with Russia, recalled: "We would talk about Crimea joining Russia, but not in our offices." Initially, he and Vladimir Konstantinov, the speaker of Crimea's parliament and a man who would go on to be instrumental in holding the referendum on joining Russia, would meet furtively in little cafés to talk about "the critical times we were in and that we had to do something. Everyone was tired. But Crimean elites were in a lot of ways disenfranchised and could not influence decision-making because Crimea was under the control of Kyiv and Donetsk [party] directors."[4]

It was at one of those Simferopol karaoke cafés that Temirgaliev and Konstantinov met with Sergei Aksyonov, a Crimean parliamentarian and the leader of the Russian Unity party, a bloc of several pro-Russian movements formed in 2009. Together, they decided that, with Russians securing the peninsula, it was time to hold an extraordinary parliamentary session to appoint new leaders. For that, they needed a quorum.

According to Temirgaliev, the impetus to hold a parliamentary session initially was not just autonomy from Ukraine—to say nothing of joining Russia—but to use the occasion to wrest power from the Donetsk branch of the Party of Regions that had dominated the Crimean parliament for years. That—and not just fears of separatism—alarmed the Tatars. According to Temirgaliev, they began to haggle for a larger share of seats in the new parliament.

On 26 February, as the session was beginning, the rally outside swelled, with the Tatars mobilizing up to 7,000 people. A counter-protest of about 3,000 pro-Russian demonstrators was already there. Temirgaliev's, Aksyonov's and Konstantinov's efforts to assemble a quorum were running short: as the start of the session kept being pushed back, they were still lacking about ten deputies. Pressure outside was growing: whereas the Tatars wanted representation, the pro-Russian protesters were demanding to join Russia. Temirgaliev and Konstantinov could promise none of these things, not least given how hard it was for deputies to push through an enraged 10,000-strong rally just to get to the parliament building.

Then Refat Chubarov, the head of the Crimean Tatar community, burst into speaker Konstantinov's office, warning that he wouldn't be able to hold off his people if a parliamentary session was held. Clashes had already erupted outside. As one crowd heaved against another, the Crimean Tatars broke into the building. Chubarov and Aksyonov stepped in to break up the fighting. Two people had died—one of them crushed to death, the other of a heart attack.[5] "It was the first time that Aksyonov had shown himself as a true leader," Temirgaliev would recall.[6]

Still, deputies were too afraid to show up for a vote. Without a quorum, the session was cancelled.

By then, the Russian military had fanned out across the peninsula, in effect seizing it with a purpose to be determined later—but ostensibly to prevent precisely the kinds of bloody clashes that had nearly taken place in front of parliament. But those clashes played a role in etching out a new purpose for the Russians: helping Crimean pro-Russian political parties and their sympathizers seize parliament and coaxing deputies to show up and vote by guaranteeing them protection.

The man whom Defense Minister Shoigu had sent to facilitate this more delicate, political operation was Oleg Belaventsev, the general director of Slavyanka, a commercial defense sector service company controlled by the Defense Ministry.[7] While some sources have described him as overseeing the security of the peninsula during the operation, others say it was rather that Belaventsev acted as the go-between between local political movements and Moscow, between local self-defense militias and Russian troops, as each sought to work out a feasible plan for Crimea's status.[8] Security and politics went hand in hand, not least as pro-Russian deputies felt they could not vote the way they wanted, because they feared repercussions if and when the new pro-Western government in Kyiv retook control of the peninsula.[9]

Finally, between 2 a.m. and 4:30 a.m. on the morning of 27 February, some fifty commandos of Russia's newly created Special Operation Forces Command,[10] accompanied by local self-defense militias mustered by Belaventsev and Shoigu, quietly seized both the building of the supreme council and the council of ministers. According to Temirgaliev, the heavy lifting was done by professional, well-armed Russians; the local self-defense militias were as much as anything there simply to camouflage the commandos' presence. "These armed guys with blue eyes controlled [the building]. Everything was equipped for a lengthy siege."[11]

That morning, with the building secured, Temirgaliev made an announcement that local self-defense militias had taken control of the building, and that he would be giving interviews only to Russian journalists. When a group of Ukrainian journalists tried to get access, they were chased away with a stun grenade.

The less professional local (and Russian volunteer) self-defense militias played their secondary—albeit no less crucial role—outside the building. By Temirgaliev's estimates, they amounted to about 500 men. These "persuaders" reached out to the remaining deputies by phone or personal visits, insisting that they come and vote. Some of them even got visits from armed men in Cossack uniforms, traditional whips on their belts, who picked them up right at their offices and demanded they go straight to parliament. One of the men doing the persuading was none other than Igor Strelkov.

Konstantinov, Temirgaliev and Aksyonov managed to gather fifty-three deputies, out of the total of 100. They were made to hand over their phones to keep them from accidentally leaking images showing the faces of the Russian soldiers. Temirgaliev, who just a day before, when facing down crowds of 10,000 people, had believed he was doomed, suddenly felt like it was Christmas.

Their mission was a success, but that, it seemed, was the easy part.

Now that they had a quorum, two exceedingly problematic questions loomed on the agenda: whom to elect as prime minister, and how to formulate the question put to plebiscite for the referendum. Through Belaventsev, Konstantinov reportedly coordinated both questions with Moscow. But Moscow was not yet clear on what agenda it was willing and able to support—that, in turn, depended to a large extent on how confident the new Crimean government felt. Claim autonomy from Ukraine? Declare full-fledged independence? Join Russia? Or all of the above, in quick succession?

First, Sergei Aksyonov—about whom Moscow reportedly had qualms given his widely alleged ties to organized crime[12]—was elected prime minister. But the real question was what, exactly, people would be voting for.

Initially, Konstantinov and Aksyonov's pro-Russian constituencies settled for a vote to reinstate the Crimean constitution of 1992, the same one revoked by Kyiv. This granted the peninsula a degree of autonomy within Ukraine that, given the union's voluntary nature, meant de facto independence.

Yet this was clearly not enough. "During our sessions Crimeans started demanding to raise the question [about joining Russia]. I kept telling them—we are, I don't know how we are, but we are going there. I had thought that this would be one of those softer transitions towards statehood without violation of any international norms, when [after the referendum] we would sign an agreement with Russia," Konstantinov would recall.[13]

After the first session on 27 February, when a quorum had been reached and Aksyonov had been elected prime minister, it would take a whole week for a formulation specifically addressing unification with Russia to be agreed. Once again, the problem appeared to be with Moscow. The Kremlin seemed to oscillate between determination and timidity. In one phone call, Grach, head of the Crimean Communist Party, whom Moscow had initially backed as a leader for the peninsula, recalled being put through to Putin himself, who told him "we are on course for unification." But once Aksyonov was at the helm, according to Konstantinov and several government sources, it turned out that the Kremlin wasn't yet ready to give the green light. Meanwhile, on the Ukrainian mainland, the anti-Maidan movement that had initially been written off as groups of drunks bussed in and paid for by the Party of Regions started gaining momentum. On 1 March, local pro-Russian activists seized regional administration buildings in Donetsk and Kharkiv, amid similar attempted raids in Odessa and a dozen other cities. These protesters were calling for everything from federalization to joining Russia outright.

"As we understand it today, the decision wasn't an easy one," Konstantinov would recall. "When we first announced the referendum, it was clear that Russia would help, wouldn't abandon us. But what exactly did that mean, not abandon us? No one knew then that there would be an agreed formulation about unification."

Those in the Kremlin who supported Crimean unification were in a clear minority, according to multiple government sources with whom I later spoke. According to Konstantinov, the Kremlin was asking him to wait a while—to accept de facto independence while the international community calmed down and forgot about the issue. But pressed on by the momentum of the moment and his own newly empowered local constituents, Konstantinov refused, demanding from the Kremlin nothing short of Crimea being returned to Russia.

What, then, was holding Putin back? According to Russian reports, the president spent an hour and a half talking to Barack Obama on 1 March, trying, in vain, to get some kind of guarantee from the White House that the Crimean referendum would be recognized. Instead, Washington announced that it would seek to "isolate Russia further" for the actions it had already taken in Crimea.

Putin felt cornered. If he stuck to the soft transition of independence and then unification, a serious risk of armed conflict remained—after all, Ukraine had already struck down Crimea's autonomous constitution once. Who was to say a newly emboldened, pro-Western government wouldn't do so more forcefully? And if it did so, would the future of the agreement securing the Black Sea Fleet's basing on the peninsula be in doubt? Indeed, might those alarmist voices suggesting that sooner or later it would be NATO, not Russian ships docked at Sevastopol, be right?

But if Moscow moved immediately towards unification—vindicating Washington's assumptions that Russia intended to annex the peninsula all along—he was courting much harder sanctions.

Retreating now—with his forces having already secured Crimea—would gain nothing. He would be regarded as having lost.

There were no good options, only one bad one.

"We understood that Kyiv would never recognize our referendum with the initial formulation [about autonomy from Ukraine], and we needed to change it," Konstantinov would recall. "And the people wanted to join Russia. But we could not do this until we got the signal from Moscow."

On the night of 3–4 March, Crimean lawmakers, with near constant coordination with the Kremlin, began scrambling to come up with a formulation that would do the least damage. "It was a round the clock meeting," one government official recalled.

On 4 March 2014, in the middle of these feverish deliberations, Putin held a press conference in which he was asked if Crimea joining Russia was a possibility. "No, it is not under consideration," he said. "And I believe that only citizens living on this or that territory, under conditions of free expression of their will, under secure conditions, can and should determine their future."[14]

Ever undecided until the last minute, on the whole Putin's remark was a lie. But if ever a lie was so painstakingly molded to resemble the truth, it was this one. The People's Deputies of Crimea had not yet formally determined what they wanted to do, and so, technically, neither had Putin had to make a decision.

The following day, on 5 March, the wording of the question to be put forward to plebiscite was finally agreed: "Are you for the unification of Crimea with Russia as a subject of the Russian Federation?" The referendum was scheduled for 16 March, pushed forward from a later date given both Moscow's and Simferopol's fears of a Ukrainian and international backlash.

Up until the last minute, Konstantinov and local deputies feared the worst. Konstantinov remembered having a nightmare: "We come to Moscow, and we're told, 'you know, we're not going to accept Crimea into the Russian fold after all.'"[15]

II

On a 14 March flight from Moscow to Simferopol, two days before the Crimean referendum, a bearded, leather-decked biker got off the plane, surrounded by a coterie of similarly clad men. Fellow passengers instantly recognized Alexander Zaldostanov, the leader of the Night Wolves motorcycle club, and began throwing questions at him. He was there to "defend Crimea" from violent Ukrainian ultranationalists, he said, and if need be, he would bring more men.

Zaldostanov was so easily recognizable because his biker gang would often be seen accompanying Putin during much-publicized excursions on a Harley Davidson trike. The unlikely symbiosis had thrived for nearly a decade, as a quintessentially rebel group, one that aped American counterculture tradition during the end of Soviet Union, metamorphosed into a bottom-up pro-Kremlin movement. Zaldostanov, a dental surgeon who would take on the nom de guerre Khirurg, or Surgeon, founded the first Night Wolves motor club in 1989. But during the Putin years it underwent a fundamental conversion, tilting from rebellion to hosting Christmas parties for children and orphans, and by 2012 winning millions of rubles in government grants.[16] As one Night Wolf described the change, "if in Soviet times the Wolves appeared as a challenge to the regime, then by the beginning of the 2000s it was time to support [our] country." As Russia faced what the bikers felt was degenerate Western propaganda aimed at undermining the nation's status and values, "the club started existing for the sake of patriotic aims."[17]

On some level, this made perfect sense and even chimed with the club's initially purported nonconformity: one rebelled, in a sense, by taking the nonconformists under your wing, the orphans, the outcasts on the margins of society, the ones who had been deceived and betrayed by the West. The Night Wolves were in effect ahead of the curve, adopting what would become Putin's new agenda long before the Kremlin itself—from imperialist support of Russians in Crimea to upholding traditional family values.

In 2009, Zaldostanov was trying to organize a biker show in Sevastopol but ran into trouble with the Ukrainian Security Service, or SBU, who were understandably suspicious of a patriotic club that spoke about Crimea as a part of Russia. "We got a call," one of the Night Wolves recalled later, with a great deal of reverence. "Come on over to the Moscow bike center. So Khirurg went to the Sexton [Bike Center]. And Vladimir Vladimirovich Putin shows up. We didn't go to him, he came to us." Putin signed off on a bike route and gave Khirurg a Russian flag, expressing the hope that it would protect him on his journey, as though it was some kind of amulet, as though by his physical touch alone he was hallowing their mission. Using the Russian word for "roof," a piece of criminal slang that came to mean extra-legal protection, the Night Wolf concluded, "Putin was literally our *krysha*."[18]

This relationship went both ways. The biker group was bent on ingratiating itself with the Kremlin, but this provided a populist perk for the government, too. The following year, Putin, clad all in black, showed up at their bike show in Sevastopol, riding a Harley Davidson Lehman Trike, brandishing both the Russian and Ukrainian flags.[19] By then, co-option of radical nationalist and patriotic groups had become part of the Kremlin's playbook in managing potential opposition, but with a government-friendly group like the Night Wolves, which not only never criticized the government but went out of its way to seek its blessing, the Kremlin had no need to tame them. Instead, the symbiosis was based on something much simpler: it made Putin look cool. With friends like these, your enemies didn't matter.

Later that year, Zaldostanov addressed Putin at his yearly telethon, clearly angling for an agenda that Putin had, as of yet, no interest in endorsing:

> I had the honor of riding a bike with you. There were 50,000 people at the show. Once you said that a person who doesn't want unification with Ukraine doesn't have a heart, and a person who wants unification doesn't have any sense. Wouldn't you agree that the heart can replace reason sometimes, but reason can never replace the heart?

"Sasha," Putin said with endearing informality, knitting his brows, "that's pretty convoluted. I don't really understand the question." He explained that his own comment had been about the breakup of the Soviet Union, not about unification with Ukraine. In his characteristic style, Putin did not answer Zaldostanov's question. But he waxed lyrical, for two minutes, praising Zaldostanov's bike club and the show they organized in

Sevastopol for its discipline, professionalism and patriotism. "I take my hat off to you," the prime minister—for Putin was still prime minister at that time—said to the leader of the bike gang, who sat in the audience with his gold chain, his ponytail and his leather jacket, and beamed.[20]

Just as deftly as Putin evaded the question about Ukraine and Crimea—for there is no indication that he was harboring any such plans in 2010—he endorsed Zaldostanov the person. And, unwittingly, his cause, too, as Putin's heart did indeed seem to replace, for a moment, his reason.

Four years later, when Zaldostanov boarded that plane, he hadn't needed to be asked to do so.

* * *

Russia has a long history of leaning on volunteer fighters in its imperial adventures. In the 1870s, as the Russian Emperor Alexander II caved to popular sentiment and declared war on Turkey, thousands of volunteers, tacitly condoned by the tsar, flooded to the Balkans to fight alongside Slavic nationalists there. The most notorious were the Cossacks, a centuries-old ethnic and military community that had served the tsar since the eighteenth century. Fiercely independent, their symbiosis with the state ran so deep that the tsar held the honorary title of Supreme Ataman, or Cossack chief. In the mid-1800s, they were managed by the Main Administration of Irregular Forces—although the community was so powerful that it successfully resisted a number of state attempts to control and subordinate it, even gaining the privilege of avoiding, in some special cases, the compulsory military service to which most of the Russian population was subjected.[21] In 2012, Cossacks rose to the fore among other patriotic groups in an enthusiastic bid to help the Kremlin fight off foreign and "subversive" forces from within. From their headquarters adorned with the trinity of a mace, a portrait of Putin and an icon, a Cossack community in eastern Moscow launched several campaigns in 2012 and 2013 to "clean up" the streets and intimidate political protesters. City authorities embraced their zeal at first, but backed off when their activities grew just a bit too enthusiastic—such as when Cossack groups started storming galleries and exhibits of controversial artists and attacking feminist protesters.[22] Many Cossacks, of course, were among the first to flock to join the ranks of self-defense militias in Crimea and Donbas, but Ukrainian Cossacks fought on both sides of the conflict. Now, much as it had in 1870, when an emperor reluctant to engage in another costly war depended heavily on volunteers, the Kremlin exploited mass mobilization from below: many Russians, particularly those with nationalist views and who had served in the military, were outraged that, in the name of an avowedly pro-Western democratic revolution, the rights and the very lives of fellow Russians in Ukraine were under threat.

Two days after the 26 February clashes in Simferopol, Defense Minister Shoigu had 170 enthusiastic veterans of the wars in Chechnya and Afghanistan delivered to Crimea aboard an Ilyushin-76 military transport aircraft. Shoigu's longtime friend, the head of the Afghan Veterans' Union Franz Klintsevich, was an eager supporter of the cause and of Shoigu.[23] It was win-win—Shoigu got to recruit additional, deniable civilian muscle who needed little motivating to take part in a delicate task, while Klintsevich and his people were given a unique opportunity to demonstrate their patriotism and fight for a cause they believed in—all useful metrics in climbing the socio-economic ladder under Putin.

These were not only veterans, after all—there were also boxers, private security guards, bikers, members of patriotic groups and ex-convicts—in other words, many who were yearning for social, legal or spiritual redemption. The men, with Shoigu's aid and support, were housed in a Crimean sanitorium, where

Klintsevich reportedly instructed them on what they had to do. The situation was becoming critical, he said: foreign intelligence agents had infiltrated the peninsula, and militants from the ultraright Pravy Sektor movement were due to arrive any day. "This is a humanitarian act," he was filmed by one of the volunteers as saying, "to establish contacts, offer aid and support." The men were instructed to surveil movements of the Ukrainian army and, most importantly, instruct Crimeans about what to do in case tensions escalated. The volunteers were divided into groups of fifteen to twenty people who spread out into various Crimean towns and settlements. It was these volunteers who, acting under the guise of local residents—but also joined with them—took part in the seizure of Ukrainian military facilities.[24] In addition to the regular soldiers of the Russian armed forces, they were the other "little green men" that I would see at Perevalne.

Klintsevich never denied that veterans were fighting as volunteers in Ukraine—he described them as feeling it was their "inner duty" to do so. But while he lobbied, as a parliamentarian, for a foundation to aid Russian volunteer fighters in Ukraine, he maintained that neither the Ministry of Defense, nor the State Duma defense committee or any other government structures were in any way connected with "these people" and that the question was never discussed on the official level.[25] The following year, though, Russian journalists would uncover that Klintsevich and his veterans were on a long list of people for whom the Kremlin would organize three secret awards ceremonies in March to covertly laud them for their services in Crimea.[26]

Beyond such government-instigated ventures as Klintsevich's, more came in groups or as individuals, often without needing to be asked, to be welcomed and joined by friends, relatives and fellow activists on the peninsula. Zaldostanov was perhaps just one of the more colorful and easily recognized examples.

In Russia, party lines of "what the boss might like" were passed down by word of mouth in veterans' unions, government-funded sports clubs and private security organizations, while former Spetsnaz fighters, emboldened and jealous of their well-equipped, silent and polite former comrades on their television screens, jumped at the opportunity both to fight for a good cause and possibly get a cushy job afterwards.[27]

But in Crimea, as well as in Eastern Ukraine, the election of Aksyonov, and his and Konstantinov's success in securing Moscow's pledge to annex Crimea, caused a fundamental pivot among local activists and the Russian-speaking population at large. If up until then they had felt abandoned by both Kyiv and Moscow and saw no point in political organization oriented towards either,[28] then Russia's sudden decisiveness gave them permission to act. Crimeans and Eastern Ukrainians who had supported Russia passively until then suddenly had enormous additional incentives to do so actively.[29]

Putin, many residents and activists in Simferopol told me then, would be a "godsend."

"Everyone here deifies him," a pensioner who had, together with her community, given up on trying to get the local Ukrainian authorities to fix the roads, told me. From her vantage point, support from Putin and the far wealthier Russian nation would in turn allow them to get better government services. The way she described it, "we've never had a president who actually does something for his people."

But while the presence of Russian troops and volunteers in Crimea might have reassured some, it reinforced the fears of Balkan-level violence among other Russian-speakers and activists. Their argument was that if even Moscow, for years reluctant to interfere, had decided to send its best men, then surely it meant that Ukrainian ultranationalists were indeed out for blood. The argument was entirely circular, but nonetheless powerful for all that.

III

The bodies had been removed, but the smell of ash and smoldering human flesh lingered in the burnt-out shell of Odessa's trade union building. Flowers, bloodied clothes, the belongings of forty pro-Russian protesters who had burned alive, barricaded inside on 2 May as they tried to hide from pro-Maidan activists bombarding them with Molotov cocktails, comprised a makeshift memorial in the building, where grown men milling about wept out loud.

I had been wandering around the city for a day, putting off sitting down and trying to write about what had happened there, to untangle who started what without setting off the belligerence of either narrative—the Russian one about NATO-backed fascists murdering Russians and the Western one about Russian aggression killing Ukrainians. Nor did I want to hole myself up in the confines of my seedy hotel by the train station.

Here and there, roving gangs armed with makeshift weapons patrolled the streets, dressed in shabby clothes with no markings, making it impossible to tell the pro-Russian militia from the Ukrainian ultranationalist Pravy Sektor. As I would later see, except for the language they spoke, they were indistinguishable from each other in those early days. These were interspersed with ad hoc protest rallies—pro-Maidan and pro-Russian in equal measure, peopled by civilians, men, women and children—of the kind I would see in the streets of any Eastern European city. But while Odessa was perhaps the most culturally diverse, the pro-Russian rallies were the more populous.

It was at one of them that I met Anatoly Kuznetsov, a soft-spoken, deeply religious father of two small children who worked as an archivist at the local library. He, his wife and her friend had turned up to the demonstration, and when I chatted to them, they couldn't let me go—it was not safe, they said, look at those gangs, you don't even know which side they are on. Anatoly insisted that instead of my hotel, I spend the night at their flat—of course there would be enough space (meaning, in reality, that of the two rooms in their tiny, cluttered, dilapidated apartment, this family of four would feed me a three-course dinner and set aside one whole room for me).

We wandered the city, hopping from one rally to the next, dodging the gangs, and Anatoly spoke at length about how he felt about Russia, Ukraine and the looming war. His fatalism was both disarming and frustrating:

> I don't want to be called a separatist. We don't want to secede from Ukraine. But we hope Russia won't leave us in our sorrow. We are weak. We are not as aggressive as they are. The West just needs Ukraine to fight Russia with. Whoever is stronger gets to dictate. And Russia just needs Ukraine to be Ukraine.

For him, he said, "Russia is a guarantor of the Orthodox faith."

But Anatoly seemed to be exaggerating his own insignificance somewhat. He seemed to believe, like many at those rallies, that history was driven by dark forces beyond his control, by strategies devised behind closed doors by cynical men who spoke a foreign language. If he, a mere Russian archivist from Odessa, had to choose in whose hands he would place the fate of his family, he'd go with Putin, because the Kremlin, self-interested as it was, at least spoke his language.

He didn't seem to understand the powerful effect of his and thousands of other people's decision to simply turn up to protest rallies. The scale of the crowds that would then be splashed across television screens in Kyiv and Moscow affected the decisions of countless others—to pick up a gun and cross the border, to deploy a mechanized brigade or to launch an anti-terror operation.

In the course of two months, the popular rallies made up of Kuznetsov and thousands like him, whether average citizens or paid activists or Russian tourists, indirectly led to the influx of Russian armed men onto the mainland; to Ukraine's anti-terrorist response, and to the civil clashes that would spill over into lethal, animal brutality—like the one in which a building where pro-Russian demonstrators took refuge had been set on fire.

* * *

On 3 March, while legislators in Simferopol were still feverishly deliberating with Moscow about what kind of referendum to hold and whether Russia would accept Crimea, pro-Russian protesters in Odessa, copying the tactics of pro-EU Maidan demonstrators in Kyiv and Western Ukrainian cities, tried to storm the regional parliamentary building, demanding a referendum that would grant them greater autonomy. They were led by Anton Davidchenko, the leader of People's Alternative, a pro-Russian movement. Two days earlier, Moscow had moved to rush a bill through the upper house of its parliament, the Federation Council, authorizing the deployment of troops to Ukraine if necessary. The move buoyed pro-Russian groups across Eastern Ukraine and encouraged the remnants of Yanukovych's Party of Regions to rally. Much as in other cities, Odessan activists and protesters led by Davidchenko held a "people's vote" on Kulikovo Polye, a central square in front of the local trade union building. There, Davidchenko issued a series of demands on federalization to the new government in Kyiv. His supporters raised the Russian flag, and some shouted "Novorossiya," or New Russia, the name once given to the regions north of the Black Sea under the Russian Empire, and what pro-Russian separatists christened their new project. While Davidchenko was careful to avoid calls to join Russia outright, his demands were clearly an ultimatum: "If our demands are not met, then on 9 March we will gather again and act differently."[30]

Just that day in Donetsk, former businessman and longtime activist Pavel Gubarev stormed and seized the headquarters of the regional administration. Two days earlier, at a street rally in the town's central Lenin Square, demonstrators had held an ad hoc "election" choosing Gubarev as the "people's governor." He would be arrested less than a week later by the SBU, but in that time, Gubarev pushed for a referendum to join Russia.[31]

Such protests and seizures of government buildings would rip through eleven cities in the southeast of Ukraine in the early days of March. Loosely organized Russian-leaning groups, as well as locals who felt betrayed by the central authorities in Kyiv, suddenly gained a new momentum across Eastern Ukraine. From December until then, the Party of Regions had been mustering counter-protests against the Euromaidan, paying demonstrators and organizing the rallies. They were joined, of course, by Russian volunteers. Dismissed as "tourists," these were widely suspected of being agents of Moscow,[32] but given the chaos of what was happening in Simferopol at the time, and the manner in which Russian volunteers flocked to the peninsula, there is little evidence suggesting these "tourists" were in any way centrally coordinated. Nor did they play any decisive role at the time.[33]

The mass uprisings sprouting with new fervor in early March were inspired largely by the events in Crimea and the hope of Russian support, encouraged by Moscow's threats to deploy troops. But decisions taken by the new government in Kyiv, itself provoked by Moscow's belligerent rhetoric and its shadow invasion of Crimea, fueled distrust, animosity and separatism in the East. The first move had come on 23 February, right after Yanukovych fled Kyiv: the Rada, Ukraine's parliament, repealed a law that gave the Russian language, as well as other minority languages, official regional status. Protests against that move across the East caused acting President Oleksandr Turchynov to veto the decision, but this still left the status of the law in limbo. The damage had been done: the issue of Russian-language rights now became so deeply enmeshed with separatism in the public imagination both in East and West such that new laws to accommodate the two camps merely ended up alienating both.[34]

The day after that, Ukraine's Interior Ministry disbanded the Berkut riot police who had returned to their home towns after their unsuccessful attempts to suppress the Euromaidan protests in Kyiv. As military scholar Michael Kofman argues, had Kyiv wanted to help the Russian cause, it could hardly have done better. By passing the language laws, doing nothing to muzzle Pravy Sektor and cutting loose Berkut, the new Ukrainian government had provided Russia with potent, fresh fodder for its propaganda campaign, as well as hundreds of disgruntled trained streetfighters, ready to fight the new regime that had sacked them.[35] In April, of the self-defense militias that ended up storming the SBU building in Luhansk, at least forty-two were former Berkut officers from other regions.[36]

If Gubarev was pushing for Donetsk to join Russia, then elsewhere in the regions locals and activists simply saw the new authorities in Kyiv as a hostile force that was at best refusing to take their interests into account, demonstratively demonizing them at worst. Local fringe activists and the remnants of the Party of Regions took to the streets demanding referenda on autonomy and federalization, but they didn't display the kind of uniform stance on joining Russia characteristic of Crimea. More importantly, they were joined by ordinary residents who shared no specific political agenda but who were simply afraid and distrustful of the new authorities in Kyiv and welcomed politicians who at least spoke their language.

On 10 March in neighboring Luhansk, about 500 pro-Maidan activists gathered in the city square. A counter-protest numbered about 5,000. Led by two local parliamentarians, Alexander Kharitonov and Arsen Klinchayev, the latter group stormed the administration building and broke into the office of the governor, Mikhail Bolotskikh. But when they finally got him to come out and address the people, it turned out no one wanted to listen to him.

They wanted to be heard themselves.

"When the Russian Spring started happening, people in Luhansk didn't want to join Russia, not even close," Klinchayev told me, years later:

> They just didn't agree with the events in Kyiv. People were looking at the TV and they had never been to Kyiv before and didn't want it to come to them. People didn't understand why taking a regional government building in Lviv was good but in Luhansk, it was a crime.

The mood in the streets then could hardly be described as planned or orchestrated.

"This has been going on for several days now. Our government [the new government in Kyiv] doesn't want to talk to us," Nina Gorbunova, a protester in front of the building, said:

> But today, I think they'll hear us, and see the people that want some kind of order in the country. Look at what's happening in Kyiv—and they call them patriots! Well if they're patriots, what does that make us? Ukrainians?! Who lives on this land?! Who was born here?!

Seeing her companion on camera, another protester rejoined,

> What's really upsetting is that no one hears us, no one takes into account the will of the people here in southeastern Ukraine. When Western Ukraine was tearing down monuments, throwing its mayors out, it was called the will of the people. Well, we want peace and order, too. And in our administrations, we want people whom we elected ourselves.[37]

* * *

Of the eleven cities where pro-Russian protesters tried to take government buildings, they succeeded in only two. The separatist movement did not take hold in Odessa. The very day Davidchenko tried to issue his ultimata, fellow deputies literally dragged him from the podium where he was ranting, emotionally, about Kyiv not wanting to listen to them, during a regional council session. They feared that his pro-Russian platform and aggressive rhetoric would bring the same violence and division to Odessa that was sweeping other regions.

That sentiment of being ignored and maligned by Kyiv remained strong among demonstrators in Odessa. Language laws, however benign, were perceived as yet another muzzle on people who saw themselves as more passive than they actually were. Understating their own agency, like Anatoly Kuznetsov, they saw the events in Kyiv, embellished by Russian propaganda, as far more threatening than they really were. And while they didn't want division and interference, they also craved protection, for someone strong to take their side.

Back in Odessa, the port town's particular diversity heightened the precarity. Kuznetsov and many regular civilians cherished that diversity and were also wary of violent clashes. Further east, the pro-Western Maidan movement hadn't really taken root, but in Odessa, while not as robust as in Western Ukrainian cities, pro-Maidan rallies were sizeable and initially more vocal than the pro-Russian rallies. The local authorities had at first steeled themselves in January against pro-Maidan demonstrators seeking to seize government buildings. But once the Yanukovych regime collapsed in February, tensions grew as the pro-Russian camp felt its increasing disenfranchisement. Both camps, sensing the heightened stakes, began attracting more radical, and often more violent participants. A number of Russian nationalist groups like Odesskaya Druzhina, supported by Kremlin aide Sergei Glazyev and lawmaker Konstantin Zatulin,[38] joined rallies organized by the more mainstream pro-Russian movements like Davidchenko's, further antagonizing the pro-Maidan camp.[39]

By 2 May, with battles already raging further east, the most radical segments in both of Odessa's camps were out for blood.

In the afternoon, several football clubs—traditionally nationalist and devoted to Ukrainian unity—gathered in central Odessa, drawing about 2,000 demonstrators. But it was no peaceful rally—participants came armed with axes, metal sticks, bats and even guns. Just across the street, ready to counter what they believed would be a violent attack, about 300 pro-Russian demonstrators—many from Odesskaya Druzhina—gathered in a counter-protest, equally armed.[40]

"People came armed with anything they could get their hands on. Some had pressure bombs with dried corn," Sergei, a pro-Maidan activist who took part in the rally, told me, referring to homemade grenades packed with desiccated kernels as makeshift shrapnel. "They were out to kill, on both sides."

Six people ended up dead in the violence that inevitably broke out; when the outnumbered pro-Russians decided to set up a tent camp on Kulikovo Polye in front of the trade union building, the pro-unity protesters burned it down. In the ensuing battle of Molotov cocktails, the pro-Russians barricaded themselves in the trade union building, which quickly caught fire. Forty more people would die inside—either burned alive, or jumping to their deaths.[41]

Supporters of the pro-Russian cause who had not participated in the violent clashes, like Anatoly Kuznetsov, looked on at these events in horror, convinced now that the enemy was indeed bent on murdering Russians, and that they had no other protector to turn to but the Kremlin.

Pyotr Volkov was a friend of Vyacheslav Markin, a local lawmaker who burned to death in the Odessa trade union building. At the time, he told me that "maybe we should have spoken out louder about what the people wanted, but we could not be heard … Maybe his death will unify and awaken people." Volkov, like many of the pro-Russians I spoke to in those days in Odessa, didn't want to separate from Ukraine or join Russia. It was just that, heartened by the example they saw in Crimea, they too wanted to secure greater autonomy from a new government that they feared didn't have their best interests at heart and, indeed, was already labeling them wholesale as separatists. "I think we can decide on our own fate. But for that to happen, the people have to be heard. We have to learn to listen to people with different opinions. But we don't need help from America or Russia."

But by the time Volkov was saying those words, by the time protesters had burned alive or jumped to their deaths from the windows of the trade union building, it was too late. Pro-Maidan activists were fighting pro-Russian protesters in the streets of Odessa, and a war was already raging in nearby Donetsk and Luhansk regions, where local militants, mixed with Russian volunteer militias, had seized government buildings, stolen weapons from abandoned depots[42] and declared a people's republic.

But it had started with mass rallies, where people who felt silent or silenced turned up to fill city squares, and whose voices, in turn, were amplified in Kyiv and Moscow. Both cities heard the voices, and so did ordinary Russians and the friends of the Kremlin on whom Putin's government had relied in Crimea.

In Russia, the events in Ukraine, embellished and blasted from TV screens, galvanized deep-seated, often suppressed popular nationalist sentiments, of fighting against what they saw as Western encroachment into Russia's sphere of interest, and the need to stand up for the rights of Russian-speakers abroad.

Putin himself may not have known in early March the full role that these newly emerged friends of the Kremlin—veterans like Klintsevich, patriotic clubs like Zaldostanov's—would play. Perhaps at the time the Kremlin was delighted by the chance to lean on the popular fervor, bottom-up strategizing and private capital that was thrown behind these causes. Once the Crimea operation was successfully completed, once the referendum was concluded and the peninsula was formally brought into Russia's fold, it seemed that there would be no need for these men any-more. The groups of veteran muscle and advisors were disbanded, the militias told to go home. But what the Kremlin doesn't seemed to have banked on was that by bringing these men to Crimea in the first place, riding the wave of patriotic sentiment and channeling it to do its bidding, it had opened a tap. These Russian volunteers delighted in dressing up and pretending to be little green men, the silent, efficient soldiers who themselves had pretended to be volunteer militias. They had also come to believe that they were indispensable. Little green men they were not, though. There is a difference between friends and soldiers: the Kremlin could recall soldiers and tell them to go home, but friends have agency. The Kremlin wouldn't, or couldn't, close the tap it had opened.

4

FRIENDS OF THE KREMLIN

We were born to make Kafka come true.

Popular pun on the "Aviator's March," in which the original
skazka, or fairytale, is replaced with Kafka.

A tent, a small stage, a clear cashbox and a 5-ton truck. On a sunny July day in Moscow, a few hundred people were fundraising. Among the men loading boxes of food, clothes and military equipment into the truck was Sergei Zakharov, a resident of a town in Donbas called Kramatorsk, which local and Russian armed separatists seized and made one of the strongholds of their insurgency. Where were the goods destined for?

"Ordinary people will get this aid," he told me proudly. "But of course, some of it will go to the militiamen." The cash box, too, was filling up fast, a testament to the grassroots efforts and the civic enthusiasm of those who attended the gathering. Among the groups that organized the fundraiser was one called the Foundation for Aid to Novorossiya and Donbas, and just that month it had raised about $177,000.

This was 2014, and Russian civil society, for decades stifled by the Kremlin, was spreading its wings and flexing its muscles—in

79

this case, it was just doing so in a decidedly imperialist manner. The aid in those boxes wasn't just humanitarian—a fact the foundation was anything but coy about. Flyers and spokespeople proudly announced that they'd managed to gather gear including army boots, optical sights for AK-47s, night vision glasses and camouflage. Amid a war the Russian government didn't seem to want to wage, volunteers took matters into their own hands and at least didn't deny the obvious. A different kind of Russian civil society was indeed being born.

In the summer of 2014, Western journalists and analysts denied the grassroots nature of these rallies. Surely, the Kremlin was simply organizing them and using them as a cover for its military involvement, propping them up so that it could create the illusion of a volunteer movement?

This was true, but only in part. The Kremlin certainly demonstrated the usual double standards when dealing with this particular strand of Russia's civil society. Throughout his tenure, but particularly since the anti-Kremlin demonstrations of 2012, Putin's tolerance for those demonstrating against corruption and government lies diminished, while his tolerance for those demonstrating in support of an imperialist agenda grew. Anti-corruption protesters were thrown in jail, harassed, beaten and even poisoned on occasion, while NGOs critical of the government were labeled "foreign agents" and had their funding cut off. In fact, the Bolotnaya protests of 2011–12 saw liberals, nationalists, communists, monarchists and imperialists marching side by side. To split the opposition—and also because he had become convinced that the Americans were encouraging protests as part of a plot against him—Putin cracked down largely on the liberals and the communists but eased the pressure on the nationalists and imperialists, or any protest, for that matter, that shared his growing resentment with the West. After the annexation of Crimea, pro-separatist rallies were not just tolerated but welcomed.

That said, these pro-separatist movements were no illusion. They were being propped up, of course—just not so much by the Kremlin as by the private and the right-wing sector of civil society. Over the previous two decades, a diverse network of businessmen, think tanks and independent political activists had coalesced around a singular, imperialist agenda. Calling themselves proponents of the Russian cause, many of them had hitherto been disappointed by what they saw as the Kremlin's neglect of what in their eyes were paramount national interests. But now that the Kremlin had decided that it had been ultimately abandoned and betrayed by the West, it found a new group of friends. These new friends were the impetus for what would become Russia's shadow invasion of Donbas.

I

In January 2014, just as the Yanukovych regime was imploding, a deeply religious businessman named Konstantin Malofeyev brought to Ukraine the Gifts of the Magi, an Orthodox relic that he had got permission to transport from Greece. During his trip, an influential member of his entourage, the parliamentarian and founder of the patriotic veterans' organization Boyevoye Bratstvo, or "Combat Brotherhood," Dmitry Sablin, himself a native of Donbas, secured Malofeyev a special meeting with Crimea's then deputy prime minister, Rustam Temirgaliev. Temirgaliev, who had pro-Russian sympathies but was generally a pragmatic politician, was hesitant at first, but Sablin convinced him. Come meet us at the airport, Sablin told him, "I understand that people have different attitudes towards Orthodox values, but you will feel a certain energy."[1]

As Temirgaliev would recall later, Malofeyev and particularly the people he brought with him—apart from Sablin, there were a number of bearded men whose names he would not disclose but whom he described as senior clerics in the Russian Orthodox

Church—were very keen to meet Crimea's prime minister, Anatoly Mogilev. But Mogilev, more cautious about the political mood in Kyiv, had declined, and they met instead with Temirgaliev and Konstantinov, Crimea's parliamentary chairman. They wanted

> to talk about the events in Kyiv. At that moment, some key decisions [he was referring here to the idea of Crimea uniting with Russia] were in the air, but were never spoken of directly. Various theoretical possibilities were discussed. But I'll be honest, it was on that day when I realized that the likelihood of these events which unfolded later is very high. What if, I asked Malofeyev and Sablin, Kyiv descends into total chaos? What are we to do? They answered, "Then you will need to raise the standard of an independent or, at the least, an absolutely autonomous Crimea."

Temirgaliev, like many standing officials in Russia, including the defense minister, thought the idea was unfeasible. "There are 20,000 Ukrainian military personnel in Crimea who will be given orders [by new authorities in Kyiv]. But [Malofeyev and Sablin] said that the heads of military units needed to be approached and asked, 'Are you more Crimean or are you subordinate to Kyiv?'"

Temirgaliev knew and trusted Sablin, and shared his views. Sablin, as a mere parliamentarian, couldn't have been speaking on behalf of Moscow, and neither Malofeyev nor the rest of the people in the entourage held any official government positions. Looking back, Temirgaliev felt that the whole Crimea operation was organized extremely well, but he admits that neither he nor Sablin, a Russian lawmaker, understood exactly where the impetus came from, and who, if anyone, had sent Malofeyev and his religious team to Crimea.

Perhaps this was because, for Malofeyev and his team, at least, they were on a mission from God. Of sorts.

* * *

In 2007, Malofeyev, who saw the Russian Orthodox Church as part and parcel of Russia's geopolitical standing and its mission for the world, had founded the St Basil Charitable Foundation. A charity that initially promoted traditional family values domestically, by 2012 its budget had swollen to $40 million, and it began operating outside the country's borders, including establishing ties with the Russian Orthodox Church abroad.[2] The tour of the Gifts of the Magi was one of the foundation's crowning achievements, but for Malofeyev it was just the start of something bigger, something into which he would invest not just his money but a good deal of his spirit too. By his own account, it was there, in Crimea, that Malofeyev met the war reenactor and the former FSB officer Igor Girkin, who called himself Strelkov, although some other evidence, including Girkin's own accounts, suggests that they knew each other before. According to Malofeyev, one of his firm's PR specialists, Alexander Borodai— the man who would be spotted in Crimea before going on to become leader of the DPR—introduced him to Girkin.

"For a long time, Borodai was my consultant," he said in an interview, "and I believed him to be a brave and honorable man. Maybe that's where the conspiracy theory that I oversee and control something emerged ..."[3]

Borodai's friendship with Malofeyev also explains how he and Girkin, his other likeminded, longtime friend, would wind up weeks later in Crimea.

Malofeyev said he befriended Girkin in January in Kyiv:

There was a very unstable situation in Ukraine. There was no police, it was all focused on the Maidan [demonstrations], which were taking place less than a kilometer from the Kyiv-Pechersk Lavra, where the relics were being kept. To protect them we drew a lot of people. Girkin was in charge of security for the Gifts in Kyiv. Then he went with us to Crimea.[4]

These weren't just accidental friends, however—they were true believers in a singular cause. Malofeyev, Russian journalists revealed, would go on to sponsor a number of fundraising rallies like the one I had attended and funded several volunteer organizations that gathered aid for Novorossiya fighters.[5] He himself admitted that his charitable foundation signed an official agreement with Borodai when he was "prime minister" of the DPR—thus implicitly recognizing the de facto statelet, something that even the Kremlin would refuse to do for many years—to provide humanitarian aid.[6] Borodai all but explicitly named Malofeyev as the source of the money that he was giving Strelkov for his operations.

Conventional wisdom holds that ideas, inspiration and orders were passed down to the likes of Malofeyev by the Kremlin with the aim of getting private citizens to do the dirty work that the government could then deny. But a closer look at Malofeyev's activities and connections shows that the vector also went in the opposite direction—from the bottom up.

In the early days of February 2014, soon after the meetings in Crimea, the businessman, together with several likeminded (but unnamed) associates, was alleged to have prepared a report containing his vision for annexing Crimea and several eastern regions of Ukraine and had it delivered to the Kremlin.[7]

In it, Malofeyev and the other authors posited that the European Union was preparing for the disintegration of Ukraine and planning to "absorb" the entire country "element by element," or region by region. To prevent this from happening, Russia must preempt their efforts. Acting within "legal means," Russia must "play up the centrifugal tendencies of various [Ukrainian] regions, with the aim, in one form or another, to ... annex its eastern regions to Russia." The report detailed efforts to stir up pro-Russian groups in Crimea and Kharkiv, and continue doing the same elsewhere in Eastern Ukraine—all of which coincided spectacularly with what appeared to have had happened after it was penned.[8]

The report was leaked in February 2015, a year after the events it described, by the oppositionist investigative newspaper *Novaya Gazeta*. Its editor, Dmitry Muratov, said the paper got its hands on a copy of the report and verified its authenticity independently. Malofeyev claimed it was nothing to do with him, while the Kremlin, in its usual fashion, declined to deny or confirm.

Malofeyev may have denied penning the report, but a birthday panegyric from the prominent nationalist ideologue Alexander Dugin, aired by Malofeyev's own television channel, Tsargrad, celebrated its spirit: "Malofeyev was the only one who began to actively and consistently, vividly and decisively advocate for the Russian Spring. In word, deed and in all possible and sometimes even impossible ways."[9]

Starting in February 2014, "Russian Spring" became the blanket term for the pro-Russian uprisings in Eastern Ukraine and in particular for the domestic wave of volunteers. As a riff on the Prague Spring, or the Arab Spring, it was coined by another prominent Russian nationalist ideologue, Yegor Kholmogorov. It was meant to signify the awakening of Russian national identity—especially the identity of those Russians who lived on the other side of the border with Ukraine.[10]

Thus, while Malofeyev may have denied the authenticity of the report attributed to him, his own television channel publicly lauded him for supporting pro-Russian uprisings in "word, deed, and in all possible and sometimes even impossible ways."

But one of the surprising aspects about Malofeyev's alleged report is the seeming ease with which it was brought to the Presidential Administration some time in February. This institution, arguably the central one in Putin's personalistic government, is constantly barraged with appeals, initiatives, proposals and demands, most of which never get more than the most cursory glance. That Malofeyev's report made it onto the desks of key officials suggests an existing connection, and one that the Kremlin seemed equally eager to exploit. Indeed, the two—for great minds think alike—seemed to have met each other half way.

It is widely believed—though not explicitly documented—that Malofeyev was somehow roped into financing a covert Kremlin project in order that the state could cut costs and enhance deniability. A businessman known for his ruthlessness, Malofeyev was alleged to be at the center of a fraud case, with half a billion dollars in debt written off in exchange for his supporting a patriotic project. Malofeyev, needless to say, has denied this.[11]

This somewhat cynical interpretation is not necessarily untrue, but it misses another, equally important dimension. Malofeyev was not just doing what the Kremlin wanted but also what he believed in. This was not a man who needed to be forced into supporting the "Crimean project."

One of Malofeyev's formative experiences was defending the Russian White House, the seat of parliament, when Boris Yeltsin used military force to dissolve it in 1993. The president's constitutional standoff with the Congress of People's Deputies had been brewing for months. His own vice president, Alexander Rutskoi, opposed his widely unpopular privatization reforms, as did a majority of his parliament. The deputies also opposed the terms of the Belovezha Accords—the document that formally ended the Soviet Union. But what it ultimately came down to was presidential power over democracy: parliamentarians wanted to put a curb on the temporary powers they had granted Yeltsin, not least rule by decree, while Yeltsin wanted to keep them in order to push through his reforms and ensure that the breakup of the Soviet Union was not contested.

Malofeyev, then working as an aide to a parliamentarian, heard on the news that somebody in the basement was handing out weapons to anyone who wanted to defend the White House.

"And we were all joyful, ran down to the basement, thinking we'd get weapons, only to find a sleepy policeman who [chased us away]."

Yeltsin's tanks shelled the building, and after six days of conflict in which 147 people were killed, this professed democrat got his way. The Congress of People's Deputies was dissolved and replaced with a new, weaker parliament, the constitution was rewritten retrospectively to make what Yeltsin did legal, and arguably Russia's budding democracy began to wither before it had had a chance to take root. Malofeyev, who was in the building at the time, would later recall that this was when he lost his faith in humanity—certainly in politics:

> Everything that Yeltsin was doing was illegal ... When I saw all those bodies in the White House ... I realized that this was such a cynical and terrible story that I definitely didn't want to have anything to do with it ever again. After finishing studies in constitutional law, I left politics and went into business.[12]

But the disillusionment—shared by many of those who had supported the parliament in its standoff with Yeltsin in 1993—never left him. He turned not just to a high-level banking career but also to God, as part and parcel of a redemptive quest.[13] Since his student years at Moscow State University, Malofeyev worshipped at the Church of St Tatiana, with a congregation consisting of students, professors and the Moscow intelligentsia. It is likely that in those circles he met and became close to Metropolitan Tikhon Shevkunov. Father Tikhon became widely popular for two books—*Lessons of Byzantium: Death of an Empire*, which was made into a TV film in 2008, and *Everyday Saints* from 2011. But it was another connection that lent Shevkunov a particular mystery and power: when the latter book was released, rumors began to swirl that Father Tikhon had met the future president, Vladimir Putin, in 1999, and gone on to become his personal confessor. Both Father Tikhon and the presidential spokesperson have neither confirmed nor denied this, referring to it obliquely.[14] But whatever the exact nature of his relationship with Putin, that undoubted closeness, and Father Tikhon's popularity, were symptomatic of the ideological wave that swept the country from around 2012. It was built around the belief in the spiritual roots of the Russian people that transcended borders, in the natural, holy symphony of Church and State, and perhaps even in the Byzantine tradition, which elevated the emperor as the vicar of Christ on earth. (Although this "caesaropapism" was officially and vehemently looked down upon in Russian political culture, despite the parallels.)

It seems that Malofeyev, too, became swept up by some of these beliefs. For an investment fund manager moving hundreds of millions of dollars, an ideology that managed to reconcile power, faith and money, to demonstrate how they can be channeled towards an overarching spiritual destiny, must have proven a compelling narrative as to how to do something profound with his life. "Both poverty and wealth come from God," he said in a 2013 interview.[15] Whether it was Shevkunov who turned on and tuned in Malofeyev to caesaropapism or whether their acquaintance naturally flowed from that spiritual and ideological alignment is hard to say, but friends and co-workers alleged in 2012 that Father Tikhon had become a mentor for Malofeyev long before the events of Donbas.[16] Malofeyev and Shevkunov have both denied this closeness, but that they knew each other well is undisputed. Shevkunov has admitted that on several occasions Malofeyev's St Basil Fund (of which Shevkunov is a trustee) financed his Sretensky seminary,[17] and the two would repeatedly speak at the same conferences, with names like "Moscow: The Third Rome," organized by Malofeyev's charity.[18]

Alongside his spiritual path, Malofeyev embarked on a banking career in mergers and acquisitions. In 2004, he decided to invest and obtain a stake in a friend's baby formula company,

Nutritek. The following year, he founded the private equity firm Marshall Capital Partners. Baby food is a curious choice, one almost exuding moral piety in a man who managed to combine such virtuous endeavors with questionable machinations. It was through a series of ruthless maneuvers—which would bring down the law on him—that he obtained a loan destined for building baby food factories. Instead, he apparently used that loan to buy up a stake in the telecoms sector.[19]

It was probably Tikhon Shevkunov who introduced Malofeyev to Igor Shchyogolev, a journalist turned presidential aide. After Shchyogolev became minister of communications in 2008, Malofeyev went on to invest nearly $1 billion in the telecommunications giant Rostelecom. He became so influential in the sector that he was known as the shadow "deputy telecoms minister."[20] It was likely through those dealings that Malofeyev became acquainted with Sergei Ivanov Jr, the deputy chairman of Gazprombank, a former stakeholder in Rostelecom. There was nothing surprising in the fluid conflation of Russian business and politics, but what was significant was that his father was Sergei Ivanov Sr, the former KGB officer and close Putin ally who would go on to be head of the Presidential Administration.[21]

For all of Malofeyev's connections, his success as a businessman was questionable. Nutritek went bankrupt, while the bank that offered the loan—VTB—filed a complaint against Malofeyev with a London court, and then in 2011 Malofeyev's Marshall Capital was raided in connection with a criminal case launched by Russian authorities. But none of this meant that his star couldn't continue rising in other ways.

II

Russian investigative journalists have widely alleged, though never documented or confirmed, that it was Sergei Ivanov Sr who asked Malofeyev to assist the government in securing Crimea and even, perhaps, parts of Donbas.[22] If this is true, it was unlikely to be a relationship in which a statesman simply gave direct orders to carry out a mission in exchange for the Kremlin forgiving Malofeyev's debt and shady business dealings.

Instead, based on what we know about Malofeyev, Ivanov and the various figures in between, we can reconstruct how their "public–private partnership" likely took shape. Rather than being tasked with a mission, Malofeyev appears to have been shopping an idea around—while the Kremlin was buying.

Aside from the general ideological zeitgeist uniting patriots, fervent Christians and former soldiers, the key link that seems to have brought the businessman and the Kremlin together was Sergei Ivanov.

The hawkish former defense minister is not known as a particularly pious man. But even if not on full display, a convergence of faith and statism seems to have played a major part in his political career. As head of the Presidential Administration since 2011, he presided over one of the most dramatic alliances between the Kremlin and the Russian Orthodox Church in recent history. In 2012, at the height of the trial of Pussy Riot—three artists who staged a punk rock performance on the altar of Christ the Savior Cathedral and prayed to the Virgin Mary to rid the country of Putin—Ivanov said the state would use "the full force of the law" to defend the feelings of the faithful, while pointing to the key role of cooperation between state and church in maintaining the peace in Russia.[23] Given that the prosecutors appear to have been inclined to treat the punk musicians relatively leniently until the Kremlin backed an outraged Patriarch Kirill, this was a clear statement that the state would back the church, so long as the church supported the state. Ivanov's own religious feelings, however, were somewhat more guarded: "A truly faithful man," he said in a speech given to university students in 2016, "does not advertise his confession. I don't like ostentatiousness."[24]

But more defining of Ivanov's political career seems to have been a disappointment: in 2008, he had been passed over in favor of the more liberal Dmitry Medvedev as Putin's anointed presidential successor. This drama of vanities ensured that the snubbed Ivanov—though rewarded for his troubles with an influential Kremlin post—sought to redeem his track record. "Malofeyev was ideologically driven" to invest in Novorossiya after Crimea, one Kremlin insider put it, "but Ivanov just wanted to curry favor."[25]

There are two links connecting Malofeyev with Ivanov. One is business, the other is religion. In 2010, Malofeyev, as mentioned, had begun buying stock in Rostelecom, in part through Gazprombank, whose deputy chair was Sergei Ivanov Jr. At the time, his father was the deputy prime minister in charge of telecommunications. There was even some speculation that Malofeyev's Marshall Capital and Gazprombank were buying up Rostelecom stock on behalf of Sergei Ivanov Sr, but his son strongly denied this.[26]

But as Malofeyev's path has demonstrated, ideology is no foe to careerism, and in this light, the second, religious link, proved all the more potent. Both Ivanov and Malofeyev were acquaintances of Father Tikhon (Shevkunov), the alleged spiritual advisor to Putin himself, and sources have told reporters a shared intellectual interest in religion drew them together.[27]

If Malofeyev was driven by spiritualism, then Ivanov's support of the annexation of Crimea seems to have come from a consistent adherence to statism. A veteran of the KGB like Putin, and a hawkish former minister of defense, Ivanov's calculus on Crimea seems to have aligned with that of Security Council secretary—and former KGB officer—Nikolai Patrushev. Ivanov, however, was more guarded and pragmatic in his public statements—rather than attributing snubs against Russia to a premeditated NATO plot, as Patrushev often did, he tended instead to defend Russian actions by saying it was only doing what other Western countries did.[28] But behind the scenes, he was growing more outspoken: the United States had created a coalition against Russia and had deceived it, but even if they tried to destroy it, Russia wouldn't give up Crimea in a hundred years, several Russian insiders described Ivanov as saying passionately at an expert forum in October 2014.[29]

But in January 2014, and more so in February, it was clear that in addition to the military and security assets deployed to secure Crimea, Kremlin officials and ministers were enlisting their friends voluntarily to support a cause that was growing spectacularly popular in business circles, among right-wing and religious intellectuals, and even the working class. Such was the case with the Afghan veterans brought to Crimea by Shoigu's friend Klintsevich, but help would come from wealthier sources, too. The Russian government seemed too timid to directly muster the financial and administrative means for the new authorities in Crimea. But a whole assortment of government-connected charitable organizations, including Malofeyev's, rose to the occasion.[30]

Were these direct orders? Was coercion applied? Likely not. As early as 2012, Ivanov, then acting as presidential chief of staff, was already involved in Malofeyev's business ventures. On at least one occasion, he moved to protect Malofeyev's interests in his official capacity, writing to the cabinet to insist that a key colleague of his keep his job.[31] This would suggest that Ivanov was already on Malofeyev's side long before the events of 2014 were set in motion.

Instead, the most plausible scenario is a series of conversations among likeminded people: between a businessman eager to invest his resources in a grand mission, and a government official just as eager to make it happen, even if only to present Putin with a fait accompli. Making Malofeyev's legal problems go away may simply have been a bonus—though not the driver—of the tacit agreement. In other words, this was at least in part a bottom-up initiative, as if the very chain of command were inverted: requests for permission went up to the Kremlin for its approval and blessing, sometimes after the fact, instead of orders and instructions being passed down to flunkies to execute. Indeed, this went all the way up and down the hierarchy. "Strelkov pitched the idea of Novorossiya to Malofeyev, and Malofeyev took it to Ivanov," a former associate of Surkov's told me.[32]

But if Malofeyev had the money and the willing accomplices to execute his vision, his voice alone wouldn't have been enough to sway Kremlin policy. For that, he needed friends—backers of the cause who could support it not with money, but with righteousness and faith, the kind of faith that becomes infectious when it reaches critical mass, infectious enough to sway the Kremlin.

III

On 28 February 2014, a conversation took place that was intercepted and later leaked by the Ukrainian Security Service. Two men discussed dire financial straits. One was Sergei Glazyev, a Kremlin aide whose imperialist rhetoric had increasingly been coming into vogue. The other was Konstantin Zatulin, a parliamentarian and the head of a think tank called the Institute for Commonwealth of Independent States, who had dedicated his entire career to supporting ethnic Russian groups abroad:

> "I want to say, on other regions ... We financed Kharkiv, financed Odessa. I've put the brakes on requests from other regions for now because I haven't solved the financing issue and now I've already paid the Cossacks—they were promised money by ten people but no one has given it to them yet. So, the financial issue is starting to get tiresome."

"What do you mean paid? Who paid?" asked Glazyev.

"No, I paid."

"Oh, you paid?"

"Of course. Well, they are not big sums. Two thousand, three thousand. But I've got four requests already, here's Chaly's for 50,000 hryvnia."

"Well, go ahead and write up these expenses, I will pass it on."

"Because when you go to this guy, and he's looking at you as though you don't have enough to build yourself a third dacha. It's like someone drew it up with his left hand."[33]

The transcripts were presented as irrefutable evidence of direct Kremlin involvement. At the time, Zatulin was a deputy of the State Duma, while Glazyev was an aide in the Presidential Administration, whose remit was advising the president on policy towards Ukraine. Although Glazyev denied the recordings were real, Zatulin confirmed it was him—adding that his words were taken out of context. But in the race to find the smoking gun of Kremlin involvement, what was missed was the significance of the content of the conversation. Two men with different degrees of influence in the Kremlin were discussing the difficulties of scraping together a few thousand dollars for a covert influence project.

The dynamic here is significant: it was Zatulin, further removed from the halls of power than Glazyev, who had been funding separatists *out of his own pocket* and then asking Glazyev to reimburse him. Furthermore, at stake were relatively small sums of money: for example, 50,000 hryvnia—the Ukrainian currency—was worth less than $6,000. What these conversations reveal wasn't that the Kremlin was involved, but rather that Zatulin and Glazyev were trying to scrape together funds to support a pet project that each had vehemently pursued for two decades. This was another bottom-up initiative for which they were hoping to get the Kremlin's full support.

"[Zatulin] believed in this," said a former Russian official familiar with the Presidential Administration's Ukraine policy. "He was running around with this idea of dividing Ukraine into two parts in the 1990s."[34]

Glazyev, while closer to the Kremlin, was still a self-motivated zealot, and his influence was also limited. "Glazyev was small fish," one of the idealogues of the pro-Russian movement and a Kremlin advisor, explained to me. "But he had his own money."[35]

In 1993, Zatulin had been a young historian and an up-and-coming "new businessman"—one of the entrepreneurial young Komsomol activists turned brokers for emerging private businesses. It was the same line of work that led oligarch Mikhail Khodorkovsky to found a bank that would go on to build an oil empire. With such entrepreneurs entering politics in droves, political pluralism was truly back in vogue—only under the caveat that, in the super-presidency Yeltsin created in 1993, the legislature, subservient to the Presidential Administration, had far fewer powers to actually legislate or, indeed, to seriously affect Kremlin policy. Zatulin found himself joining one of the new pro-government parties—the Party of Russian Unity and Accord, PRES, one of the many predecessors of what would, under Putin, eventually become the dominant United Russia party. PRES just barely made it into the State Duma in 1993, and Zatulin, through a mix of personal conviction and political accident, found himself managing a newly created Committee for CIS Affairs and Relations with Russians Abroad. By 1995, he had joined forces with Glazyev—one of the new economists and by then a former minister of foreign economic affairs—to found the Congress of Russian Communities (KRO), a political organization devoted to the rights of ethnic Russians in newly independent former Soviet countries. While PRES passed the 5 percent threshold to make it into the State Duma, KRO never would—not until it would be incorporated into the nationalist Rodina party in 2006.

But if the government of the Russian Federation—still crippled by the economic and political crises following the Soviet collapse—was in no position to act on any of these agendas, it was all the more critical, in the minds of politicians like Zatulin, to use their government positions to further an agenda that the Kremlin as a whole couldn't or wouldn't back.

"There has been no precedent in the world for 25 million people to suddenly find themselves without a Motherland," Zatulin said in an interview in 1995. "I already knew that the plight of Russian people in newly independent states is unenviable. But what I saw during my trips abroad as a Duma deputy astonished me! Forgotten, oppressed, often hungry people!"

Zatulin was referring to Central Asia as well as the European republics, but even then, he especially noted the animosity he had encountered in Ukraine:

> Personally, I believe that until the Russian government consolidates all of its influence in Ukraine—political, economic, cultural—we will not be able to convince the Ukrainian leadership that by basing its statehood on anti-Russian principles it is risking Ukraine's territorial integrity. As long as Ukraine acts the way it does, our first priority in our relations with that country must be Crimea, Sevastopol, the Black Sea Fleet, the issue of dual citizenship, and the status of the Russian language.[36]

That same year, 1995, Zatulin also founded the CIS Institute, a think tank with a fairly expansive agenda: the rights of Russians abroad needed to be upheld, and Crimea historically belonged to Russia. Zatulin was no loner on a fringe mission. His institute was financially supported by then Moscow Mayor Yuri Luzhkov, another fierce proponent of both causes. The notoriously corrupt Moscow leader had repeatedly called for the "reunification" of Crimea with Russia and even funneled money in support of the Black Sea Fleet throughout the 1990s and until his ouster in 2010. Zatulin also worked closely with Glazyev, and while he had started out working as an economist in a neoliberal government in the early 1990s, his views even then veered towards the revanchist. If Zatulin concerned himself with the plight of Russians abroad, for Glazyev, with more decidedly anti-Western views, Russia had to stand up to hostile global forces. Economic integration with former Soviet republics was key—and if that wasn't enough, it needed to act first to pre-empt the designs of the West. For years, weaving in and out of government jobs, he was considered to be on the fringe of Kremlin officialdom. But by 2014, other forces were propelling him and Zatulin closer to Putin's ear.

IV

While Zatulin's CIS Institute had operated since the mid-1990s and had consistently lobbied for the interests of ethnic Russians abroad for nearly two decades, and while Glazyev had consistently promoted the same imperialist views throughout his government stints, another think tank was emerging whose leader began exerting more and more influence on Vladimir Putin.

RISI—the Russian Institute of Strategic Studies—was once a sleepy research arm of the SVR, the Foreign Intelligence Service, the successor to the First Chief Department of the KGB. Situated deep in the Moscow suburbs and virtually unknown, it conducted open source analysis of international affairs and laid its analytical materials on the desks of the foreign intelligence generals it advised. The SVR was not a policymaking body back then, and, as such, RISI had next to no policymaking clout. Its analytical materials, unlike those of other think tanks at the time, were decidedly devoid of any "geopolitical fantasies," according to an analyst who worked there. Indeed, if anything RISI was something of an old spooks' home, a comfortable final berth for former SVR analysts heading out the door.

In 2009, Lieutenant General Leonid Reshetnikov resigned from his post as head of the Informational and Analytical Directorate of the SVR and was appointed head of the newly revamped RISI. On some level, heading up a think tank was a typical retirement track for a Russian general—lots of SVR veterans followed similar paths. But that same year, RISI was transferred from the SVR to the Presidential Administration. Not only did it have rather more powerful patrons, but it also acquired a new, ideological role. What was meant to be a quiet, retirement track position for Reshetnikov turned out to be an unexpected elevation.

"We were a closed institute for the foreign intelligence. As strange as it may seem, the Presidential Administration didn't have such serious analytical centers," Reshetnikov would recall, years later.[37] "The Presidential Administration lacked serious specialists, and so the intelligence services had to share. Today our founder is the President of Russia, and all of our state commissions and research is signed off by the head of the Administration, Sergei Ivanov."

But it wasn't only that Reshetnikov found himself closer to the seat of power. According to a former colleague, Alexander Sytin, who worked at RISI for over a decade, towards the end of his years at the SVR, while he was heading up research on the Balkans, Reshetnikov became a deeply religious man. And when he headed RISI, some of that imperialist-religious fervor was transferred over to its suburban offices at Flotskaya Street in northern Moscow.

"New people started appearing at the institute, growing long beards and imitating the manners and dress of White Guard officers, or how they imagined White Guard officers to look like, based on Soviet films," Sytin would recall.[38] "They would hang icons over their workstations and would cross themselves fervently over the soup served in the institute's cafeteria." Suddenly, in addition to its analytical work, the institute was also tasked with "resisting the falsification of history in the post-Soviet space."[39]

All these things—from newfound religious fervor to romanticizing Imperial Russia—had come into vogue in early 2012 when Putin returned for his third presidential term. As he grasped for something to fill the ideological vacuum that had formed during this four-year absence from the Kremlin, he increasingly began to rely on the Russian Orthodox Church to bolster his mandate to rule. Pussy Riot's protest stunt on the altar of Christ the Savior Cathedral in February 2012—and the subsequent show trial and imprisonment—reflected the increasing role of the Church and helped revive its ancient position not just as an independent institution, but as something of a handmaiden to the divine mandate of the autocratic ruler. What went hand in hand with these sentiments was a premium placed on the "Russian World"—a transnational oikumene of Russian language and Russian culture, which, according to many of its adepts, could only be restored by using Russia's might to unite Russians, Slavs or Orthodox believers around the world. These religious ideas were, in other words, also distinctly imperialist.

But it was also popular, and not something coming directly from Putin himself or from his chief of staff, Sergei Ivanov. Both Putin and Ivanov were religious but never ostentatiously so; rather, their move to back nationalism and the Church in 2012 was a turn to populism. The mass protests that greeted Putin's decision to return to the Kremlin in 2011–12 demonstrated that the ideology of "managed democracy" Putin had relied on for his first two terms had proven too transparent a lie to continue justifying his rule. He needed something more appealing to the masses—the less educated, more nationalistic, more religious and less affluent. And so he sidelined his more secular, intellectual ideologue Vladislav Surkov in 2012 and started promoting statists, conservatives and the Church. People like Glazyev began getting more airtime, while people like Reshetnikov suddenly discovered that they mattered.

This mood manifested itself at RISI, under the directorship of the spiritually awakened Reshetnikov, with icons over the workstations and clergymen often found wandering the halls as diplomats. Some of the people there to give talks, to advise or advocate were delighted by the enthusiasm with which Lieutenant General Reshetnikov distilled their ideas onto the pages of analytical notes that would land directly on the desk of not just Ivanov but Putin himself.

One of those deeply religious men who found himself welcome at RISI was Konstantin Malofeyev. Another was a retired FSB colonel who now devoted his life to war re-enactment and had made a name for himself on various internet forums for military enthusiasts: Igor Girkin, the infamous Strelkov.

That Malofeyev associated with Reshetnikov is well established: both signed a petition to the president in 2013, for example, requesting that the Orthodox faith be established as a cornerstone of the Russian Constitution.[40] As for Girkin, who later became very critical of Reshetnikov, while qualifying him as "a person I once respected," his association with RISI was revealed by Sytin. In October 2013, he wrote that Girkin appeared for several talks at the institute, and Reshetnikov would publicly refer to him as a "friend."[41]

By the time they got there, the institute was saturated with similar ideas. Reports promoted the idea that former Soviet republics should not be considered to have full sovereignty and were thus not entirely the subject of international law, while the uprisings in Eastern Ukraine were an expression of the people's desire to join Russia, rather than of a rebellion against the new government in Kyiv.

Much of the analysis was based on wishful thinking, but that wishful thinking echoed with the events developing on the ground in Kyiv. Driven by fear and hope, political analysts with a clear agenda saw what they wanted to see. "The assessment of the situation in Ukraine was spectacularly miscalculated, and they knew it," a former Kremlin official claimed. And if Reshetnikov saw what he wanted to see, then so did Glazyev, who kept trying to convince a skeptical Putin that the residents of Donbas wanted to join Russia as strongly as those in Crimea did.[42] The RISI reports fed into his logic, until the advisors and the advisees became part of the same feedback loop.[43]

In such a fervid environment, one cannot define the single node where a particular idea originated. But if Glazyev had been a proponent of similar ideas for a while, then the atmosphere at RISI was one of escalation, as these ideas swirled towards a crescendo of ultimate action. Ideas alone were not enough—they needed those with the means and the will to execute them. Petitioning the Kremlin was well and good—and firmly rooted in the Orthodox, autocratic tradition—but if the tsar dithered, or if his hands were tied, or if his responses were inconclusive, then surely those devoted to the cause of the Motherland had to believe that they were nonetheless driven by the same divine plan. If the tsar had not yet blessed them in word, then he certainly had in spirit, or in any case would.

They felt they had the mandate to act, they just needed the means. Malofeyev had the means. And Girkin would get the men.

5

THE TRIGGER-MAN OF THE RUSSIAN SPRING

We were born to make a fairy tale come true.

Aviator's March, anthem of the Russian Aerospace Forces, 1923

Igor Vsevolodovich Girkin, the man whom Dima and Sasha, the Ukrainian and Russian volunteer fighters, followed into battle, the man who, in his own hyperbolic words, pulled the trigger on the war in Donbas, did not exude the energy of battle, the determination of a covert, beleaguered mission, or the aura of an ideological renegade. In front of me was a medium-built man in his late forties with sad eyes, shivering in a parka. But then, decisive leaders—or those who at least create a strong impression of decisiveness—often underwhelm when met face to face.

Such was Sasha's impression. "When I met him, he looked to me like a charismatic but very tired man."

And such was mine. I met him outside a tent where leaders of the Novorossiya movement, including Girkin, were complaining about the Kremlin's betrayal of their cause to about a thousand likeminded protesters in Moscow in the winter of 2019. "Let's not talk now," he said, returning my handshake. His was neither strong nor weak. "Talk to one of my people," he said as he examined my card. Then he looked up and added, "We'll see what you do and we'll see."

Everything about his face, his eyes, his mouth, looked droopy and tired, defeated, almost, as if he had achieved a heroic feat by force of will alone but then couldn't shake some deeply buried sense that it had all been part of a misunderstanding that rendered the whole exercise meaningless. And no, he was certainly not going to give an interview to the representative of a Western NGO. The truth was that Strelkov, having returned from Donbas in 2014 and since then launched a campaign criticizing the Kremlin and Putin personally, had more to fear from his own government than he did from the West—even if he was identified as the key suspect in the shootdown by Russian-backed forces of Flight MH-17 and wanted by The Hague. While he was giving interviews, he was doing so with extreme caution. This was not because, one of his associates told me, he feared what the Western press would write about him. It was because he feared that what the Western press printed could get him in trouble back home. Of course, he wouldn't say much to me, pointing me instead to one of his people who turned out to be equally polite but recalcitrant.

A former colonel in the FSB, Girkin, known by his nom de guerre Strelkov, or Sharpshooter, is widely credited in Ukraine and in the West as being the first and most prominent of the deniable Russian forces the Kremlin sent to invade Donbas in early April and start the pro-Russian separatist rebellion. Ukrainian authorities have gone so far as to suggest that Girkin got his orders directly from Russian Defense Minister Shoigu—a highly unlikely connection, even if one were to assume that Girkin was directly integrated in the Russian military's command and control structures. When, soon after the Russian siege and annexation of Crimea, Girkin led a unit of fifty-two men across the Ukrainian border into Donbas and swiftly seized the town of Slovyansk, it was easy to mistake his decisiveness and the relatively professional kit of his men for the notorious Russian "little green men" who seized key positions in Sevastopol just a month earlier. Nor was it just the interim Ukrainian government in Kyiv who believed him to be a Russian officer acting under direct orders from the Kremlin—pro-Russian separatist militias in Donbas also saw in him and his unit the long-awaited Russian backup that would come to rescue them and bring them into Moscow's fold, just as they had done with Crimea.

But the reality was that both were mistaken. It's not that Girkin was not a Russian officer of the FSB, albeit a former one, who had served in the security service's anti-terrorism squad in Chechnya. He never denied that. It's the questions of whether he was acting under orders, from whom and, most of all, how he was interpreting those orders that remain a mystery. If anything, there is strong evidence to suggest that in "invading" Donbas on 12 April 2014, Igor Ivanovich Girkin, aka Strelkov, was *defying* orders, not carrying them out.

I

Sometime in late February 2014—just before the Kremlin finalized its decision to annex Crimea through a referendum on "reunification"—strange men began appearing in Simferopol, the peninsula's capital, and Sevastopol. Some, as discussed in earlier chapters, provided auxiliary muscle to the Russian troops that helped secure the peninsula, while some were helping, advising and protecting the newly elected Crimean governor, Sergei Aksyonov, and his pro-Russian Unity party. Neither Russian officials nor independent activists, they hailed from that twilight of the public and private sector: hybrid warriors with military, security or political ties who seemed to be in

Crimea of their own volition but coordinated their activities with the military. One of them was a self-described PR specialist who later turned out to be Alexander Borodai, the future "prime minister" of the self-proclaimed DPR. Another was an "emissary of the Kremlin, Igor," as he reportedly introduced himself to other, local militiamen.[1]

The presence of "Igor" in Unity's party headquarters was first recorded by the Russian journalist Oleg Kashin, who described an "intelligent-looking man with a moustache in civilian clothes" talking on the phone and issuing assurances to officers of the Ukrainian navy that there would be no Russian offensive until the following morning. The man was one of many local militia guarding the headquarters, but he seemed to stand out from the rest, not least in the way that he was regarded by his peers.

"Wow, you know him?" a militiaman asked Kashin, pointing to the mustachioed man. "That's an acting Russian GRU officer. He is appointing people to their posts. He promised to include our units into the new army!"[2]

Whether the man was in fact sent by the GRU (military intelligence) or simply managed to pass himself off as a GRU officer in order to command respect and get things done remains unclear. But in fact, the man known as Strelok, or Strelkov, would turn out not to be a current GRU officer but a former FSB one. More to the point, along with Borodai, he was affiliated to and funded by one of the chief financiers of the pro-Russian separatist movement, the Orthodox businessman Konstantin Malofeyev.[3]

Igor, the "Kremlin emissary," might have worked for several masters, including, during his stint in Crimea, the Kremlin directly. But he fervently served only one cause. Girkin's role in helping Aksyonov, aside from advising him, was organizing a division of volunteer militiamen into a professional "Spetsnaz," or special forces unit, to resemble as much as possible the elite forces of the FSB in which he had once served. With some organizational help from Aksyonov, and probably from Moscow as well, he managed to amass a "battalion" in Simferopol of more than 200 men, albeit with just 154 firearms between them.[4] According to Girkin, his was the "only" real volunteer militia company in Crimea.[5] But it is hard to corroborate such claims, and much comes down to how volunteer militias defined their own status. Either way, these militias would take over key posts across Crimea and ensured that local law enforcement and military units pledged their allegiance to Aksyonov.

Girkin's own accounts of his experiences veer on the bipolar—at times, he marvels at what he was able to achieve, at others he complains of powerlessness. In several interviews, he claimed that he personally negotiated the surrender of Ukrainian military garrisons, and he did so largely relying on his anonymity and the widespread belief that he was, in fact, a high-placed "emissary" of the Kremlin and a colonel of the FSB or the GRU. As he would describe later, staying in the shadows magnified his powers. Whatever the extent of any Kremlin mandate and the authority of those giving him orders, what seemed to matter most was what the people on the ground—Crimean and Ukrainian officers—believed:

> I started the negotiations for the surrender of the fleet headquarters
> ... For tactical purposes, it was convenient for me that everyone think
> of me as an active [officer]. But I never went around yelling that I
> was an active [officer]. I just said, colonel. And then they would draw
> their own conclusions. So, they would think, yeah, some kind of
> colonel. But only a few people knew that I was retired. They didn't
> know my name, after all.[6]

The tactic certainly worked. Other volunteers in Aksyonov's entourage began to believe that not only was the Kremlin sending powerful "advisors," but that the mysterious "colonel" was the most powerful of them all—so much so that Aksyonov was taking orders from him and not the other way around.[7] It may have been a bluff, but it generated a compelling illusion of Russian power and resolve for the Ukrainian side, too. This is how Volodymyr Zamana, Ukraine's chief of the General Staff at the time, described interacting with a man presumed to be Girkin:

> An FSB colonel, I don't remember his name, arrived in the naval headquarters of the Black Sea Fleet and invited me to defect to the Russian side, saying we all served in the USSR, we're brothers, we don't want blood, come over to us. Suddenly there was a call from Aksyonov. Generally, he said the same thing as the FSB colonel, only more profanely.[8]

Girkin's penchant for oscillating between defeatism and exaggeration of his role in the war is a tell-tale sign of his personal investment and commitment to the cause of Novorossiya, and his fervent belief that he was acting in Russia's true national interests. The reality was that Aksyonov alone could not have facilitated such a smooth, bloodless annexation without a leading role from Russia's military. According to several militia members in Simferopol and Sevastopol interviewed on the eve of the referendum on joining Russia, they were "helping" and "coordinating" with officers of the Russian Black Sea Fleet and the Russian military. When speaking to me, they did not deny the presence of Russian soldiers. Girkin may have personally negotiated with Ukrainian military garrisons, but those negotiations certainly went more smoothly when the bases were surrounded by Russian muscle.[9] The role of the militias, including those organized by Strelkov, was twofold—to prepare the ground for regular Russian troops,[10] and to serve as the local, volunteer mascots that those Russian troops would hide behind.

Given the role of the Russian military in securing the Crimean Peninsula, one can imagine his enemies seeing him as part of their advance guard. The belief that he was an integral, and possibly central element in an efficient, well-oiled machine's cunning plan propelled him to take the next step. But what followed was based far more on Girkin's beliefs and ideas of reality than the reality itself.

II

On 12 April 2014, Igor Girkin led fifty-two men across the Russian–Ukrainian border from the Rostov region southwest into Donbas. It was a grueling, 25-km march, with each of the men carrying two Kalashnikov rifles, 50 kg of munitions, 5-l water flasks filled with ammunition, and spare uniforms. At night, Girkin forbade them from using cellphones; they were vulnerable to arrest both from the Ukrainian and—reflecting their lack of any formal sanction—Russian border patrol. To avoid interception, they communicated by shining flashlights at each other—there was a perverse poetic justice that a collection of history buffs and war reenactors would find themselves in a real, twenty-first-century battlefield, relying on World War II methods.

On the other side, they were met by a local militiaman named Buiny, or Wild, who was part of the team of the self-proclaimed local "governor" of Donbas, Pavel Gubarev, and who had recently led local protesters to seize an SBU building in Donetsk, scoring some badly needed weapons for the men.[11] They were all anticipating reinforcements, weapons and professional soldiers from Russia any day now. They desperately wanted to show the Kremlin, and Putin personally, how much they could accomplish with their limited resources. If the Russian president only saw and appreciated how much they had done and what they were up against, they felt, he would deploy the full might of Russia's military machine behind them and, as he was repeatedly hinting at on television, "liberate" their region from the "Kyiv junta" and rejoin it with Russia just as he had done with Crimea.[12] In fact, Buiny had initially hoped Girkin's unit was none other than a brigade of well-armed paratroopers from Ryazan.[13]

But he was wrong. Girkin had in fact struggled to muster his unit. Following the referendum on 16 March, his Crimean "Spetsnaz battalion" was disbanded and their sizeable weapons inventory handed back over to the new authorities in Crimea. Girkin had managed to amass a small personal retinue of about fifteen men, many of them Ukrainian citizens who were also veterans of two wars in Chechnya and even Afghanistan. But they weren't enough. A number of local Cossacks came to Strelkov wanting to join his mission, but they were rejected— according to him, a lot of these volunteers were in it for their own personal gain and not interested in following orders. Others agreed to join but then deserted immediately, daunted by the unpredictability of the whole affair. "I immediately told the men where we were going and why," Girkin recalled later. "I made it clear that we would have no official status, and if we failed, no one would recognize us."[14]

With the help of the new Crimean leader Aksyonov, Strelkov managed to gather fifty-two more or less loyal veteran fighters to go to the Ukrainian mainland with him. About 80 percent of them were Ukrainian citizens.[15]

But despite the uncertainty of their mission, the ruthlessness of Strelkov and his men astonished Buiny. "You know what made the Strelkovites different from the local [militia]?" he recalled later, in apparent horror and delight. "They smelled like war, of an inexorable determination. They knew they were there to spill blood." Buiny had arranged for the men to be transported in a postal truck. Within earshot of the trembling civilian driver, Girkin casually asked Buiny, "Is he one of ours, or do we waste him?"[16]

* * *

Given their ruthlessness, one would expect that a company of men as well organized as Girkin's would have its invasion mapped out in advance. Based on first-hand accounts, though, this does not appear to be the case. It took Girkin about a week to recruit his unit, and the next steps—aside from going into the mainland—were literally plotted en route.

Upon crossing the border, Girkin asked Buiny where they should head to next. In other words, the decision about where to establish the stronghold of the Russian Spring resistance was taken within hours of actually securing it. Girkin wanted a town with maximal local support for their cause, which, given that he commanded only fifty-two men, would make it easier to secure. Without hesitation, Buiny pointed to Slovyansk.[17]

But what Girkin doesn't like talking about are the circumstances of his departure for Donbas. In fact, according to Borodai, Girkin's handler in Crimea and Donbas and the future leader of the DPR, his initial destination was not Slovyansk, but the smaller town of Shakhtarsk.[18] "When we crossed the border," Girkin would recall, "we didn't have a clearly defined plan of where we should go. I immediately set a task for myself—to find some medium-sized settlement. On the one hand, sizeable enough, on the other hand, one in which we can quickly establish people's power."[19] It appears strange that his unit made plans to go to Slovyansk right upon arrival at the border, and not sooner. And yet, all sources seem to corroborate this. Kashin, a well-connected journalist who covered the first days of the insurgency out of Crimea and Donetsk, was tipped off by a friend that Strelkov was due to arrive in Slovyansk on 12 April, three hours before it happened.[20] Given that the leader of the local pro-Russian insurgency in Slovyansk also learned of Girkin's impending arrival at about the same time, it appears simply that no such plans had existed beforehand.

Instead, the reason for such hasty planning is that the very orders for Girkin to go to Donbas in the first place were equally hastily prepared—and then promptly recalled. Here is how Borodai described what happened on the day of the invasion: "I curated Strelkov's activities, starting from Crimea and ending with Slovyansk. When Strelkov and his group arrived in Rostov a couple of days before going to Donbas, I met with him at an airport café and gave him some money for all of his planned operations." Later, Borodai says, he went back to Moscow and, at an airport there, met with five people

> who had just returned from an important trip abroad, connected to the Ukrainian events. I suggested that we treat the situation with care. They suggested to me that I recall Strelkov. I left the airport, got in the car, and rang Strelkov ... His number was not available. Later I learned that at that moment he was still on Russian territory, but had turned off his phone, having already guessed how the situation would develop and not wanting to change his plans regarding Donbas.[21]

Borodai, who served as prime minister of the DPR from May to August 2014, is an important actor in his own right, but he is also a major piece in the puzzle of the relationships between various leaders of the insurgency, their respective relationship with the Russian government and the degree of their autonomy. Like Girkin, Borodai was self-driven and described his appearance in Crimea and then Donbas as part of a "private–public partnership" with the Russian government.[22] Girkin, too, was part of that partnership, but due to its loose nature, like many of its participants, he took matters into his own hands. Borodai, as his own comments demonstrate, appeared to have been more cautious. A former PR specialist for Malofeyev, he was deeply driven by ideology but seemed more mindful of the inner workings of government–business relations, and especially how these were spun. Malofeyev was the "private" part of the equation, and according to Borodai, the "hundreds of thousands of dollars" he handed over to Girkin for his expenses before his trip to Donbas came from Malofeyev, not from the government. Given the private nature of his financing and his lack of an official role in Crimea and Donbas, Borodai had a great deal of autonomy in deciding whether to go ahead with a military operation or not. By his own admission, he was skeptical of Girkin's mission all along, and the final decision to ring him and call it off was as much his own as that of the "five men":

> After the Rostov trip I returned to Moscow with a not very positive opinion of the people representing the various protest groups in Donbas. I had concerns about how the project would turn out. First of all, I saw that the level of [local] support for our activities would not be as serious as in Crimea. Secondly, I started to understand that there would not be a repeat of the Crimea scenario in Donbas. Yes, it was a wide, popular movement, the majority of people wanted to join Russia. But in Russia itself, it wasn't yet decided whether they should get involved in all this. So we decided to wait until the results of this popular movement crystalized. That was why it was decided to put the brakes on the situation with Strelkov. But Strelkov had his own opinion, and he pushed forward.[23]

Taking Slovyansk, according to this account, was Girkin's own initiative.

On the receiving end, the self-proclaimed mayor of the city, Vyacheslav Ponomaryov, corroborated the chaos and spontaneity of the seizure of his city. By early April, he recounts, his town of about 120,000 people was overwhelmingly opposed to the new Kyiv government, and at least 300 activists had gone so far as to take up arms against it. These were locals who had the support of the city and security officials in Slovyansk, and they were eagerly awaiting the arrival of "little green men" from Moscow. He got the call that "volunteers" were on their way on the morning of 12 April—just hours before Strelkov's "battalion" arrived in Slovyansk.

"I met them, took them into the city," Ponomaryov recounted in a subsequent interview with a Russian news agency:

There were about fifty of them. We had about 300 fighters ... That very day I had a conversation with Girkin. He introduced himself as a retired FSB colonel. As a former military man myself, knowing subordination, I basically handed over control of all of the militias of the surrounding cities that I had dealt with to him. We decided that he would deal with the military aspects of defending the city, while I would deal with the administration of civilians in the city. But I still retained control of the Slavyansk militia, which was guarding the main administration building.[24]

Ponomaryov's account is noteworthy because unlike Girkin, he was in no way an "emissary" of the Kremlin or even a useful enthusiast. There is no known evidence of any contacts between him and the Russian Presidential Administration or other authorities. He was a local and led a local rebellion that may have had to rely on, but did not consist of, Russians and Russian-backed groups. Between April and June, when he was first arrested by Girkin's forces and then fired, he regularly clashed with Girkin and his men.

Ponomaryov, a businessman whose father was Ukrainian and his mother Russian, became one of the leaders of the pro-Russian insurgency not with any clear-cut goals of separatism, but in order to defend what to him and many others was a regional identity that—while different from Russia proper and more intermixed with the Ukrainian—was still distinctly Russian. Buoyed by the success of Crimea, he too was certain that Moscow would come to the defense of the local Russian-speaking population. "We didn't think it would get to that point [of war], to be honest we hoped Russia would come in and help," he recounted in a subsequent interview:

We had the example of Crimea, where "polite people" did everything without firing a single shot. We were hoping to have a referendum and a peaceful resolution. After all, we were able to agree with our police in Slavyansk, Konstantinovka and Druzhkovka. It's not that we wanted to separate from Ukraine, we just wanted to live in our own way. But when blood was spilled, everything became different.[25]

Based on Ponomaryov's first impression, it was easy to assume that Strelkov was indeed the long-awaited Russian backup—covert, clandestine and "former," because, as the Russian trope has it, there is no such thing as a "former" security officer.

Girkin was thus easily able to take Slovyansk, with minimal resistance from the city's police. It had been chosen for three reasons. His relatively small retinue needed to be sure that they could hold the area by relying on local support alone, because even though they expected Russian-back up, they knew they had to first prove the viability of their own resources. Secondly, Slovyansk was strategically located in the heart of Donbas and part of a conglomerate of pro-Russian towns that included Kramatorsk and accounted for some half a million people, many of whom, in those initial days, supported the cause. And thirdly, the name of Slovyansk, or Slavyansk in Russian—"Slavic town"—resonated with the Russian nationalist movement, which in the early days supplied the bulk of separatist volunteer fighters. The word seamlessly inserted itself into the myth of an anti-Nazi, World War II resistance that war reenactor Girkin and his supporters bought into wholesale—towns in Ukraine's east were "occupied" and needed to be "liberated." If this was Russian propaganda, then these were words that pro-Russian militia believed literally even before they came out of the mouths of the more cynical pundits on Russian television.

The town was taken, but could they hold onto it?

III

Up on the seventh floor of the regional administration building in Donetsk—then the seat of the newly proclaimed DPR—journalists scurried around in a flurry of activity as they waited for

Denis Pushilin, the republic's self-proclaimed co-chairman, to make an important announcement about the referendum for independence scheduled for 11 May. For about a month now, the building, barricaded with boards, tires, barbed wire and trash, had been occupied by a motley assortment of random men with guns—not little green men at all, more like street riff-raff playing war—but armed with real Kalashnikovs and a genuine determination to detain any perceived enemy at gun point and throw them into the cellars. The militants, brandishing their rifles and shouting "make way" as they pushed past me at the entrance and the corridors, were thuggish locals, puffed up with their new power, often drunk and far scarier than the current or former Russian "Spetsnaz" officers that had taken government buildings in Crimea. They were also dangerous because they were beginning to get worried: the certainty that Moscow would send troops to support their cause and defend them from murderous "fascists" was still there, but it was wearing thin.

Anxious to get the answers before anyone else—and confused about when the event was due to start—I found myself in front of a room with an ajar door, a heated discussion going on inside. Believing this to be the press conference, I slipped inside. A member of Pushilin's security shot me a lethal look and I realized my mistake: this was no press conference, but a session of a soon-to-be fledgling legislature. Deputies of the would-be statelets—former local officials and activists who had turned against the new government in Kyiv and joined the insurgency—were arguing about how to interpret Putin's words, what to do about the referendum and whether to hold it at all. In particular, they were discussing a directive that would have sounded fairly unambiguous had it been uttered by anyone else: "Hold off on the referendum so that dialogue has a chance." But because the words were pronounced by Vladimir Putin, the ruler to whom many of the insurgents pledged their allegiance without really ascertaining whether said allegiance was required or even wanted, they assumed a cryptic, almost mystic quality.

Finally, one of the more decisive deputies spoke out. "The referendum has to happen," he said:

> But I see a number of people seem to be in a state of confusion after Vladimir Vladimirovich's comments. This was an act of colossal support for us ... It was a proclamation to the whole world that we are holding a referendum. Thanks to Vladimir Vladimirovich's statements, people from across the world will know that the Donetsk People's Republic will express its will. It was a positioning of the Donetsk Republic as a people's republic.

Was this all a ruse choreographed by the Kremlin? Had Putin said one thing in public while unequivocal commands to the contrary were passed down through other, private channels? But then why the discussion? Had there been a secret, alternative Kremlin directive, there would be no need for the great pains taken in that room to twist Putin's words into their exact opposite, just so that they could be useful and comforting to the recipients. More to the point, if the deputies were discussing a secret Kremlin directive, it's hard to believe that one of the security agents would limit his warning to me with a stern glance followed by a roll of the eyes. He would have crossed the 3 meters that separated me from him and duly evicted, or worse, the only Western journalist in the room. But he didn't.

What was actually happening in that room on 9 May had a more prosaic explanation. Up to that point, the self-proclaimed leaders of the "people's republics" had been chaotically aping the political process of Crimea's annexation, hoping to get the same results.

On 6 April, a week before Strelkov crossed into Ukraine, about 2,000 people gathered in Donetsk's central square and demanded that the regional parliament hold an emergency session to announce a referendum. For a month, ever since the authorities had arrested the self-proclaimed "governor," Pavel Gubarev, on 6 March, pro-Russian demonstrators had been holding thousands-strong rallies demanding autonomy and increasingly more radical concessions from the new government in Kyiv. Now, protest leaders issued an ultimatum to the regional authorities: either hold an emergency session, or they would dissolve parliament in accordance with something called a "people's mandate" and assemble a new council of elected community representatives.[26] Given that no council deputies were there to hold a session on a Sunday, it quickly became clear that this would not be possible. Anywhere from 200 to 1,000 protesters broke off and stormed the regional administration building, occupying the near empty premises with relative ease. Immediately, they hung a Russian flag and the blue, red and black flag of a new proto-state, the DPR.[27]

With police and local authorities divided and in disarray, the regional government, led by the new Kyiv-appointed governor Sergei Taruta, was paralyzed. The separatists, some of them armed, had occupied his office, but on the following day, a Monday, there was no record of either Taruta or the police trying to reclaim the premises, aside from a condemnation of the insurgents' proclamation as illegal.[28] It would take Taruta a week to announce a "special operation" against the "terrorists" who had occupied the building, a day after Kyiv's acting interim leader Oleksandr Turchynov ordered the insurgents to clear it.[29] But nor did Taruta cave to their demands to hold an emergency session. And so, on 7 April, with their demands still unmet, the insurgents holding the building issued a declaration proclaiming the DPR as a sovereign state. During a session of its newly established ad hoc "supreme council," a group of self-proclaimed deputies drafted a document announcing the Donetsk region's sovereignty, establishing a supreme council and, among other things, appealing to Putin directly to help protect Donbas from the "Kyiv junta" by sending a peacekeeping contingent:

The Kiev junta is purposefully leading us to war and destruction. We do not want this and we are ready to fight for our future and the future of our children! Now the entire state apparatus is working against us. The military forces of the Ukrainian army are already being drawn to our lands, which are ordered to act against their people.

We appeal to you, Vladimir Vladimirovich, as the last hope for our future and the future of our children. Only in Russia do we see the only protector of our culture of the Russian world. Only the peace-keeping contingents of the Russian army will be able to give a convincing signal to the Kiev junta, which came to power through arms and blood. We are ready to fight and die for our ideals and for our beliefs! But without your support, without the support of Russia, it will not be easy for us alone to resist the Kiev junta and its neo-fascist system.[30]

The wording was at once aping the idiom of anti-Kyiv propaganda coming from Russian television channels while also being painfully earnest: as though the separatists were trying to ingratiate themselves with a Kremlin they genuinely believed would come to their aid. But this was where any similarities with the Crimea annexation abruptly end.

Years after the events, there is still no evidence or record of any negotiations with Moscow to coordinate the political side of the DPR's state-building in its early days, something that had kept elected members of Crimea's parliament up all night in early March. Indeed, there is not even any record of the names associated with the initial proclamation of independence. "An unidentified bearded man read out 'the act of the proclamation of an independent state, Donetsk People's Republic' in front of a white, blue and red Russian flag," Reuters reported.[31] The declaration was then posted on an obscure news site based in Donetsk called the "committee of Donetsk voters" on 7 April, but neither the document, nor the news reports about it, named any of its authors. Presumably, one of the leaders of these insurgents was the local businessman Denis Pushilin, who, according to his official site, "became a Donbas People's Liberation Movement leader" in March 2014 and was "one of those who, shouldering responsibility, made a historic decision to proclaim the Donetsk People's Republic on April 7, 2014."[32] While probably reflecting the truth, such congratulatory language was produced long after the fact. The earliest mention of Pushilin as a leader of the insurgents who either stormed the regional administration building or emerged as their political leader was on 10 April, when Russian news agencies first identified him as chairman of the DPR. Pushilin then boasted that negotiations with Moscow were ongoing,[33] but to this day there is nothing of any substance to those contacts.

The reaction from Moscow, meanwhile, was cold. Putin's spokesman declined to comment on the insurgents' proclamation, while Senator Viktor Ozerov, chair of the defense committee, immediately ruled out a peacekeeping contingent in no uncertain terms: "It is simply contrary to international principles and norms to take our peacekeeping contingent to Donetsk or elsewhere at the urging of local authorities. Russia has no right to do so unilaterally."[34]

Not only were Russian troops absent from Donbas in early April, there was also no sign of the kind of painstaking coordination with Moscow that preceded the referendum on Crimea's annexation. Of course, one is tempted to assume that there would be no record of that which is covert—but the entire history of the "covert" Crimea operation, and even Girkin's and Borodai's "covert" Moscow negotiations about Donbas, has left an abundant trail, either through intercepted telephone conversations or investigative reporting. Indeed, on 13 April, a week after buildings in Donetsk and Luhansk were captured by separatist insurgents, Ukraine's SBU intercepted a conversation between Strelkov and Malofeyev about their counteroffensive against the

Ukrainian anti-terrorist operation just a day after Girkin arrived in Slovyansk.[35] By contrast, it is significant that both uprisings in Donetsk and Luhansk were virtually leaderless until days or weeks after government buildings were seized and sovereignty was proclaimed, as it suggests there simply wasn't a plan, and that there wasn't anyone important enough for Moscow to coordinate with and talk to.

"It was just miners and truck drivers," Kashin, the reporter who had first identified Strelkov in Crimea, and who was inside the Donetsk reginal administration building on 6 and 7 April, told me. "They thought they were aping what had happened on Maidan." No one stood out from the crowd, not yet.[36]

But with an interim Kyiv government still disoriented and demoralized by Moscow's annexation of Crimea, that crowd was enough to paralyze local authorities as well. Just a month earlier, on 2 March, amid growing pro-Russian protests in Donbas, Sergei Taruta, a billionaire from Donetsk region, had been appointed governor by interim leader Oleksandr Turchynov, who had hoped that local big business could use its influence to rein in separatist sentiments.[37] Powerful figures like him and the even richer Rinat Akhmetov, who had ties to the Russian-speaking communities in the East, could have perhaps brokered a compromise of sorts. But this effort foundered. His advisor at the time, Valery Zhaldak, told me that having appointed him, Kyiv then managed to alienate Russian-speakers in Donbas throughout March and April, by failing to establish any meaningful outreach, despite the Taruta administration's repeated requests. Kyiv's anti-Russian rhetoric, while understandable in light of Crimea, did not help matters either.[38]

Amid the disarray and power vacuum, ties between Kyiv and Donetsk continued to fray. "Local police aren't so much pro-separatist as they are non-allegiance," a Western NGO worker based in Donetsk that spring said. "A lot of the police officers aren't fulfilling their duties because they feel they will not get their due. Local gangs are running the show."[39]

By Monday, 7 April, Taruta was holed up at a nearby hotel, unable to return to his office. "In effect, that's no longer a leader," Kashin, who was at the scene at the time, recalled.

Over a year later, Taruta tried to justify what happened. "It was a [Russian] special operation," he said of the seizure of the regional administration building. "If we didn't have provocateurs and coordinators [from Russia], this wouldn't have happened. Security officials couldn't do anything." But even the journalist he was speaking to had a hard time believing him. The closest thing to a special operation would be Girkin's invasion and seizure of Slovyansk—but that took place nearly a week after local separatists captured Donetsk.[40]

In neighboring Luhansk, protesters seized the local SBU office—the regional seat of Ukraine's Security Service—giving them access to more weapons than in Donetsk, but ultimately they would follow Donetsk's lead. At first, the insurgents didn't proclaim independence but issued local authorities an ultimatum to release all "political prisoners," including separatist leaders Alexander Kharitonov, the self-proclaimed governor, and Arsen Klinchayev, a former pro-Russian council member. They called for a referendum on independence and said that if local authorities didn't listen to them, then they would proclaim their own parliament.[41] But it was only two weeks later that the insurgents barricaded themselves in the SBU building, holding a "people's assembly," and elected Valery Bolotov, an unknown former Soviet airborne troops commander, as the new "people's governor."[42] In Kharkiv, protesters likewise seized the regional administration building on 6 April, but Ukrainian security authorities cleared it the following day.

And so, the following week, when Girkin brought his fifty-two men to seize Slovyansk, local separatists—miners, truck drivers, angry local residents, militant gangs itching for a fight—had already managed to incapacitate the local authorities in two Ukrainian regional seats and announce that they would hold a referendum on independence, much like in Crimea, on Sunday, 11 May.

But on that Sunday, support for the proclamation to secede from Ukraine wasn't nearly as unanimous as in Crimea. Once the ballot, unrecognized by any official body, including those of Russia, was held, 89 percent voted "yes" to a broadly worded question on whether they supported independence. But the turnout, despite boasts of 80 percent by separatist election officials, was probably closer to the paltry 32 percent given by Ukraine's Interior Ministry.[43] Separatist officials, meanwhile, all but admitted to me that they had had to coerce people to set up polling stations. "Only a few local government officials are supporting us in holding this referendum," said Boris Litvinov, a self-styled election official in Donetsk:

> Mostly it's done on the enthusiasm of the people. Sometimes we have to—not use harsh measures, no—but we have to be very insistent ... [Sometimes] it's necessary just to come and open the school (where the polling station is organized) ourselves. We are very polite, we don't break anything.

But reports of violence—especially in Luhansk—were widespread.[44]

Independent polls were equally lackluster. There was no doubt that a majority of Donbas residents favored some autonomy: 41 percent wanted decentralization and 38 percent wanted federalization. However, less than 30 percent supported outright secession.[45] Many I spoke to—the protesters turning up to pro-Russian rallies in the streets of Donetsk, residents, onlookers—didn't seem to know exactly what they wanted. "I don't know. For a start, Yanukovych should be hanged for his betrayal of us, for leaving us at the mercy of the junta," a resident of Donetsk who turned up to a protest with her friend told me. Another, older native of Donetsk was more sober: "It's not that people want to join Russia, they don't. They're scared. They just want to get under something—either under Russia, or under Mongolia, it doesn't matter."[46]

Moscow, meanwhile, would remain cryptic: Putin kept putting off commenting unequivocally on the vote; the Foreign Ministry said merely that it "respected" the results, but only in February 2022, almost eight years later, would Russia formally recognize referendums for independence in Donetsk and Luhansk.[47] And so, by early May 2014, miners, truck drivers, an assortment of local pensioners and shady businessmen, and an army of local and Russian adventure-seekers had set up their own pretend governments with flags, parliaments, defense ministries, militias, declarations of independence and even proto-constitutions with formal elections scheduled for later in the month. They just lacked the main thing, for some, perhaps, the only thing, that they had fought for: Russia's formal recognition and protection.

IV

The key to understanding why Strelkov went to Donbas, why fifty-two men followed him, and why tens of thousands of people took up arms for the cause that he espoused, may lie precisely in the kind of emotional confusion that overtook the meeting of "people's deputies" deciding on whether to go ahead with the referendum. In the post-revolutionary disarray that was Ukraine, hundreds of thousands of local officials, politicians, businessmen and people simply with little better to do feared the new Ukrainian government would take away their livelihoods, or worse. There may have been little basis for their fears, but they acted on what they believed. They took solace in the rhetoric coming out of Moscow—something about Novorossiya, a union with Russia or a return to the way things were in some distant past. But most seemed to do so without quite understanding what it meant. Most of all, having internalized the "rule by signal" model in which Putin issued vague directives that could, depending on the recipient, be interpreted as commands or mere opinions, they projected onto the Russian president's cryptic words everything they wanted to hear.

But perhaps what had fooled them was the same thing that was fooling the entire international community: for once, Putin may have been telling the truth. Something had happened that month, possibly in response to Girkin's own actions.

"Up until 26 April they [local separatist leaders] kept hammering this idea—that there would be a major Russian contingent," Dima, the Ukrainian separatist fighter, had told me. For Girkin, too, a key development took place on that day, the full meaning of which he either did not understand or would not reveal.

"Something went wrong," he recalled in an interview, "and I understood that on 26 April, when I was asked to take my mask off and give a joint interview with [then co-chairman of the DPR Denis] Pushilin." In that interview, he described his unit and said they crossed into Ukraine at the request of local activists:[48]

> I was perfectly fine with an anonymous status, the kind I had in Crimea. Most of the things I did there were not out in the public. I thought that that would be the case in Donbas—that I would remain in the shadows. My emergence in the public sphere meant that the plan had changed entirely.[49]

But was there ever a plan, though? Or did Girkin, like the local politicians in Donetsk, read the emanations of the Kremlin too much to his own advantage?

"All decisions I took independently," Girkin said about his march into Donbas. His reasoning, based on other interviews, was that in order to maintain peace after the annexation of

Crimea, it was imperative that Donbas was secured in Russia's hands as well. He ascribed this view to Crimea's new leader, Aksyonov. "He understood that Crimea without Novorossiya was a hostage in a cell without a key."[50]

If local militias believed Strelkov to be the manifestation of the "little green men" they were hoping for, then it was understandable that the new and as yet hardly functional Ukrainian government also assumed them to be the Russian Spetsnaz that they feared. If Kyiv at first looked on without a clear sense of what to do as local activists seized buildings in Donetsk, Luhansk and Kharkiv, Girkin's arrival was interpreted as a Russian invasion and triggered what became called the Anti-Terrorist Operation. At first, Kyiv, whose army was in disarray, had little choice but to rely on volunteer battalions, including although by no means confined to the ultra-right groups such as Pravy Sektor that many Russian-speakers in the East associated with fascism. Soon enough, these battalions would be incorporated into Ukraine's National Guard. By June, it would surround Slovyansk.

Girkin's calls for Russian aid would become increasingly desperate as Ukrainian artillery and aircraft pounded Slovyansk. His YouTube addresses no longer shied from criticizing the Kremlin for its lack of assistance. Due to his complaints, he was increasingly becoming a thorn in the side of the man who would become the first formal leader of the DPR, Alexander Borodai. But while Borodai had more realistic expectations of the Kremlin, Girkin seemed to believe that Russian national interests dictated reinforcement and it was a matter of time before help arrived.

It didn't—at least, not to the extent that Girkin had come to expect based on his work in Crimea. By July, Girkin took the decision to retreat from Slovyansk. On 17 July, militiamen under Girkin's command, using a Buk surface-to-air missile provided by Russia, shot down a passenger jet carrying 298 people, believing it to be a Ukrainian military cargo jet. Russia would go on to deny and, by turn, blame the shoot-down of Flight MH-17 on

Ukraine, or describe it as a set-up. But after that, it was a matter of time before Girkin was forced to resign and sent back to Moscow. Something tragic had happened that overturned his plans and his very faith in himself and, most of all, his place within the elaborate hierarchy of subordination to national interests in which he so stubbornly believed. As a military officer, it was his duty not to question the motives of the Commander in Chief but to implement his orders. But were there orders? Or merely signals so vague and inconsistent, and so mangled by the time they got passed down—from the Presidential Administration to Malofeyev, from Malofeyev to Borodai, from Borodai to Girkin—that their original intent was irredeemably lost? Each, along that vague chain, projected his own assumptions about what the "national interest" really was and what that they thought they were being encouraged to do from above, and so they acted, from below, on their own impulses, thinking them to be the Kremlin's intent.

Whatever happened, if for the first few months after his return to Moscow in the late summer of 2014 Girkin loyally kept a portrait of Putin in his study, by the fall that portrait was conspicuously gone. "Igor Ivanovich tried to be loyal for a long time. He is by character a typical patriot ... [with] complexes typical of Soviet security officers," Konstantin Krylov, a close associate of Girkin, told me years later:

> These people believe they know better than others, that they have a right to hold in contempt the average person's views. And at the same time he is used to thinking that the bosses know better, that certain sacrifices in the name of the government are inevitable. But everything has its limits. When those same bosses start acting in a way that cannot be explained, then you have to admit that ... there are traitors and thieves in the government.[51]

6

THE BETRAYAL

It's a shame they didn't bail us out.
Didn't send no reinforcements after all
Only two of us are left here
You and I have been fucked over
All our brothers have been killed,
Ammunition's a disaster,
But we're holding onto our post

Boris Grebenshikov, "You and I Have Been Fucked Over"

In Moscow, in the shadows of the State Duma building looming over us across the street, Arsen Klinchayev, the Ukrainian businessman and former MP who led one of the first, unsuccessful seizures of a government building in Luhansk before getting arrested and kicked out of Ukraine, met me at a café and tried to sell me on a new Donbas. With the right care and financing, he said, it could become the new Switzerland of the East.

Whether to help him with his pitch, or from loneliness or boredom, he had brought his pet bunny rabbit along, and I feared we would get evicted because the rabbit was shitting all over the table. But then again, "it's a living creature, it will get lonely at home."

Klinchayev's demeanor combined the confidence of a ruthless businessman, with his gold chain and watch, with the desperation of a freedom fighter. A former member of the Party of Regions, the pro-Russian faction behind ousted President Yanukovych, he was trying to convince lawmakers and Kremlin officials that Donbas was still important enough for Russian strategic interests to give it more money.

It was 2018. For all the confidence, there was something hollow about his patter—as if he had been led on, let down, and didn't believe in his own sell anymore.

"Gradually I have come to understand that we are pawns in a big game, the rules of which we do not understand," he told me. "There are twenty-seven opinions. Just like twenty-seven Kremlin towers. Everyone takes their opinion to Vladimir Vladimirovich on how to solve the problem in Donbas and Ukraine. In that battle, Surkov won out, defeated everyone. He was against Novorossiya. He defeated the Glazyev people. He defeated the military structures."

I

By the time Moscow started getting involved in the new separatist governments in mid-May, Borodai was having serious doubts about what he'd gotten himself into. But then again, he'd had them for a while.

"Serega, that you?" he called up a field-commander in mid-May, based on an intercepted phone call released by the Dutch Joint Investigative Team as part of its fact-finding mission into the downing of Flight MH-17:

"Yeah."

"It's me, Sasha. Where you sitting? At the base?"

"Yeah."

"Well, you keep on sitting there. Now, listen. We've got a serious fucking situation here. An event, fuck me, of quote 'government importance.' We're going to set up a government today. So, I've got an order for you, or a suggestion, or whatever you want to call it. You sit there, quietly. You don't go anywhere, you don't do anything, if anyone asks you to comment you say you support everything. Moscow has a big surprise, for fuck's sake. You know who the prime minister is going to be, Serega?"

"Mm, doesn't matter," Serega says.

"Well, it matters to me. Because it's me, goddamn it," Borodai sighs heavily.

"Well congratulations!" a boozy Serega drawls sarcastically.

"Why I would ... Oh, *fuck* all this. FUCK."

"Comrade Prime Minister!"

"Oh *fuck* ..."

"Well, I'm subordinate to you now ..."

"Guy from Moscow looks at all this, says, I wash my hands of it. Fuck."

"Listen, I can't talk much, really tired."

"Ok, Serega. You go get some sleep."[1]

On 16 May 2014 (Borodai himself claimed it was 13 or 14 May), the third assembly of the Supreme Council of the DPR appointed Borodai as prime minister. Girkin was officially made minister of defense.[2] Someone in Moscow, according to the intercepted phone call, either approved or initiated the vote. Borodai, however, described being so distressed by his own appointment that he spent the day smoking two packs of cigarettes and cursing incessantly. "I couldn't sleep for days. I didn't want this," he would recall later.[3]

He hadn't banked on taking the reins and instead believed he would remain in the background. But it seemed everyone was trying to wash their hands of the separatist movement—to pass it on, like a toxic potato, to the next guy. The "guy from Moscow," Putin, and Borodai himself—no one wanted responsibility for the emergence of a new breakaway state, but everyone believed it was too late to stop it. Indeed, the newly minted prime minister of this breakaway state, one whose independence from Ukraine Moscow had, at that point, no intention of recognizing, had begun to have misgivings at least a month earlier, even before Girkin's invasion was underway. There was no point, he had said, in pursuing the project if the Kremlin hadn't decided whether it even wanted to get involved. But Girkin, according to him, didn't want to wait.[4]

At least a part of Borodai's seeming frustration with Girkin's impatience can be attributed to their closeness. The two knew each other quite well. Like Girkin, Borodai would take it upon himself to fight wars that he felt the Kremlin was unable or unwilling to fight, but should. A philosophy major, he would go on to make a career for himself as a political consultant, flitting around the halls of power and business, and perhaps imagining himself a competent occupier of both. In his youth, he had become acquainted with a close friend of his father, the nationalist philosopher Lev Gumilyov, and absorbed a great deal of his mystical beliefs about ethnic destiny and the cosmic forces driving a select few "impassioned" people to make history. "The civil war between the White and the Red that started in 1917 never ended," he would recall. "It continues to this day, and there are reasons for that."[5]

Borodai was nineteen when the Soviet Union collapsed, and, much like Malofeyev—another fan of Gumilyov's—was eager to pick up an AK to right the wrongs of what he believed was a new, undemocratic regime acting against the interests of the Russian people. There was no lack of opportunities. Nationalist sentiments flared across a fraying empire, and in 1990 Moldova, which bordered Ukraine to the west, became one of several Soviet republics to assert its independence and sovereignty—both legally and culturally, by declaring Moldovan the state language and curbing the status of Russian. In response, the regional council of the predominantly Russian-speaking enclave of Pridnestrovie (the Russian name for the region of Transnistria) likewise declared its own independence, establishing the self-styled Pridnestrovian Moldovan Republic (PMR). Civilians mobilized into volunteer militias to stave off nationalist Moldovan forces. War broke out, but Moscow was silent—paralyzed by the collapse of its power all around, it chose neutrality. Gorbachev, while still in power, had ruled Transnistria's declaration of independence null and void, while the Soviet army maintained official non-involvement. This neutrality remained under Yeltsin, despite the fact that the 14,000-strong Soviet 14th Guards Army stationed in Transnistria was tacitly supporting the volunteer militias by allowing them to plunder its depots and closing its eyes as its soldiers defected to the separatist cause. To Borodai—and to many of the nationalist-minded middle- and senior-ranking Russian military officers who made up his and his father's circle at the time—Moscow's inaction was a travesty just short of treason. "I finished my second year of university, and, on my own initiative went over there. I was taken into a [volunteer] battalion. We were ready to go all the way to [Moldovan capital] Chisinau."

Although Borodai didn't know it then, at about the same time, a twenty-two-year-old history graduate named Igor Girkin hopped on a train with a friend to join a Cossack battalion to fight on behalf of the PMR, for largely the same reasons. They wouldn't meet until 1996, following the first Chechen war, when they were introduced by a fellow veteran of Transnistria, Olga Kulygina, who would go on to fight in Donbas. By then, Borodai was working as a war correspondent for Russian news agencies, and as an opinion columnist for the nationalist *Zavtra* newspaper. Together with Girkin, they would travel to Dagestan and write about ethnic conflict there.[6]

While Girkin had gone on to join the army and then the FSB, Borodai joined the ranks of political consultants and spin-doctors that flourished in Russia during the 1990s and early 2000s. In 2002, around the time when nationalist-leaning journalists and pundits were joking about what they would do when they came to power, a prominent political technologist, Stanislav Belkovsky, published a fake leak[7] in a nationalist publication claiming that Borodai had been appointed deputy head of the FSB for information policy. The joke was intended as a present for Borodai's thirtieth birthday, but it stuck. Girkin, who had actually served in the FSB, couldn't stop mock-saluting Borodai for weeks afterwards.[8]

There was more than a bit of wishful thinking in the joke. These two had fought wars their own country had refused to fight, to whom the whole anarchy of the 1990s was a wrong that still somehow needed to be righted. To Borodai, Yeltsin's decision to send General Alexander Lebed to the PMR in 1992 and head up the 14th Army and broker a peace agreement was actually a capitulation, because it was intended to prevent the militias from going forward. "Our tattered armored vehicles had inscriptions on them, 'to Bucharest,'" Borodai would recall. "You know that saying, if you can't stop a herd of sheep, then you have to lead them? Well, we weren't a herd of sheep, but that's how they tried to stop us."[9] Technically, Borodai was referring to the events of 1992 in Moldova, where Moscow presented itself as the champion of the insurgents in order to contain them, but, speaking in 2017, he was just as likely describing Donbas.

II

In late April 2014, the participants of the pro-Russian movement that had moved from the Crimea Peninsula to mainland

Ukraine started noticing a subtle shift in the signals they were getting from Moscow. Whereas before, militants were hearing encouragement and off-the-record promises about "little green men" arriving to finish what these volunteers had started and bring Donetsk and Luhansk into Russia's fold, the signals stopped. They held their positions, they fought against Ukrainian pro-government forces, and they kept hoping that Moscow wouldn't let them down. For those higher up, the change was more pronounced. Girkin described how he was asked to give an interview without his mask on. And while a signal to go public, viewed from one angle, could have been an encouraging sign about shifting what was an essentially covert phase of a mission into a public one, Girkin was anything but encouraged. He understood it to be a sign that the Kremlin was cutting him loose, preparing to wash its hands of the mission and blame everything on him, if necessary.

Girkin and other sources close to the Kremlin described the shift as "sudden," and while there would be many more incremental changes in the Kremlin's gradual abandonment of the initial Novorossiya project as a whole, 26 April 2014 is widely considered the date when the Kremlin made its first, most pivotal decision: not to deploy troops to mainland Ukraine, if there ever had been any such plans in the first place.[10]

"I don't know what it was," Girkin said in a subsequent interview. "But I was told rumors that the [Russian] Security Council [headed by Patrushev] convened on 26 April and decided not to send troops to Donbas."[11]

The fervent, wishful expectation that Putin would deploy troops to Donbas in March and April 2014 was widespread not just among the rank-and-file enthusiasts who went to fight, but also among many senior Kremlin and military officials. "A lot of top brass would come to me later, justifying why they couldn't send troops in April," said a former Kremlin official, suggesting that despite all their will to do so, the decision from the top was to hold back, and even the top brass felt bad enough about it to feel they had to make excuses.[12]

In other words, until that point, the expectation that "little green men" would soon arrive in Donbas had gone viral. An associate of Girkin who traveled regularly to Donbas as a volunteer described the "Russian Spring" as a pyramid:

> For every man with a machine gun who went there, there were ten people who helped, supported him, gave him money; for each of those there are a hundred who approved, and for each of them, a thousand who wrote an approving [social media] post. It was a massive uprising. I wouldn't call it all-Russian, that's too much, but basically any active people who didn't have an important reason to stay home ended up going, from Muscovites and St Pete residents to guys from Siberia and Cossacks.[13]

At each level of the pyramid, the actors operated under a common assumption—fed by TV rhetoric and statements from the most fervent supporters of Novorossiya like Glazyev, Zatulin and a whole swath of ultraconservative parliamentarians—that it was inevitable that the Kremlin would send troops to "liberate" Donbas, just as it had done with Crimea. It was just a matter of time. Genuine fears of Balkan-style violent reprisals from the Ukrainian National Guard fueled the flames, but these fears were also embellished and magnified in the media by the pro-Novorossiya commentariat in Russia with the hope of compelling the Kremlin to act. Cementing the belief was a 1 March ruling by the Federation Council, the upper chamber of parliament. On the initiative of the Duma, the lower chamber, it authorized the deployment of troops to Ukraine to protect the Russian-speaking population.

Bolstering the prospect of an invasion—which the West feared and the separatists longed for—was a massing of troops around the Ukrainian border. By mid-April, analyses of satellite images and Western intelligence reports suggested that up to 40,000 troops were stationed within an hour's march of Ukraine, backed by fighter planes, helicopters and artillery.[14] With Moscow insisting these were normal exercises, they seemed intended to keep everyone in a state of anticipation, especially as the preparations for past invasions, such as that into Georgia in 2008, were masked as such maneuvers.

However, while the Kremlin had taken ownership of the political transition in Crimea, there was no consensus behind the scenes over whether it even wanted the same for Donbas. Directives, if there were any, were vague. "I can say with all certainty—[the Kremlin] didn't have a plan to capture Donbas," Borodai would recall of his trips there in the spring of 2014. "[They talked to me] because they wanted to understand the situation."[15]

According to Girkin, even Malofeyev, who was passionately behind the Crimean annexation, had misgivings about going further into mainland Ukraine, and Girkin, in his own words, "had to convince him." Perhaps, in Malofeyev's case, his initial enthusiasm for annexing regions of Ukraine's mainland—if the report he allegedly authored is to be believed—was checked by the actual developments on the ground, and by a cooler attitude to his endeavors from the Kremlin. In any case, Girkin had to go looking for a new patron. While he did not directly deny that Malofeyev gave him money for the mission, he said it was no longer necessary, and that it was Aksyonov who provided the funding and the arms for his subsequent move into the mainland.[16]

Malofeyev's misgivings suggest that even as early as March and April there was no definite Kremlin support for extending the Crimean scenario to mainland Ukraine—at most, a skeptical tolerance of the Russian activists, businessmen and officials backing the separatist groups in Donbas, and a potential preparedness to come to their aid if absolutely necessary. Crucially, though, there was for a while a belief on the ground that Putin was still smiling on Russian adventurism in Donbas—but this would soon be brought into question.

"You see, if there was no support at all, not even passive support," Girkin would recall,

> then fifty men with machine guns wouldn't have been able to cross the border back from Crimea [into mainland Russia], let alone into Ukraine. If we had waited just a couple of days, we wouldn't have been able to go ... And then something happened—and what was at least passive support disappeared.[17]

If the shift was sudden, and came down to Putin signaling, in one way or another, that the separatists should assume that they are on their own, then what circumstances had compelled him to make those signals?

"This remains a mystery to me," said one Kremlin advisor, a proponent of Novorossiya with ties to the separatists and senior Kremlin officials. "The legend is that Putin's meeting with the president of Switzerland changed his mind,"[18] but that meeting took place 7 May, after the noticeable policy shift in late April.

Instead, three factors seemed to be becoming increasingly significant in the Kremlin's calculus. The first was Ukraine's military response, virtually non-existent in Crimea and thus, especially as Kyiv hardly had a functioning government yet, not expected in Donbas. Yet on 15 April, interim President Turchynov launched what he called an "Anti-Terrorist Operation," one that would rely predominantly on nationalist volunteer battalions.

The second was that it had become clear that support for the pro-Russian cause was not nearly as strong as in Crimea. The referendum—even as separatists had to use muscle to get people to vote—was unimpressive, and Moscow refused to recognize it. Even before then, insurgencies had failed to take hold in Kharkiv and Odessa, two cities many had expected would actually be hubs for pro-Russian activism, and there was a growing sense that whoever was advising the Kremlin—RISI, the FSB or the host of political technologists who backed the cause—had been led on by their own wishful thinking and miscalculated the strength of the insurgency.[19]

The third factor was the Western sanctions. The EU and the US imposed a series of sanctions over Crimea throughout March, with the last serious sanctions—involving a US ban on export licenses for defense products or services to Russia—issued on 27 March. While seven Crimean officials were sanctioned on 11 April, days after the 6 April seizure of government buildings by pro-Russian separatists in Luhansk, Donetsk and Kharkiv, that did not deter Girkin's march into the Ukrainian mainland on 12 April. The next serious sanctions would come only on 28 April, when the EU and the US banned seven individuals and seventeen companies linked to Putin from traveling or trading with Western countries and further restricted Russia's access to military goods.

Washington formally imposed this third round of sanctions over Moscow's failure to fulfill a 17 April agreement in Geneva on resolving the crisis. That agreement included a pledge to disarm "all illegal armed groups" and return "all illegally seized buildings."[20] But at that point, even if Moscow had the will to remove separatists from the buildings they occupied in three Ukrainian cities (it did not), actually doing so would have involved using Russian special forces on Ukrainian territory. After all, at that particular point in time, most of those separatists were Ukrainian citizens inspired by Moscow but not directly under its command.

The 28 April sanctions were likely discussed with Putin ahead of time. From his perspective, although Moscow had signed onto them, the Geneva requirements were neither fair nor possible. If it was legal for pro-Western mobs to seize buildings in Kyiv and

Lviv ahead of the Maidan Revolution, the Kremlin believed, then so too was the takeover of buildings by anti-Maidan protesters in the East.

To Putin, that Washington was willing to punish Moscow for its failure to do something that was out of its power seemed to confirm his worst suspicions, that the United States was essentially using Ukraine to weaken and undermine Russia. And if that were the case, then putting a stop to the separatist movement would only embolden Washington in its hybrid war against Russia, given that it would mean sending Russian special forces onto Ukrainian soil to arrest or shoot the separatists it had inspired and tacitly supported.

Putin felt he was in a bind. Crimea had demonstrated that the Kremlin and its army was perfectly capable of decisive action—of securing an entire peninsula and enabling a parliament to vote to join Russia—swiftly and secretly, with the help of the local population. However, in the Donbas the risks were higher, the opposition greater and the support weaker. If he launched a full-blown military intervention, he would trigger a tougher Western response and quite possibly find himself trying to prop up a regime with no real constituency. Yet if he backed away entirely, he would show weakness to the Americans and to his own nationalists. He could neither advance nor abandon the Donbas project.

III

The first visible sign that Putin was trying to distance himself from the separatist groups that had installed themselves in Donetsk and Luhansk came on 7 May 2014. Following a lengthy meeting with the president of Switzerland and OSCE Chairperson-in-Office, Didier Burkhalter, Putin called on rebels to suspend the referendum for independence they had scheduled for 11 May and announced that Russian troops had been pulled back from the Ukrainian border.

"We appeal ... to representatives of southeast Ukraine and supporters of federalization to hold off the referendum scheduled for May 11, in order to give this dialogue the conditions it needs to have a chance," he said.[21]

The about-face stunned Russian and Western observers alike. In Moscow, the move was seen as a result of "intensive bargaining" with the West, in the words of one Kremlin advisor. A day earlier, Ukrainian authorities had moved to release the "people's governor," Pavel Gubarev, a longtime pro-Russian activist who had been jailed in March. Perhaps Putin saw in concession a chance to deescalate. The meeting with the Swiss president was an opportunity for Putin to explore reviving the stalled Geneva Agreement of 17 April—which Russia had signed on to but found itself unable to implement—by agreeing to an expanded role for the OSCE.[22]

Putin's comments, however, were shrouded in so many conditions, including demands that Kyiv halt military operations and "release all political prisoners," that it sounded more like he was holding off on making a decision rather than taking a stance. That was one of the reasons why both the separatists and the Ukrainians refused to believe him. The Kyiv-appointed governor of Donetsk, Taruta, saw the move as a ruse: Putin was trying to convince his Western partners that he couldn't control the situation, when he was merely choosing not to.[23] On the other side, the pro-separatist Russian lawmaker Konstantin Zatulin, echoing the wishful thinking of the separatist leaders I would witness the following day in Donetsk, said Putin's words were intended for Burkhalter himself, rather than a signal for the separatists, and didn't amount to any change in policy at all.[24] Indeed, as an ideological patron of the pro-Russian movements in Donbas, Zatulin may have been the source of their rationalizations.

The move flummoxed the separatist leadership, the militias and their supporters. Having already spilled blood, many felt they didn't really have a choice but continue to fight, and many justified their increasingly desperate fight with the hope that while Moscow would send troops to back them if they succeeded, it would also have to do so if Kyiv moved in to crush them.

Putin certainly wanted to distance himself from the movement and was clearly doing so, but there is a reason for the ambiguity in his messaging and his actions. Aside from Kremlin officials like Glazyev, lawmakers like Zatulin and Sablin, and businessmen like Malofeyev, the separatist movement also had powerful backers in the FSB, albeit with a different agenda.

To date, no names have been leaked, and the question of exactly with whom Aksyonov, Girkin and Malofeyev coordinated their activities in the Donbas remains speculative. However, senior Kremlin aides such as Glazyev and Surkov did not have the remit to release weapons to the separatists or send the special forces operators who would soon start advising the militias. That would be either the Defense Ministry or the FSB. But it is widely understood in Moscow circles that Defense Minister Shoigu was initially opposed to the military intervention in Crimea, and to a potential one in Donbas, while Patrushev—the powerful Security Council chief and former head of the FSB—was enthusiastic about the Crimean operation, at least.[25]

Since 1998, the FSB had a special Fifth Service for Operational Information and International Communications, responsible for conducting intelligence activities in former Soviet republics, including Ukraine. In February 2014, its officers took a particular interest in the Maidan Revolution and even visited Kyiv.[26] At the time, there was no evidence their interest went beyond intelligence gathering, but since then, the FSB has become notoriously aggressive in Ukraine. The first signs of this came in July 2014, when an intercepted phone call recorded two separatist fighters in Donbas discussing their chains of command: one turned out to be getting orders from the FSB and the other from the GRU, the military intelligence arm of the General Staff of the armed forces. This kind of competitive activity is quite usual in modern Russian security politics, as agencies with overlapping remits seek to demonstrate their own value to the Kremlin. While the GRU controlled the Spetsnaz special force, though, the FSB seemed to have a greater overall role in the Donbas. In another intercepted call, a militant is heard asking the chief of the Southern Military District, Andrei Serdyukov, for weapons, only to be told that it is an FSB general who approves such matters. That general, a certain Vladimir Ivanovich, featured in several other phone calls in which Borodai and another field commander presented their wish lists of support, apparently unsuccessfully.[27] It seems, then, that it was the FSB more than any other agency or official that was approving the transfer of weapons and, in some cases, helping the separatists coordinate offensives.

With Patrushev, its powerful former chief, heading the Security Council, this essentially domestic intelligence agency—seemingly equivalent to Britain's MI5 or the FBI, albeit in practice much more extensive and aggressive—was becoming increasingly eager to drive Russian foreign policy.[28] Those FSB officers gathering intelligence in the "Near Abroad," though, were prone to a certain cognitive bias that had its roots in the Soviet Union: they didn't believe that popular movements could be genuine, instead of a nefarious plot by their counterparts in enemy governments. It was no wonder, then, that much of what they observed in Kyiv in 2014 they attributed to a well-planned coup instigated by hostile powers with the goal of undermining Russia. Having made that connection, many believed it was up to them to use the same methods, co-opting popular movements to fight the West's hybrid war.

But some of those officers themselves went native, becoming part of the pro-Russian popular movement that their superiors in the FSB—the generals—had mistakenly thought they could co-opt.

"Our men are dying [in Ukraine]—the Alfa, Vimpel [special forces]. They can fight, they are able," one FSB major who attended a pro-Novorossiya rally told me. "Putin—give us orders! We need just one day and Ukraine will be ours. We have 300 men in Donbas. We just need a command. To fight, to conquer. Like in Georgia."[29]

It was no surprise, then, that it was a former officer, Girkin, who took the initiative both on behalf of the pro-Russian movement and on behalf of Russian national interests, which, according to the FSB, meant countering a malign threat from the West. He was driven not so much by any orders as much as by a culture that had permeated the security community.

"Yes, Girkin was an enthusiast," said one Kremlin advisor with ties to Malofeyev. "But he couldn't have done what he did without some serious protection. And that must have come from the FSB."

Putin, himself a former director of the FSB, could not put a decisive stop to a project that had such strong emotional investment from the FSB without alienating them. His very power as president rested on their loyalty to him—and thus on his loyalty to them.

But it wasn't just the FSB. In 2014, to stop the separatist movement would mean firing every FSB and army general who had encouraged his men to move weapons and advisors across the border to Ukraine, and arresting thousands of volunteers and former and current mid-rank security and military officers who joined them. It would also mean censoring (and possibly prosecuting) an army of policymakers and media pundits who, initially encouraged by the Kremlin to compete for its favor, had railed against a fascist Ukrainian "junta."

To do all of these things meant that Putin would be admitting to having made a series of catastrophic mistakes and could soon be facing a nationalist junta of its own, led by the one force he relied on for his power. This was something he could not risk. But nor could he risk what some of the hardliners, particularly in the FSB, but also in the military, were advocating: a full-scale invasion into Donbas to support the separatists. The costs, in terms of international isolation, were just too high. For the Kremlin, that left it in an impossible middle ground: propping up the separatists with guns and advice, while at the same time reining in their separatist ambitions and replacing them with something else, but quite what, the Kremlin had yet to decide.

IV

In mid-May 2014, Moscow began the years-long effort to establish its control over the separatist statelets while distancing itself from and removing the freelance enthusiasts that had set them up. First on the agenda was sweeping away the "miners and truck drivers" that had made up the initial grassroots movement in hopes of installing something or someone more manageable. To control the politics, one first had to take control of the muscle, even if one did not yet know, as Moscow likely didn't, what political direction it was going to take.

In the second half of May, a new militia, the Vostok Battalion, began arriving from Russia and filling its ranks from those among the local militias. Among the fighters were men from Russia's Northern Caucasus republics, Chechnya and Ossetia, and they were often much better armed than the local Russian and Ukrainian separatists.[30] On 29 May, Vostok seized the rebel headquarters in Donetsk. The new militia cleared away the barricades of tires and rubble surrounding the building and kicked out the irregulars who had occupied it since April.[31]

The battalion, it turned out, was a resurrected force of Chechens and veterans of wars in the Northern Caucasus, recruited by the GRU[32] with the mission of restoring order among the militias—or rather of imposing Moscow's authority. Headed by Alexander Khodakovsky, a Ukrainian veteran of the Berkut special police, the battalion was also soon made up of local Ukrainian volunteers rather than Russians, but its Russian roots made it clear it was the first attempt to impose some kind of control on the militias.[33]

The efforts to clean up and manage the separatist militias intensified over the month of June, along with an influx of weapons and men. But rather than serving the existing commanders, many of these men were actually being brought in to replace them. Even so, these new commanders still didn't seem to have any clear objectives, aside from imposing order. This bred confusion. After all, even Vostok was soon made up largely of local Ukrainian fighters, many of whom still believed that their goal was defending and establishing the independent state of Novorossiya.

A July phone call between Alexander Lyashenko, the commander of Makeyevka, and another field commander, with the nickname Mongol, illustrates fighters' frustrations in understanding where their orders were coming from and what their objectives were.

"I have a question, do you have a fucking phone number for fucking Strelkov?" Lyashenko asks.

"No, not really."

"Is there a way to reach him? I mean, to just find out, where are we going with this? I'm asking as a commander of Makeyevka."

"We're going towards centralization," Mongol explains slowly. "People are arriving here with a mandate from Shoigu, local field commanders are being thrown the fuck out from their divisions and replaced by people from Moscow."

"Hm ..."

"But this doesn't apply to Makeyevka."

"But you tell me something, I'm just trying to fucking understand what's going on, so I know who do I report to?"

"You're going to report to the minister of defense."

"Who is that?"

"Strelkov as the minister of defense reports to Borodai as the Commander in Chief, just like in any country. You get your orders from Strelkov. No one else is in a position to give you any orders. Well, as prime minister, Borodai can give you orders directly too, and you'd have to carry them out."

"Hm. Ok, I get it."

"But yeah, basically you don't move a single soldier without Strelkov's orders. Otherwise, yeah, we're moving towards centralization, towards a serious war. But the local field commanders are being culled because they're out of control. Looting, raping, killing, playing politics. And you know this better than I do, Sasha."[34]

It would seem, from this, that a "mandate from Shoigu" meant that the current and former Russian army officers who headed up militia units coordinated with the Defense Ministry, or, more likely, the GRU. Ostensibly, this kind of coordination could mean better discipline in preparation for war with Ukraine. But from the vantage point of Girkin, the defense minister, whose relationship with Khodakovsky had become increasingly tense and who in June had gone as far as warning Putin against giving up on Novorossiya, this was far too optimistic.

The likelier explanation was that this new coordination was intended to hold the militias back. For a month now, Girkin and many of his fighters had sensed that Moscow was distancing itself from the separatist idea, and they saw its subsequent actions through that prism.

But the more Moscow seemed to cool to their agenda, the greater the effort the separatists made to persuade it to send troops, weapons and aid. A series of intercepted telephone conversations from June and July 2014 paint a complex picture of increasing desperation in the rebel leaders' requests for help from the Russian government. But the story they tell is not just one of desperation, but also of confusion—a mounting disconnect between assumed strategies that the rebels were operating under and the calculi of whoever was coordinating them in the Kremlin. They are interesting too in that they are not part of a fabricated narrative. Some presumed Girkin's public statements were part of a ruse in which the Kremlin was making him pretend to be an independent actor over which it had no control, but the intercepted calls reveal just how tense the relationship was and how limited the support he was getting.

A phone conversation on 8 June between Girkin and Aksyonov's assistant, and then with Aksyonov himself, published by the Joint Investigation Team, was widely cited as proof that Girkin was getting help and instructions from the Russian government. Aksyonov, after all, was by then a Russian regional governor. But the actual substance of that conversation has Girkin almost begging Aksyonov to get badly needed weapons.

The conversation begins with a man named Mikhail, purportedly an assistant to Aksyonov, returning a call apparently placed by Girkin earlier.

"Sergei told me you wanted to connect to pass on some information," he said.

"Well, what information ..." Girkin began dejectedly, "it's already obvious that if there's no massive help soon, then, well ... Whatever it is we're getting now—this one teaspoon per hour—it's not playing any role at all." The separatists were vastly outnumbered, he said,

> and if I've managed to dig in, then if the [Ukrainians] start launching assaults on other cities, at this rate they'll quickly squash them, and then me [and my men] too. If they don't resolve this issue with Russian help, air cover, with artillery support, then we won't be able

to hold on to the East. We won't hold on for certain. What we've got now just helps us keep our pants up.

This last part, about not being able to hold the East, was said with a bit of a dramatic flair, as if Girkin was talking about the entire Eastern Front during the Nazi advance, and indeed many of the separatists had convinced themselves of this mythology to the point that they often took it literally.

"I see," Girkin's interlocutor said, with the tone of a man who could only sympathize but do little. Girkin continued:

We need anti-tank artillery, we need anti-air defense, because MANPADS are no longer sufficient, and we need specialized crew, already trained, because we don't have the time to train them. I've got four tanks positioned by Semyonovka, [Ukrainians] are shelling [our] positions for the third day already. I don't have a single anti-tank gun to fight back with. And it's like that everywhere, [against] the whole Ukrainian army. And that's what needs to be passed on [to the top]. Because sooner or later a decision is going to need to be made. But it may be too late by then, because much of the militia will be destroyed by then, and the front line will have moved east of Donetsk.[35]

Aksyonov's assistant could only sigh at this, but he clearly did pass on Strelkov's words to "the First," their nickname for Aksyonov, because fifteen minutes later Aksyonov himself called Strelkov back.

Aksyonov rushed through his report.

"Hello, Gir. Well, you're acting in your own style again. So I was there on Tuesday, where I needed to be, but all these visits, yesterday, today, you know how it is," he said apologetically:

Today at 22 I got a connection with them, with those who make the decisions, so those who were here working with me, you know them, they got the full picture. So we'll talk at 22, I'll inform you. And there's been a coordination center on this situation set up.

"Ok, I'll connect with you at that time," Girkin said. "But you understand the situation ..."

"I understand," Aksyonov interrupts, speaking in a hurry, at times sounding almost frustrated. "Listen, I was there on Tuesday where I needed to be, and explained that if we don't take steps ... we will lose our markets."

That didn't sound like it made a lot of sense to Girkin, though.

"But we'll lose everything."

> I'm telling you, we'll lose *markets*, we understand what we're talking about. And the person there called another person right in front of me ... They're getting documents ready. If I hadn't seen the situation with my own eyes it would have been harder to refuse me. But I did, so the commands were made right in front of me.[36]

Maybe Aksyonov was trying to reassure an increasingly impatient Girkin, but there is also a sense that each are speaking of different things. The *markets* could be a code for rebel-held areas spoken by a government official aware of the need to remain cryptic, or they could be an indicator of how Aksyonov was trying to sell the need to defend these territories to the decision-makers in Moscow. Perhaps he needed to convince a skeptical Girkin to get off his back for a project that both understood was proving a much harder sell in the Kremlin than either anticipated. But in any case, whoever *they* were that Aksyonov was referring to—senior generals in the security agencies or Putin himself—their reluctance to get involved in Girkin's affairs was evident by the increasing efforts he was taking to convince them otherwise.

Girkin—or the people who had given him false promises—was being cut loose.

V

Amid Moscow's efforts to establish its authority over the militias, by June it became clear that it was also seeking to establish political control. Putin's First Deputy Chief of Staff Vladislav Surkov, a rival of Glazyev's, emerged as the key handler, or "curator," of the separatist governments. Publicly, at least, the separatist leadership presented this in the most positive light: that after months of sitting on the fence Moscow was finally listening to the separatists and beginning to take them seriously.

"I dare say that the Russian leadership is absolutely accurate in its understanding of how to solve the problems of the Donetsk People's Republic," Borodai said with quite a degree of bravado in a 17 June interview. "They are ready to help on the highest level. I also know and respect the presidential aide Vladislav Surkov, who always offers the Donetsk People's Republic serious support. Without exaggeration, Surkov is our man in the Kremlin."[37] But that man was there to solve a different problem: the problem that the DPR and Lugansk People's Republic had become for Moscow. To that extent, he was co-opting the movement rather than helping it, heading up a herd of sheep in order to stop them.

* * *

The rebels' "man in the Kremlin" was indeed a charmer. A dark-eyed half Chechen with links to the underworld, a poet and a novelist, for over a decade Surkov had artfully concocted a compelling narrative of himself—and indeed of the Kremlin as a whole—as a powerful, manipulative demiurge, using dark psychological arts to control domestic policy, and to manage an opposition that often didn't even know it was being managed. When he re-emerged on the scene during the Russian Spring, the longtime first deputy chief of staff seemed like the perfect choice to manage what both Russians and foreigners widely regarded as a cunning Kremlin plan to steal a chunk of Ukraine under the guise of a manufactured popular movement.

But what that demonic, all-powerful narrative concealed—and perhaps the real reason why the Kremlin needed that narrative so much—was just how little was actually under the Kremlin's control. In hindsight, it also concealed what many of those who had dealings with Surkov—Girkin included—would come to know all too well. To some who had worked with him, he left the impression of an inefficient manipulator who too easily promised all things to all people, leaving waste, disappointment and scandal in his wake.[38]

Once a manager in the jailed oil tycoon Mikhail Khodorkovsky's Menatep empire, Surkov became first deputy chief of staff in 1999. One of his first tasks was to manufacture a Kremlin-compliant nationalist opposition party to draw votes away from the Communists, whom Khodorkovsky had been funding, and, indeed, which served as the main reason for his imprisonment that year. Thus was born the Rodina, or "Motherland," party, headed by the nationalists Dmitry Rogozin and Sergei Glazyev—the latter going on to be one of the foremost mentors of the Russian Spring. As a Kremlin project, Rodina, however, was a failure; its members, as would often happen when Surkov tried to manage things, turned out to be too outspoken and ultimately cut the puppet strings themselves.

In 2004, the Kremlin suffered a painful blow when Ukraine's first Maidan—the street protests that became the Orange Revolution—wrested the presidency from Kremlin favorite Viktor Yanukovych and handed it to the pro-Western Viktor Yushchenko. It was a blow not just because the Kremlin feared losing influence over its neighbor, but because it more broadly came to fear what it believed could be a similar, Western-engineered "color" revolution in Russia. To help prevent this, Putin tasked Surkov with preventing this scenario at all costs.[39] To that end, Surkov began grooming an army of pro-Kremlin youth movements dubbed Nashi, or "Ours."

In 2008, when Putin vacated the presidential seat in favor of his anointed protégé, Dmitry Medvedev, Surkov stayed on in the

Presidential Administration, maintaining his virtual carte blanche over domestic politics and remaining in charge of the pro-Kremlin youth movements. In that role, however, he reportedly grew close to Medvedev and even came to support some of his liberal reforms. That—together with the ultimate failure of the Nashi movement in preventing exactly the kinds of mass protests the Kremlin feared—would prove his undoing.

In the winter of 2011–12, Putin's decision to return to the presidency dashed hopes for genuine liberal reform that Medvedev had, rather unknowingly, fostered in the newly emerging urban creative class. The result was an unprecedented wave of anti-Kremlin demonstrations known as the Bolotnaya protests. But despite hundreds of thousands of people rallying in the streets, Putin managed a comfortable victory—with some vote rigging and manipulation, of course—in March 2012. The master-manipulator Surkov's role in all this was as confusing as it was tantalizing: even as his army of pro-Kremlin demonstrators harassed and clashed with the protesters on Moscow's streets, Surkov unabashedly praised those who were calling Putin a thief and a thug: "The best part of our society, or, the more productive part is demanding respect," he said in a newspaper interview in December 2011. "You can't just condescendingly wave off their opinion."[40]

At the time, his comments were taken as part of some cunning manipulation, but in hindsight, it seems more likely that they were sincere. Surkov was siding with Medvedev and his liberal reforms, and that was too much for Putin's comfort. That spring, whether because of the failure of his Nashi movement to prevent the protests or because of his closeness to Medvedev, he left his post and moved on to work in Medvedev's cabinet as first deputy prime minister. While he would return to the Presidential Administration the following year, it was merely as Putin's aide, for by then Sergei Ivanov had taken his old seat as first deputy chief of staff. Surkov's power as the "gray cardinal" of domestic politics began to wane, and much of his domestic policy portfolio was handed over to Vyacheslav Volodin. He favored a more straightforward approach to mustering pro-Putin support, courting the populist base of factory workers, civil servants and rank-and-file police and security officers, rather than the creative class.

Surkov's remit, like that of Glazyev, now became managing the "Near Abroad," and especially the Russia-backed independent statelets of Abkhazia and South Ossetia in Georgia, and to an extent Transnistria in Moldova. But if Glazyev was passionately involved in the Novorossiya project—in recognizing and then annexing parts of Ukraine—Surkov's heart never really seemed to be in it. While he claims to have chosen handling the Ukraine project himself, he did so while, in his own words, already feeling "alienated" from the system he was serving.

"I realized [in 2013] that there is no room in the system for me," he described rather cryptically in a subsequent interview:

> Of course, I created this system, but I was never a part of it. It's not the system's problem, it's my problem. I felt alienated. I just can't do something longer than for five years ... I almost left then, but then returned. I got a unique opportunity to choose a project, so I chose Ukraine. Intuitively. I just felt that it's going to be big. I figured out even before everything started happening that there would be a real battle with the West. Serious. With casualties and sanctions. Because the West would not stop at anything. And we wouldn't [stop] at any cost.[41]

Surkov's own words are often riddled with mysticism and contradictions—in the same interview, for instance, he describes in detail how he practices a form of "non-thinking" meditation as he struggles to empty his mind—while his political stances have notoriously shifted. Standing up to a hostile West has probably been his most consistent policy as a statesman, but the tactics and machinations applied on the domestic arena and in his management style have been kaleidoscopic, only further lending to his theatrical image of the sophisticated, subtle political impresario. By the time he took on his new portfolio in 2013, he seemed to be doing so out of ennui, hopeful for a chance to be revived by something grand, to pull on the strings of history, rather than out of any genuine ideal or belief. His job was to keep Ukraine within Russia's orbit at all costs—a goal in which he likely believed—but by the end of 2013, all options of doing so seemed equally bad, and he probably saw this too.

He bumbled along this path throughout 2013, flexing the muscles of Russian soft power in Ukraine and, according to a trove of leaked emails, organizing cultural events there, and fielding endless emails from various pro-Russian politicians asking for money.[42] While presented as more evidence of Russia's coordinated interference, on closer reading the leaked emails instead depict a tired man looking for opportunities that would wake him up, lazily and cynically stringing along a whole host of Russian and Ukrainian political hangers-on petitioning Surkov for money, influence and love.

As such, Surkov was a real contrast to his colleague in the Presidential Administration, the "lone shooter" Glazyev, who firmly believed in an independent Novorossiya. Whereas throughout late 2013 and early 2014, Glazyev robustly promoted and directly funded separatist and pro-separatist Russian groups in Donbas, often out of his own pocket, Surkov tended to work more subtly and favored "great game" politicking, rather than rabble-rousing. He also seems to have been opposed to any direct annexation or even recognition of the separatist territories.

"I don't understand quite how Surkov saw [Novorossiya], because in all the times I've spoken to him, he sounded like he believed in all of the Kremlin's talking points about Ukraine, about Russians in Ukraine," said a veteran Kremlin advisor with ties to the separatists. "And yet there he was, stalling the whole idea."[43]

Sometime in April and May, as the arrow of the Kremlin's compass on what to do with Ukraine shifted, Glazyev was moved aside and the project of managing whatever it was that the separatists had created in Donbas landed squarely on Surkov's desk. According to that advisor, the decision to sideline Glazyev reflected a decision to exclude two policy options for which supporters of Novorossiya had lobbied and separatists had fought: direct Russian military intervention in support of the separatists and formal recognition of the new statelets. While the Donbas portfolio had been in Glazyev's hands, for instance, there had been talk of appointing a prominent Russian parliamentarian as prime minister of the new DPR. This was allegedly none other than Dmitry Sablin, the man who had traveled to Crimea with Malofeyev in February.[44] That idea was scrapped, and by appointing Surkov, the Kremlin was, in a way, washing its hands of the matter. Instead of a prominent Russian politician heading the DPR, the role fell to Borodai. "He was chosen simply because he could work well with Surkov," said the Kremlin advisor. "He was cynical, he was a political technologist, he understood the game."[45] Meanwhile, the decision to rule out an armed intervention was cemented on 25 June, when the Federation Council annulled a temporary decree passed on 1 March allowing the deployment of the Russian armed forces.

It was easier for the Kremlin to indicate what it didn't want than what it did. "Surkov's job was a form of penance," a former Kremlin official told me. "He was given the job, as I understand, for backing Medvedev instead of Putin. To atone for his sins, he was given a job in hell."[46]

But what was that job, exactly? If Glazyev had been sidelined, what were the Kremlin's objectives now that rebels they had inspired controlled a good chunk of Ukrainian territory? Even the new "curator" doesn't seem to have known: "Surkov had to improvise in the absence of a plan," said the advisor, who had worked for him in the past.

"The Kremlin didn't want to recognize Novorossiya, they didn't want to send troops, they didn't want anything, and Surkov had to figure out how to fix it."[47]

VI

Along with Glazyev, Malofeyev was also sidelined: it was signaled to him that his financial support of the separatists was no longer acceptable. "He tried to argue his case at first, to rally support in the media, but ultimately accepted the loss."[48] From then on, his charitable organizations would continue financing the statelets, but only in the form of humanitarian aid. With Glazyev and Malofeyev off the scene, the heads would start to roll that summer. They would continue doing so—sometimes literally—over the next four years, but in July and August they were the only evidence that the Kremlin was scrambling to contain a problem that had gotten out of hand.

By June and July, as Surkov tried to coordinate the politics of the new governments, intercepted phone calls between him and Borodai demonstrated all the constraints of Surkov's new role as improviser-in-chief. With few resources, little power and no plan from above, his best bet seemed to be delegating as much responsibility—if not resources—downwards so as to avoid taking any responsibility himself. The conversations are informal, advisory in nature, with Surkov at times apologizing to Borodai for too many suggestions, asking him at one point to decide for himself whom he wants to appoint to a post and when. In other words, rather than Borodai receiving "orders" from Surkov, what he seems to have been getting was support and facilitation. Surkov, for his part, acknowledges how dire the "civil war" has become, and sounded like he himself felt no one, least of all him, had much control over the situation. "I wish I was a minister," he says at one point.[49]

On 3 July, Borodai had a lengthy conversation with Surkov in which the latter was hinting at a reshuffle. "There's a certain Antyufeyev coming your way, I told you about him," Surkov tells Borodai after a lengthy exchange about the state of affairs. "But, Sasha, there's one thing I've got to tell you right away. They want state security posts. But I told them that Khodakovsky heads state security."

"I'm not against it," Borodai says. "I think that Khodakovsky himself might give up his post gladly."

"Well, you see how it goes. You decide. If he gives it up, then he gives it up. If he doesn't want to give it up for whatever reason, then just have them create another security service. Nothing wrong with that."

Observers often attribute Surkov with the skills of a chess grandmaster, plotting out cunning schemes to stay two steps ahead of whoever it is he is controlling or inveigling. But his last suggestion reveals something entirely different: an improvisation, and a potentially dangerous one at that, where a weary Kremlin official, dismayed by all the chaos Borodai has described, proposes *two* identical, rival security structures in a self-proclaimed republic. What could possibly go wrong?

Meanwhile, Girkin, the defense minister, was losing his hold on Slovyansk and making a painful decision to retreat. Morale was low as hopes for Russian intervention grew thin. On 25 May, Moscow had officially recognized Ukraine's presidential elections, which, for some separatist leaders, spelled the beginning of the end. "It was a heavy psychological blow for us," Pavel Gubarev would recall years later. "How could this be? It was as though Russia crossed out everything we had sacrificed for in Donbas."[50] At the same time, Ukraine's counteroffensive against Girkin's forces was strengthening. "The Ukrainians were careful, they were testing the waters, waiting to see how far we would go and how far Russia would go," Girkin would recall. "The first month, there was no artillery bombardment [of Slovyansk]. They would bomb towns, but left Slovyansk alone until the end of May. But seeing that Russia is not reacting ... shelling became more aggressive, while armored vehicles and aircraft were more heavily used." At first, volunteer battalions from Pravy Sektor and the National Guard, heavily made up of volunteer fighters, staged the main attacks, but by June Ukraine's regular armed forces became involved. By 3 June, Slovyansk's separatist militias, largely volunteers armed with whatever they could get their hands on and some hand-me-downs from Russia, faced the full brunt of Ukraine's army and aviation.[51]

According to the accounts of former separatist fighter Alexander Zhuchkovsky, the separatist militia defending Slovyansk numbered 2,500 men. In total, Girkin's forces in Donbas by then had up to 1,800 artillery weapons supplied by Russia, but this support was neither centralized nor systematic. It came through businessmen with army connections, with the tacit approval of the authorities. Beyond that, many weapons were simply collected from the battlefield or bought from Ukrainian soldiers. The existence of this kind of ad hoc weapons supply has been well documented: in one incident, separatists and local civilians took six armored vehicles from the Ukrainian 25th Airborne Brigade without a fight.[52]

This reliance on scavenging and buying Ukrainian arms illustrates the desperation of Girkin's forces more than their resourcefulness. By the end of June, Girkin claimed, his forces in Slovyansk were outnumbered 1 to 15. Although Girkin was no stranger to dramatic exaggeration and this number should not be taken literally, it reflects the way his militia were no match for the Ukrainian forces, however unprepared and disarrayed they often were.

On 16 June, Girkin made a desperate public statement:

Yes, we can hold Slavyansk for another month and a month and a half, but sooner or later we will still be destroyed. There is only one alternative to all-out war or to giving up Novorossiya—it is the immediate recognition of de-facto Novorossiya, Lugansk and Donetsk People's Republics and giving them real, massive and immediate military support. I address Russia as a commander of militia of Donetsk People's Republic and as a patriot of Russia and the Russian people.[53]

The following day, Girkin issued what seemed to be a warning to Putin, accusing Russian officials and oligarchs of "systemically sabotaging" the separatist project. Abandoning the Novorossiya project entirely would be disastrous for Putin, he claimed, placing him on the path of Slobodan Milošević.[54] While he was not yet openly accusing the Kremlin of giving up, and Russian officials of betrayal and treason, as he would in a few months, this bit of emotional blackmail was as close as he could come while still "in office."

On the night of 3–4 July, Girkin made the decision that he had to retreat from Slovyansk. By all accounts, the separatist leadership and his Moscow coordinators had ordered him to stay, but with the city surrounded and as it became clear that Moscow was not going to help, he felt he had no choice. He hesitated right up to the last minute, hoping for an eleventh-hour intervention from Moscow, but it never came. On the following day, his forces broke the siege and headed southwest to the other separatist stronghold of Kramatorsk.

Reputationally, the retreat cost Girkin dearly. Even the pro-Russian commentariat in Moscow had grown weary of his pleas and criticized the self-styled commander for counting on Russian aid—a clear indication of how frustrated Moscow was becoming with him. The same pundits would come down hard on him for his abandonment of Slovyansk, as if he had any real alternative.

It was not the only major failure. On 17 July, when Girkin had taken up command in Donetsk, his rebel forces, operating a Russian-supplied BUK surface-to-air missile, shot down what they thought was a Ukrainian military cargo jet. Instead, it was a civilian airliner operated by Malaysia Airlines, heading for Kuala Lumpur from Amsterdam. All 283 passengers and fifteen crew were killed. Girkin, and then the Kremlin, artfully denied their involvement, blaming the incident on Ukraine, NATO, anyone but themselves. But the damage was irreparable: regardless of intent, Russian action or inaction had killed nearly 300 innocent civilians in no way involved in the conflict. If Russia's annexation of Crimea and support of rebels in Donbas wasn't enough, the incident, and especially Moscow's refusal to take responsibility and properly investigate it, put it on a diplomatic collision course with the West. Girkin's reputation was tarnished beyond repair.

A catastrophe of such proportions might be expected to have immediately spelled the end of the separatist project, or at least its leadership. But Borodai and Girkin held on to their posts until early August. On 8 August, Borodai quietly left his post, replaced by local Donetsk businessman and the head of a volunteer fighter brigade, Alexander Zakharchenko. A week later, Girkin was equally quietly dispatched to Moscow, with Zakharchenko explaining his resignation by a "new place of employment." Vladimir Kononov, rebel commander of Shakhtarsk, took his place. In Luhansk, Valery Bolotov, the man who emerged as leader of the original local insurgency, was replaced by the commander of the armed militia, Igor Plotnitsky.[55]

According to two sources close to Girkin, his departure was part of a negotiation process: in return for leaving Donbas peacefully, the Kremlin had promised to send troops after all.[56] But there were other, more critical factors. According to a Kremlin insider, Putin "had grown tired of Girkin's blackmail and pressure to send troops. Such a decision could only have been made at the very top."[57]

The Kremlin seemed to be trying to control the situation and washing its hands of it at the same time.

PART TWO

... AND HOW THE KREMLIN LOST IT

7

THE NORTHERN WIND

"I'll have you standing in front of a military prosecutor," said the activist, a local leader of an NGO that lobbied on behalf of Russian soldiers and conscripts, when she called me back, "if I see even a word of what I told you in your newspaper."

I had been trying to piece together a story that wasn't making any sense, and had called her for comment.

Sometime after 15 August 2014, Saratov resident Lyubov Maksimova stopped receiving calls from her son, Ilya, who was a contract soldier serving in the 76th Pskov Airborne Division, unit number 74268. During their last conversation on 15 August, he had called to tell her that he was leaving for exercises in the field, somewhere in Rostov region. "He used to call every day before that," she told me. But then his calls stopped and she couldn't reach him. Her calls to his unit in Rostov went unanswered, and officials from the military recruitment office refused to give her any information.

In late August 2014, the parents of Russian paratroopers from several divisions started to worry. Ostensibly, their sons were serving in peacetime, and while accidents happened, they generally had little to worry about. But suddenly pictures of mysterious burials began popping up on obscure local media websites. Here and there, soldiers began arriving home in zinc coffins, accompanied by an eerie silence from their commanding officers.

On 21 August, Colonel Andrei Lysenko of Ukraine's National Security and Defense Council announced that Ukrainian troops had captured two armored vehicles belonging to unit 74268 of the 76th Pskov Airborne Division just outside Luhansk.[1] That same day, Ukrainian bloggers published photographs of the names and personal items of the crew, who were nowhere to be found. Among the belongings left behind were those of Ilya Maksimov.[2] It wasn't the first allegation that Russians were fighting in Ukraine, but it was the first piece of evidence of not just Russian nationals or Russian kit, but of regular, serving soldiers of the Russian armed forces.

On 25 August, journalists in the Pskov region uncovered two fresh graves belonging to soldiers from the 76th Division, after a funeral attended by about 100 people the same day.[3] At the cemetery, the journalists were approached by men in black and under threat of violence ordered to leave the city.[4]

After getting an anonymous phone call in the middle of the night in which a man who refused to identify himself told Maksimova her son was under arrest in Ukraine, she decided to go public with her story. Shortly after that, another unidentified man called her husband's number and passed the phone over to her son. Ilya spoke briefly, only to say that he was alive and well on a training ground in Rostov across the border from Ukraine. "I don't know anything else," she said.[5]

Lyubov Maksimova, as well as the activist, had every reason to be terrified when they spoke to me. If Ilya was captured in Ukraine, he could be jailed for twenty years for terrorism. But under Russian law, he could face up to seven years for desertion—after all, there was no legal basis for him to be in Ukraine, fighting in an undeclared war. Maksimova was already getting questioned by police, who said that the FSB was interested in his case. It was a gentle reminder to her and to anyone else asking too many questions that she needed to stick to the official story—that Ilya was in Rostov on exercises, and that, as the Defense Ministry had repeated time and time again, there were no Russian armed forces in Ukraine.

I

The Northern Wind began to blow in August; it blew through the fall and into the deepest winter of 2015; it routed the Ukrainian forces at Ilovaisk and fanned the flames in the battle for Debaltseve in February 2015. No one was to speak of it, no one was to know for sure, but the long-expected Russian troop reinforcements had finally begun to arrive.

With its poetic flair, its cloak-and-dagger hint of covert special ops, the tantalizing fiction of a powerful, northern empire that would step in and solve all their problems, "Northern Wind" was a code word used among separatists and their nationalist supporters in Russia, among them the former officers who liked to drop the reference while speaking to me. It denoted the covert Russian invasion of mainland Ukraine that properly began around 15 August 2014.[6] Sometime in July, Russian Spetsnaz reconnaissance groups started making their way into Donbas, and in mid-August, Moscow deployed battalion tactical groups (BTGs) amassed from an assortment of regular brigades and divisions, including paratroopers from the 76th Airborne.

Although in December 2015 Putin did admit there were some "Russian military personnel" in the Donbas "resolving various issues," Moscow has never admitted that it had any substantial regular military troop presence in Ukraine up until its full-scale military campaign in Ukraine in February 2022. Thus, there is no official date for the start of its covert invasion in 2014, no clear threshold between what was essentially a civil war involving foreign non-state actors (as many civil wars often do) and an actual inter-state armed conflict. Military expert Igor Sutyagin names 11 August as the date when the Russian armed forces commenced their large-scale armed incursion into Ukraine, consisting at the time of ten BTGs drawn from both paratrooper and mechanized brigades.[7] He gives no sources, but that date is broadly in line with other evidence that Russia was no longer sending just weapons and small Spetsnaz reconnaissance teams but full-scale invasion forces. On 15 August, DPR leader Zakharchenko announced the "joyful news" that a substantial reinforcement had arrived from Russia, consisting of at least 150 armored vehicles, thirty tanks and, most important, 1,200 servicemen "who had undergone training in Russia."[8] Less than a week later, Ukraine's Security Council would announce the capture of those Russian armed vehicles manned by Russian soldiers, including Ilya Maksimov. And on 25 August, Ukraine's Security Service captured ten soldiers who were part of an airborne battalion dislocated to Rostov and then ordered to march into Ukraine along with a column of infantry fighting vehicles.[9]

This was the first time that irrefutable, documented evidence had appeared of regular Russian troops in Donbas. Moscow, however, began not only denying its military involvement, but disavowing its own soldiers. The Defense Ministry wouldn't officially comment on the capture of Russian soldiers, but news reports citing anonymous defense officials said the soldiers "got lost." Of the ten captured in Ukraine, nine appeared publicly and two gave media statements. "We don't know when exactly we crossed the border, there were no signs or posts," said one of them, Sergeant Vladimir Zavosteyev. Another, Yegor Pochtayev, said it was their commanders' fault that they got lost. "They were leading us."[10]

Zakharchenko, obligated to conform, at least in part, to Moscow's fiction lest the blessed Northern Wind ceased to blow, could hardly contain his glee. He admitted to the presence of Russian regulars but continued to describe them as volunteers. They "preferred to spend their vacation not on a beach, but among us, among our brothers who are fighting for their freedom," he said. The Russian Defense Ministry was none too pleased with this—not least as it would have been illegal under Russian law—and while it refrained from dignifying the remark with an official comment, a senior defense official, speaking off the record, called it a "mistake."[11]

By the end of August, Russian troops in Ukraine numbered about 6,500, with about 42,000 troops rotating close to the Ukrainian border on the Russian side.[12] This seemed like a substantial contingent, especially compared to Ukraine's entire armed forces of 130,000 at the time,[13] but there was in fact a very limited number of troops that Russia at the time was prepared to deploy.

Russia's persistent denial of its involvement in Ukraine has often been viewed as a cunning subterfuge, but in reality, it limited and undermined not just Moscow's control of the situation in Donbas, but also its conventional military invasion. In June 2014, the Federation Council had revoked a temporary law passed in March, which allowed the deployment of forces to Ukraine to protect the Russian-speaking population. This was in line with the Kremlin's decision that spring to put an end to talk of a full-blown military deployment. And yet, by August, with Ukraine's forces gaining ground, it became clear that the separatists could not retain their positions without substantial Russian help. The decision to use BTGs rather than entire regiments reflected the constraints Moscow was operating under. By its own decision, it had ruled out the legal deployment of armed forces. Under Russian law, only contract soldiers and volunteers were allowed to be deployed abroad without a formal declaration of war. That meant cherry-picking all the professional soldiers it could muster from a whole assortment of brigades across Russia. Sutyagin argues that the Defense Ministry had considerable challenges in amassing the required groups, with an average BTG numbering between 700 and 900 soldiers,[14] such that most were having to be cobbled together from multiple brigades that had not had the chance to train together.

These challenges underscored Moscow's half-heartedness and its persistent reluctance to commit any more military or political support than was necessary to prevent the Ukrainian army from wiping out the separatists and to allow them to maintain their positions. While the separatists might hope—and the Ukrainians and the West, fear—that the Northern Wind would expand rebel-held areas deeper into Ukraine, perhaps even establishing a land bridge with Crimea, in hindsight it became clear that such plans, even if they existed in Moscow, were incompatible with their calculus at the time. Only with its full-blown invasion of 2022, which was accompanied by an air campaign, did Russia move to establish the land bridge. But by then, it was a war with entirely different objectives and on a wholly different scale.

In June and July, Ukraine's armed forces together with the National Guard and a number of volunteer battalions pushed east into rebel-held areas, retaking Mariupol in the south and Slovyansk to the north. They were trying to regain control over the border, encircling Donetsk and Luhansk and cutting them off from supplies and reinforcements from Russia. As Girkin and his forces retreated from Slovyansk, Kramatorsk and other towns to the northwest of the region to the capital of Donetsk, the center of the conflict shifted there as well. The fiercest fighting raged at Donetsk Airport throughout the summer months. Prior to its actual invasion, Russian units positioned in Rostov region regularly bombarded Ukrainian positions with rocket launchers.[15] But even though the Ukrainians suffered from disorganization and low morale, occasional shelling of their positions and limited supplies of new weapons for the separatists were not enough to stave off the government's summer counteroffensive. The Ukrainians steadily pushed eastwards, and despite Russian reinforcements, they managed to retake some two-thirds of the rebel-held areas.[16] For the separatists, it became imperative to hold key strategic towns along the Ukrainian–Russian border to prevent their being cut off, never mind dreaming of new offensives pushing further west. That was why the Northern Wind was so critical.

A massive counteroffensive by separatist militants and the Russian BTGs that had come to their aid started on 24 August. Joint forces surrounded the towns of Savur-Mohyla and Ilovaisk in the northeast of Donetsk region. On the night of 27 August, they captured the southern town of Novoazovsk on the Black Sea coast.[17] As the Ukrainian forces circled around east along the Ukrainian–Russian border to cut off the separatist strongholds at Donetsk and Luhansk, they found themselves kettled between rebel forces to the west and the Russian army across the border to the east.

The Russian troops were not tasked with expanding the rebel-held territories so much as defending what they had left, maintaining separatist control of the territory between Donetsk and Luhansk and the Ukrainian–Russian border to the west and countering Ukraine's attempted encirclement. On 29 August, after days of the deadliest fighting the conflict had seen to date, the Ukrainians were forced into a humiliating retreat from Ilovaisk. They had sought to recapture the city from separatists but became encircled with the arrival of Russian reinforcements. Nearly 400 Ukrainian soldiers were killed in the fighting.[18]

In the chaos, disinformation and carnage of the battles following the Russian invasion, the only logical explanation at the time for Russia's sudden decision to send in conventional forces, both from the separatist point of view and from the Ukrainian and Western one, was that by propping up the separatist statelets, Moscow was seeking to help them expand and establish themselves as independent states. This logic presumed what seemed obvious: that the separatists' strategy was the same as Moscow's.

Up to a point, it was: it had become clear both to the separatists and their backers in Moscow that the rebels could not hold on in the short term without Russian involvement. Moscow could not risk the domestic political debacle that would ensue, had it allowed the separatists it had backed in spirit to be defeated by Ukrainian forces. But in the longer term, their goals diverged. If it was clear that the separatists were seeking to expand their statelets at least to the borders of Donetsk and Luhansk regions to secure independence, less evident was how exactly Moscow saw the conflict playing out.

Speculation continued well into the next year of Moscow's and its separatist proxies' planned new offensives to secure more territory. But on 5 September 2014 representatives of Moscow, the separatists, Ukraine and the EU had signed the first of two agreements to establish a ceasefire and end the conflict: the Minsk Protocol. Russian BTGs continued to fight alongside the separatists well into the spring of 2015, though. Between mid-January and 18 February, separatist militias and Russian troops waged a battle to retake control of the strategic salient of Debaltseve, with some 500 people killed according to initial estimates, mostly civilians.[19] With the Ukrainians' withdrawal from Debaltseve, the contact line between government forces and the rebels settled into the position it would largely retain up until 24 February 2022. The second iteration of this ultimately futile roadmap to a settlement, the Minsk Package of Measures, in some ways put this disposition on paper.

The peace plan, committing all signatories to establishing autonomy for the statelets *within* Ukraine, essentially ruled out the possibility that Russia would recognize the territories, let alone annex them. But given that Ukraine signed it under duress—in the midst of the heaviest fighting the conflict had seen—it was inevitable that the Russian troop presence was seen by Kyiv and the separatists as part of a more complicated plan. Force federalization on Ukraine so that Moscow could control it through its proxies? Snap up more territories and create a land bridge to Crimea? Everyone, it seemed, knew exactly what Moscow was after. Everyone, that is, but Moscow.

II

Long before the Northern Wind, when the armed activists who stormed government buildings in the East were first coming into their own, buoyed by hopes that Moscow would defend them but already beginning to doubt Moscow's trustworthiness, one of those activists, a young, passionate Ukrainian-Russian fighter named Alexander Zakharchenko who had found himself at the helm of a self-declared government, raised up his eyes at a prominent Russian sympathizer, and asked, "Will you come and stand up for us?"

* * *

In the fall of 2016, Zakhar Prilepin, a Russian novelist and political activist of the National Bolsheviks group (Natsboly), consigned all of his real estate to his wife and children, emptied his bank accounts and, his pockets packed with cash, hopped on a train to Rostov and then to Donetsk. There, he formed a battalion of a few hundred men—mostly guys from the Luhansk region and wandering remnants of defeated and dispersed Donetsk people's militias as well as some Natsbol activists—and took up the post of advisor to "Batya," or Dad, as the leader of the self-proclaimed republic, Zakharchenko, was known. Having spent a night traveling, he rented the first house on the outskirts of the city his realtor could find and went to sleep. In the morning, Prilepin learned that his house stood next to Zakharchenko's on one side and was just 200 meters from the Prague Hotel, where his battalion was stationed, on the other.

"I felt just wonderful. A new life was beginning. A new life that promised new discoveries, new meetings, and death. Lots of things," he wrote in his fictionalized account of his experiences.[20] While the work was a novel, it was the only way for Prilepin to sincerely address a topic that even in Russia could not be openly discussed: the deployment of Russian troops. While he had to gloss over a number of details, his impressionistic narrative serves as an invaluable account of the interplay between irregular and regular forces.

In a subsequent interview, Prilepin, the descendent of an aristocratic military caste who himself had served several years in Russia's notorious riot police, the OMON, gave a more expansive explanation for why he decided to create the battalion:

> It's a feeling that your motherland needs you to do something. There is a feeling of responsibility not just for the people of Donbas, but for Russian people, for Russian history ... There's a war, and the end goal is to for it to end with a victory for Donbas. I personally don't have an end goal, especially since the battalion doesn't have them. The battalion carries out orders issued by the command.[21]

But the most interesting question is under whose orders he was fighting—and what exactly those orders were.

By the time Prilepin arrived in Donetsk, a curious diarchy had formed within the armed forces of the DPR, albeit not by design. Some units answered directly to Zakharchenko, but others to a Russian army general. And while the army general was nominally subordinate to Zakharchenko, in reality he reported to Moscow.[22]

After the broad entrenchment of the line of contact and the stated goal of a ceasefire in the spring of 2015, fighting dwindled and with it the need for substantial reinforcements. To be more exact, the separatists still felt there was a need for them, but Moscow felt the threat to the statelets was no longer so serious that it warranted the substantial financial and political cost of an open-ended deployment. Moscow significantly reduced its troop presence in the Donbas. While Russian officers continued to head up some battalions, give tactical advice and monitor the situation, the bulk of the fighting was done by local, Ukrainian citizens or Russian volunteers.

The war of 2014, in other words, had created a more or less "professional" army on the ruins of what was initially a volunteer militia. "When the militia was just beginning to form, it was like a commune of Cossack outlaws," a rebel fighter recalls. "In late 2014–15 it began to form into an army. By the end of 2015 the militia was entirely dismantled and replaced by a regular army— the People's Militia. It consisted of ideologically driven soldiers who were willing to fight for their [republic's] independence to the end."[23]

The People's Militia of the DPR was formally inaugurated in November 2014, but it had existed since April, when Girkin took over de facto command of the various separatist militias that had arisen over the month. He managed to establish something of an ad hoc command and control structure during his tenure as defense minister. By the time he resigned in August, a general architecture of the statelet's defense forces had already been set up, but centralized control and discipline was still a problem— the ideologically driven soldiers and warlords that commanded them were united in their general strategy of independence but divided in the tactics of how to achieve it.

The Northern Wind and the signing of the Minsk Protocol changed that, but only slightly. Formally, the soldiers of the People's Militia, who numbered about 35,000 troops by 2017,[24] answered to the commander in chief of the DPR, republic head

Zakharchenko. But informally, all the units of the People's Militia save one—Zakharchenko's own elite Republican Guard—actually came under the command of a rotating series of serving Russian generals.

"The main advantage of a regular army was centralized command," recalled a rebel fighter. "The disadvantage was that any initiative was suppressed. A militia is about initiative. They quashed this initiative."[25] The rebel fighter—speaking on the record to a Russian daily newspaper—did not admit who, exactly, was doing that. Russia vehemently denied the involvement of any of its officers, but among separatists and former fighters it was an open secret.[26]

In his fictionalized account of the war, Prilepin described some of these Russian generals as "pensioners" serving out the last of their terms in Donbas—either as a punishment and convenient way to get rid of them, or as an incentive for a cozy addition to their pensions. By downplaying their weight, however, Prilepin may have been accommodating official Russian accounts, because according to Kyiv, many of them were serving commanders in the prime of their careers. For example, "Sedov," the Russian commander in charge at the time according to Kyiv's National Security and Defense Council, was Colonel General Andrei Serdyukov, the chief of staff of Russia's Southern Military District.[27] He went on to head Russia's paratrooper forces, commanded Russia's military contingent in Syria in 2019 and then openly played a senior role in Russia's 2022 invasion of Ukraine.[28] Either way, these officers were in practice beholden to Moscow, not to Zakharchenko, and the separatists looked up to them with a great deal of misplaced hope. As Prilepin wrote:

> The Donetsk people believed that these Russian advisors are smart, these Russians will bring sense to things, the Russians have a white emperor who looks at the world with transparent eyes and the world pines away ... But then the surprise passed and it turned out that the

blood of these newcomers was also wet, that they squabble, do dumb things, and go whoring. For every one sensible outside officer there were three strays who got sent here because everyone was sick of them up north.[29]

The relationship between the Russian general in effective charge and Zakharchenko was cordial and based on a mutual understanding, according to Prilepin: the army corps held the main positions along the line of contact while Zakharchenko's Republican Guard picked up the slack along the front.

Nominally subordinate, the general was actually there to hold Zakharchenko's forces back from any ill-considered initiatives of their own. Batya, Prilepin wrote, simply could not launch an all-out offensive, and his forces made do with taking what positions they could that were not under the Russian general's and the army's purview.[30]

As the wife of a former rebel fighter said to me: "The units headed by Russian officers were hardly allowed to fight."[31]

III

What, then, of Zakharchenko and his battalions?

Alexander Zakharchenko, the man who had emerged as leader of the DPR after Borodai's and Girkin's forced resignations, was the son of a Ukrainian miner father and a Russian mother. A native of Donetsk, its archetypical child, he went into the mining business himself, first as a mine electrician, then as a businessman. In December 2013, just as the anti-Yanukovych protests gained ground in Kyiv, he headed up the Donetsk branch of the Oplot organization, a sort of veterans' club that sought to aid former police and military officers and their families. The group, created in 2010 by former police officer Yevgeny Zhilin in Kharkiv, was involved in a number of activities, from helping veteran families financially to countering the popular rehabilitation of the far-right Organization of Ukrainian Nationalists (OUN). But Oplot also had a sports offshoot, a mixed martial arts fight club. During the Maidan demonstrations, Oplot helped organize the infamous *titushky*, the pro-government thugs who attacked protesters and defended police. By February 2014, Zhilin bragged that the organization had 350 fighters and thousands of supporters across the country.[32] And when the Russian lawmaker Konstantin Zatulin was overheard asking Kremlin aide Glazyev to reimburse him for spending about $50,000 to fund eager anti-Maidan protestors in Ukraine, he mentioned Oplot as one of the potential recipients.[33]

As he described it, Zakharchenko seemed driven by a passionate, local Donetsk nationalism that he was willing to die for. "Every day, I used to go down into the mines," he told a Russian reporter in October 2014. "My mother, my wife, would wait for us. And everyone understood that the one going down into the mines might never be seen again. The thought of death sits deep within every miner and his loved ones ... [As fighters, the thought of death] gives us strength."[34]

Passionate, emotional—and also naïve, to the point of gullibility—was how one of his associates described him to me. Zakharchenko trusted easily and as easily followed those who seemed to share his beliefs.[35] Prilepin described him as having an inimitable laugh: "Only children can laugh like that."[36]

On 26 April 2014, not yet hardened by war—and never even having fought, unlike the volunteer militias he would soon be commanding—Zakharchenko led twenty Oplot fighters to take over the Donetsk city council building. This was just a week after a similar mob had taken control of the Donetsk regional administration building nearby, and Zakharchenko must have thought it was time to ride the momentum. "Our first aim is to issue our demands [to hold a referendum on the status of Donetsk region] to the Kyiv authorities," he told journalists. "We will remain here until our demands are met."[37]

Whatever else can be said of him—and much was—Zakharchenko really did stick to that promise. But as military commandant of Donetsk city and then as head of the statelet's self-declared Interior Ministry, Zakharchenko began to clash with Girkin. Both were idealistic, passionate and headstrong, but one was a Russian with his own vision, and one was a Donbas local. "To us, you simply smell different," Zakharchenko claims to have told Girkin that summer—apparently, Girkin was planning to demolish several apartment blocks on the outskirts of Donetsk to make it more defensible, but Zakharchenko wouldn't let him.[38]

Sometime in the summer, Borodai took Zakharchenko to Moscow—or to Rostov, according to Girkin's account—where they met with Russian officials who signed off on Zakharchenko's elevation. Borodai, who took credit for grooming Zakharchenko to replace him, said the Kremlin liked the fact that he was a local Donbas man and was also easy to control.[39]

For the time being, at least, it seemed that the almost canine trust that Zakharchenko placed in those who were willing to share his vision, as well as his popularity, charisma and local roots, appealed to a Kremlin that had grown tired of what it saw as Girkin's whining and emotional blackmail.

In Zakharchenko, Surkov, then manager of the new statelet's politics, saw a man "who would sign any piece of paper they put in front of him," Girkin would later bitterly claim.[40] The paper that the Kremlin evidently wanted him to sign was the Minsk Agreement on 5 September, then Minsk II on 12 February 2015. Zakharchenko was taciturn when describing the process, trying to convince journalists—but most of all himself—that he did not betray anyone by doing so.

"We were expected to sign the line [of contact] after which we would have to return all of our gains [to Ukraine]. I refused to sign that," he said in October 2014, weeks before being elected prime minister of the self-proclaimed republic:

It would be a betrayal of the people that live there. But I'll say more—I just wrote a letter of resignation. I can't betray my people. I didn't sleep all night. We were trying to figure out what to do and we decided not to retreat. But if I don't leave my post, then I will be a traitor. Because they will force me to sign that line.[41]

But Zakharchenko never resigned. Almost simultaneously, his deputy, Andrei Purgin, denied that Zakharchenko had written any such letter.[42] The following month, in November, the statelets held elections that no one—not even Russia—deigned to officially recognize, making Zakharchenko prime minister of a state he didn't want to lead and that no one wanted to exist.

His battalions pressed on, and the Russian forces that invaded that summer continued to back them. After the signing of the first Minsk Protocol, Zakharchenko would brag about capturing thirty-eight settlements (while claiming, of course, that it was the Ukrainian side that was the first to violate the ceasefire in each of those instances). But in the end, as much as he tried to expand his self-declared state, by February the Kremlin had forced him to sign the second Minsk Agreement, to establish the line of contact and—what to Zakharchenko was indeed a betrayal and what would likely, four years later, cost him his life—put an end to the Novorossiya project as he knew it.

Why did Zakharchenko, in an apparent emotional outburst, or a threat, or a bit of the same emotional blackmail that had earlier led to Girkin's removal, announce his own resignation, only for his own "officials" to immediately deny it? And why, four months after being forced to sign a document that he could barely stop himself calling a betrayal, was he forced to sign yet another one? Why did he brag about his battalions taking new positions, even as he walked his boasts back, insisting they were not ceasefire violations, but merely responses to Ukrainian shelling?

This was a man caught between a rock and a hard place, dependent on the Kremlin's support but increasingly mistrusting it, fighting back to the extent that he could against a policy imposed on him against his will by his patrons in the north.

IV

The Sergei Prokofyev International Airport of Donetsk, Ukraine, was refurbished in 2011, just in time for the UEFA football championship, and now boasted a glossy new terminal. When I arrived there, on my birthday on 1 May 2014, I was impressed with its swish, breezy, contemporary flair, the efficiency of its border patrol that put JFK to shame and, at just 10 km northwest of Donetsk, its convenience. But then the Ukrainian border guard looked carefully at my passport and frowned, picked up the phone and ordered me to wait, until I was led by an armed officer into a basement room. There, I was interrogated by six masked men clutching assault rifles, who alternated between accusing me of being an agent of the Russian FSB or the American CIA. But such was the necessity of war, because by then Russian irregulars and weapons were fanning out across Eastern Ukraine, joining local armed separatists to seize government buildings and announce a new proto-state. The confusion and suspicions of the airport's contingent from the SBU, the Ukrainian Security Service, were understandable, if uncomfortable for me.

In the coming months, a combination of separatist and Russian shelling and Ukrainian air attacks leveled several terminals to the ground, including the new one. A band of pro-Russian separatists, armed by Russia, had occupied the airport, just as their accomplices had done two months before in Donetsk, Luhansk, Kharkiv, Slovyansk and other cities, and Ukraine had lost patience. After an ultimatum, the National Guard went in to clear the airport, Mi-24 helicopter gunships shattering one of the glass terminals with gun and rocket fire. According to separatist estimates, Ukrainian forces killed as many as 100 insurgents and civilians and seized the airport overnight. But it was no final battle—control of the airport took on a symbolic meaning divorced from its strategic value (for what strategic value could it have, when aviation strikes rendered its runways unusable and it was permanently closed?). Battles continued over the summer, and who held the airport became a point of pride and principle.

On 5 September, representatives of Russia, Ukraine and the EU, as well as the de facto leaders of the Donetsk and Lugansk People's Republics, signed the Minsk Protocol, the initial peace plan and ceasefire. Two weeks later, they signed an additional protocol requiring each side to withdraw heavy weapons 100 km from the line of contact. The map showing the exact line of contact was never published, but it was leaked by Ukrainian sources.[43] According to the map, Donetsk Airport remained squarely within rebel territories. And yet, Ukrainian armed forces remained holed up in its terminals. It was their airport, after all. They had built it. Not the Russians.

* * *

Zakharchenko, as his own remarks to the Russian interviewer suggest, was livid that he had had to sign that piece of paper. The war, for him, was a simple matter of life and death, and every inch of captured territory the Russians were forced to give up to the Ukrainians was like giving up his own flesh. "He would take out his gun, point it at his head," Prilepin would recall. "He would just sit there, looking at the gun. And then ... well, then he just took back that territory. Just dug in and said, 'I'm not going to sign anything.'"[44]

While Russian regular troops had been brought in that August, the interim period between Minsk I and Minsk II was only the start of Russia's attempt to bring rebel militias under its own command—and even that control would be exceedingly limited. In September 2014, self-driven rebel commanders like Zakharchenko, Mikhail Tolstykh (Givi) and Arsen Pavlov (Motorola) still had a lot of leeway in the kind of offensives they chose to launch.

Aside from an assortment of small towns along the contact line that separatist warlords tried to secure, three key positions emerged as the sites of heaviest fighting. These were either ones that the separatists refused to give up to the Ukrainians after the signing of the first ceasefire or that the Ukrainians refused to surrender to the separatists: Donetsk Airport, Mariupol and Debaltseve.

From the separatist vantage point, Donetsk Airport seemed, at first, a straightforward mop-up operation. Unlike other towns, the airport was, according to the memorandum map that all sides had signed, clearly on rebel-held territory, albeit bordering the line of contact. Following the signing of the document, shelling continued to break out in the area, and some of Zakharchenko's forces decided to set up a checkpoint in the vicinity of the airport.

One of the men leading the operation that September was Akhra Avidzba, with the nom de guerre Abkhaz. His Pyatnashka Brigade was one of three or four volunteer militias (the others were the Somalia and the Sparta Battalions) under Zakharchenko's command that had been dislocated to the airport. This Abkhazian nationalist activist had come to Donbas to follow in the footsteps of his father and uncle, both of whom fought in the bloody Abkhazian separatist insurrection in 1993 against Georgia, which had just two years ago seceded from the Soviet Union. The Abkhazians were an ethnic minority with a separate language and culture whose communities straddled the newly created border between Russia and Georgia. When the Soviet Union broke up, many of them not only refused to recognize the new border, but also the sovereignty of the new Georgian state over them. For Avidzba and many of the Abkhazians who flocked to Donbas as volunteers, whether into the Vostok Battalion or his Pyatnashka Brigade, this new war was a continuation of an old one. It was a war fought for minority rights, between newly sovereign post-Soviet governments like Georgia and Ukraine and those minorities stuck inside them that disagreed with how the borders had been imposed on them without their consent.

In early July, Avidzba's brigade had quartered itself about half a kilometer from one of the airport's terminals. At the time, he said, the buildings had been occupied by a small Ukrainian force. "They gave it up without a fight, and then look what they did to it," he said, showing ruined buildings to a Russian TV reporter. When Avidzba tried to establish a checkpoint just southeast of the airport in late September, his brigade was confronted by Ukrainian troops supported by two BMP infantry fighting vehicles. "We called Zakharchenko, and in twenty minutes he sent in his tanks with forty infantrymen."[45]

The second battle for Donetsk Airport had begun. Over the coming months, the fight over what was essentially no longer a strategic but rather a symbolic and emotional object had become so protracted that by December, Kyiv and Moscow each dispatched a general to the scene to broker a *separate* ceasefire for the airport alone.[46] The way Ukrainian troops and the volunteer battalions—among them the ultranationalist Pravy Sektor and OUN Battalion[47]—steadfastly held on to the airport (despite their leadership in Kyiv having signed it away to the separatists in the September Minsk Agreement) led to their becoming mythologized as cyborgs—first by the separatists, who marveled at their superhuman tenacity, and then the Ukrainians. "The cyborgs fought as if the fate of the war was being decided in that cursed airport," the journalist Sergei Loiko, who was embedded with Ukrainian forces at the airport during the battles, would later write. "At the same time, none of the cyborgs could really explain why he fought to the point of frenzy. If we discard the clichés, the explanations essentially amounted to the answer: I fight because I fight."[48] But even amid the ferocity with which each side fought for this symbolic objective, at its heart it was still about logistics and agreements. Even while locked in bitter conflict, each side seemed to be equally respectful of this universal reality. Absurdly, yet wonderfully, during a brief ceasefire in December, as the OSCE oversaw a rotation of Ukrainian troops to and from the surrounded airport, separatist military trucks would drive to and fro, carrying Ukrainian soldiers and supplying them with food and water.[49]

But that ceasefire broke as the separatists launched an attack just days before the New Year and continued to mount assaults over the next three weeks. After a final battle on 22 January 2015, Ukrainian forces retreated from the airport, as separatists paraded captured soldiers through the streets of Donetsk.[50]

With that defeat, it had become clear that the peace agreement signed in Minsk the previous September was finally dead.

V

The scholar Samuel Charap rightly names the battle for Donetsk Airport as the main reason why the first Minsk Agreement ultimately crumbled.[51] But renewed separatist offensives were actually launched in multiple directions after September 2014, in apparent defiance of Moscow's efforts to fix the line of contact and secure the ceasefire. By October, Zakharchenko had doubled down on his resolve to regain lost territories despite the ceasefire he had just signed. "Kramatorsk, Mariupol, Slavyansk—they will be ours," he said on 23 October. "We intend to return them. So I can't rule out further military action."[52] Indeed, separatist officials had been talking about retaking Mariupol since late August,[53] when it was already becoming clear that Russia and the West were angling for a ceasefire and a peace agreement. For a morally embattled Zakharchenko, this new offensive may have seemed like the only way to square the "treacherous" agreement he felt forced to sign with what his conscience dictated.

Still, according to Western sources, until November there was relatively little large-scale fighting going on.[54] It was with the renewed battles for Donetsk Airport that month that rebels began launching more substantive attacks along the line of contact. That suggests that in those months at least, the involvement of Russian armed forces had waned.

But towards the end of the battle for the airport, that seemed to change. The fighting was not just about the airport anymore. In mid-January, rebels launched a renewed assault to wrest back control of the strategic transport hub of Debaltseve, which Ukrainians had recaptured from the separatists the previous summer. On 21 January, Ukrainian President Petro Poroshenko announced that Russia had deployed some 9,000 troops into Ukraine, with 500 tanks and other equipment.[55] That same day, Russia's OSCE envoy Andrei Kelin issued a desperate bid for talks over the continued fighting in the airport.[56]

The rising tensions were part of a vicious circle: a failure to maintain a ceasefire led both sides to push for renewed talks, which in turn also led both sides to try to gain more territory to strengthen their negotiating positions ahead of these talks. This in turn made the talks even more critical—and harder to resolve. The Russians were trying to curb Zakharchenko's enthusiasm and said they had gotten the rebels to pull back from the line of contact.[57] Instead, Zakharchenko seemed emboldened enough by the new influx of Russian troops to announce a renewed march on Mariupol on 24 January.[58]

Moscow, it seemed, was becoming frustrated with the failure of any ceasefire to hold and was being pulled again into the kind of military commitment that, after August, it had been trying to avoid. After months of watching the rebels they backed violate the ceasefire they had all signed, the only way to end the intensifying fighting seemed to be to send in troops so that the rebels could finally win.

A big question is whether Moscow was being disingenuous with its half-hearted attempts to rein in the separatists. There is little doubt that had the Kremlin been truly determined to stop them, it would have done so, one way or another. This made it easy at the time to jump to the conclusion that Moscow was simply using its proxies to deflect blame, leading them on to do its dirty work and then denying it was a party to the conflict.

Yet this fails to explain the considerable efforts Moscow undertook to get the separatists on board with the ceasefires, as well as its evident hesitancy to send additional troops until the last minute in January. It is also clear that Zakharchenko's livid opposition to Minsk could not have been anything but genuine.

Rather, the explanation for Moscow's military involvement—however costly in terms of sanctions—lies not so much in what it could gain by helping the separatists, but in the costs of cutting them loose. Having led pro-Russian separatists to believe in the spring that they had Moscow's support, and then scaled down that support, to stand back and watch them get slaughtered by Ukrainian forces could have cost Putin his hold on power at home, or at the very least seriously tarnished the legitimacy he had gained by the annexation of Crimea. It is often forgotten that many of the demonstrators who protested against his return to the Kremlin in 2011–12 had not been pro-Western liberals, but nationalists, imperialists and even monarchists. For over a decade, the Kremlin sought to clip the wings of this contingent by creating an assortment of fake nationalist parties. But however disparate and weak they were in peacetime, a bloodbath in which ethnic Russians were dying in Ukraine thanks to the Kremlin's incompetence and inaction could have ignited not just these nationalist forces, but their supporters in the security and defense community, the FSB and GRU officers who backed Girkin and separatists like him. For Putin, it was paramount that these people continued viewing the West as their true enemy, and not the Kremlin itself.

Even so, the war was costly. At the time, caving in to the demands of the separatists and backing them fully by annexing them was deemed costlier still. Russia needed a peace plan that would, as much as possible, balance all of its mutually conflicting interests: exit the war, save face and maintain its influence in Ukraine.

8

THE NEGOTIATORS

"You *must* try the Napoleon here, it's *delicious*," said the Kremlin advisor to a group of Western NGO mediators, over a duly expensed dinner at the advisor's favorite Moscow restaurant. Not too close to the Kremlin, and not ostentatiously posh—after all, it would be in bad taste to spend international grant and tax dollars on somewhere truly extravagant like Café Pushkin (unless, of course, you were an NGO executive)—but, with its plush leather upholstered chairs and its array of classic pastries, the venue was exquisitely beautiful nonetheless. It was the spring of 2018, but the conversation was the same as it had been for about three years now—how to break the stalemate over the Minsk Package of Measures. The Novorossiya project was dead. The Russian Spring had turned into an endless winter. The shooting war in Donbas had long died down to a simmer, albeit with a steady supply of casualties on both sides of the line of contact. That meant that the main theater of war had moved to the more comfortable venues of Moscow and DC Beltway offices, to convenings of policymakers and pundits secure in their belief that their armchair words could move troops and sign treaties, to boozy international conferences and opinion pages. Narratives were the weapons—"hybrid war," "reflexive control," "active measures" and other hazy buzzwords were thrown around by each side in a bid to ... do what, exactly? No one seemed to know. Each side, it seemed, was determined to deflect its mistakes onto the other, onto anyone else, really, but themselves.

"Girkin?" scoffed the advisor:

> Who went over there and started this headache in the first place? They were the ones who started this mess. They didn't succeed, and now we are cleaning up their mess. They aren't responsible for it, we are. And if they're so worried, well, they are Russian citizens, why don't they do something productive here?

The remark—and numerous ones like it I had heard from officials and policymakers in Moscow—was not so much a statement of defiance, or of a conscious bid to continue imposing on Ukraine a peace package that it had clearly signed under duress. It was one of impotence, the frustration of someone forced to clean up another's mess—but deep inside fully aware that he is complicit in creating it. The Kremlin had made a mistake, but quite which mistake?

I

It is no surprise, under the circumstances, that both Putin and former German Chancellor Angela Merkel take the credit for being the first to initiate talks for a new ceasefire at the start of 2015. It is also no surprise that each side would insistently blame the other for why these talks ultimately failed.

From Merkel's perspective, the growing encirclement of Ukrainian troops in Debaltseve risked a wider war close to Germany's borders. Adding to the pressure were American plans to send weapons to Ukraine, a move she feared could aggravate Russian belligerence and spiral into a proxy war in Europe.

Everything was being done to prevent the kind of catastrophe that would occur on 24 February 2022—and, as if in a Greek drama, everything would lead up to it.

Putin, too, was finding himself in an increasingly tense predicament. Previously brokered ceasefires weren't holding. The leader of the DPR, Zakharchenko, a man expected to be more pliable than his adventurous predecessors, was proving to be anything but. First, he threatened new offensives beyond the line of contact, in direct defiance of the first Minsk Agreement in September, and had to be pressured to take his statements back and say he meant something "peaceful" instead.[1] Then, he threatened to resign and had to be coaxed to stay on. The presence of Russian reinforcements sent in to keep the rebels from being overtaken by Ukrainian troops at Donetsk Airport were being taken by Zakharchenko as permission to further defy the ceasefire and launch new offensives. On 23 January, just days after news of new Russian troops crossing the border, the self-proclaimed leader announced his refusal to take part in any more truce talks and instead planned to "attack right up to the borders of Donetsk region."[2]

Putin could not openly blame the separatists for the collapse of the ceasefire: to do so was tantamount to cutting them loose, and there were already a lot of dissatisfied grumblings in Moscow from the "patriotic" contingent—and from a disgruntled Girkin—about Moscow's "betrayal" of Novorossiya. But nor was Ukraine truly adhering to the peace plan—despite the September memorandum, Ukrainian troops had held on to Donetsk Airport and continued shelling rebel positions from there, starting the battle that ultimately ended the truce. Simply deflecting blame onto Ukraine would only get Moscow so far: the need to bail out its unruly proxies each time they got themselves into a new battle was costly militarily, politically and—as sanctions bit—financially.

After talks failed in December, Putin wrote directly to his Ukrainian counterpart Poroshenko on 15 January, proposing the immediate mutual withdrawal of heavy weapons from the line of contact.[3] It didn't seem to go anywhere. On 7 February, Merkel and French President François Hollande sought to revive the peace plan with a new draft, and the following day he scheduled a summit to discuss it for 11 February, once again to be held in Minsk.

That evening, Putin, Poroshenko, Hollande and Merkel arrived in the Belarusian capital for what they hoped would be a meeting to iron out inconsistencies in the old memorandum and get the sides to put their signatures on a new framework to implement the peace plan.

From the moment it started, at about 6 p.m. on 11 February, to when a document was finally signed, took about sixteen hours of grueling talks. It was a cumbersome affair, reflecting the irreconcilable differences between Russia and Ukraine that would hound the peace plan for years after. At the heart of it was Ukraine's understandable refusal to lend any legitimacy or recognition to the self-proclaimed leaders of the separatist territories. With Russia, for its part, insisting it was not a party to the conflict, this made even the very logistics of the summit difficult. The four state leaders and their delegations met in the grand Palace of Independence, the official residence of the Belarusian president, closer to the outskirts of the city. But the representatives of the separatist statelets—who would be joined by their "leaders," Zakharchenko and Plotnitsky, only on the following morning—were housed in the Dipservice Hall events center, a fifteen-minute drive away in the city center. These representatives, part of a trilateral contact group from Ukraine, the statelets and the EU, would be the actual signatories of the peace plan, but the document they were signing was being hashed out 6 km away.

THE NEGOTIATORS

One of the main points of contention was when to implement the ceasefire and what exactly it would entail: all that hinged on the battle of Debaltseve, where thousands of Ukrainian troops were surrounded by separatist and Russian forces. Of the sixteen hours of the talks, half were reportedly about Debaltseve: Poroshenko, for some reason, insisted that there was no encirclement, despite arguments to the contrary from both Putin and Hollande. Even so, Ukraine didn't want an immediate ceasefire; nor did the separatists, for understandable reasons: with the battle in Debaltseve still raging, each hoped they could still cement their gains.[4] In the end, the Europeans were the only ones pushing for an immediate end to the fighting.

But after a night of boozy talking, interspersed with a few bouts of Putin and Poroshenko shouting at each other in Russian—and sometimes even leaving the hall to talk in private—the sides managed to work out a few compromises that required considerable concessions from all sides. Russia's insistence on "direct" talks with the separatists was replaced with vague language to the effect that "a dialogue is to start."[5] Furthermore, local elections in the separatist areas—something that Moscow was insisting on, to help legitimate its clients while also getting them off its hands—would be limited to territories behind the demarcation line spelled out in the September memorandum. In other words, any new territorial gains the separatists made since then wouldn't be counted. The demilitarized zone was extended at the insistence of Hollande, who prevailed upon Putin to consider the provision.[6] But the most problematic concession was made by Poroshenko: Ukraine would not get control of its border with Russia until after local elections had been held and autonomy had been granted to the statelets. Only then would Russia withdraw the troops that it officially denied were there and give up control of the border.[7]

Towards about 7 a.m., after eleven hours of talks, a draft called the Package of Measures for the Implementation of the Minsk

Agreement was ready—except for the small matter of getting the contact group across town to actually sign it.

After about 8 a.m., just as exhausted journalists were expecting a signed agreement, the Russian reporter Andrei Kolesnikov noticed a perplexing scene: Kremlin aide Vladislav Surkov rushed out of the conference room and headed out to Dipservice Hall. Next to leave was a clearly unhappy Poroshenko.[8] Just a few minutes earlier, one of the members of the contact group, OSCE special envoy Heidi Tagliavini, had shuttled from Dipservice Hall to inform the state leaders that Zakharchenko and Plotnitsky refused to sign the document.[9] They were unhappy with a lot of things, but in particular with the provision requiring them to remove their heavy weapons to the front line from the previous September, creating a 140-km buffer zone. All of their recent gains—some 600 km of territory—were in effect to be ceded back to the Ukrainians.

There are somewhat differing accounts of the commotion that followed. According to German sources, Putin withdrew to a special room set up for him on the third floor and spent about two hours on the phone with Zakharchenko and Plotnitsky until he got them to agree to sign. But in the Russian account, those talks were not so simple. Putin did indeed withdraw to the third floor, but he was joined there by Merkel and Hollande, and reportedly repeated to them several times, "I cannot put pressure on [the separatists]." In response, Merkel issued an ultimatum: the separatists had ninety minutes until she and the French president would leave the palace and the talks would be over. Putin agreed with the ultimatum, and it was passed on to the separatist leaders. Then the Russian president was left alone for a while, until finally all of them gathered back on the first floor to wait for the response from the separatists. With just two minutes left until the deadline, Putin rushed out of the room and returned moments later: Surkov had called him, he said. "They signed everything."[10]

The final document had neither the signatures of Putin nor of Poroshenko, as if neither side ultimately wanted to take responsibility for what each already suspected would be a failure. Instead, it was signed by former president Leonid Kuchma, then Ukraine's representative to the trilateral contact group, and by the Russian ambassador to Ukraine, Mikhail Zurabov. Heidi Tagliavini represented the EU. The signatures of the self-named leaders of the statelets, Zakharchenko and Plotnitsky, were mere appendages: their names were preceded by no status, not even a description of who they were. But whatever it was they had all managed to agree on, for now they had bought some respite and could finally call it a day and have a nap.

II

Two problematic premises cloud our understanding of what the Kremlin wants. The first is what exactly we understand to be "the Kremlin." As a collective of people driven by the same objective, it is meaningless: if anything, a closer look at the decision-makers involved illustrates a pattern whereby they might be following a vague plan but are ultimately driven by their own, often different, and often personal motives. To view the Kremlin as a monolith is possible only when one narrows the notion down to the person of Vladimir Putin, a tsar informed by the various voices of those around him but ultimately pursuing his own decisions. But given the leeway he allows various actors in deciding what his grand plan is and thus projecting their own personal ambitions onto their state activities, his decisions are shaped by his courtiers far more than one would expect in an autocratic system.

But therein lies the second problematic premise: that the Kremlin's ultimate aims are fixed, and can therefore be ascertained and countered. Yet Moscow's behavior since its annexation of Crimea in March 2014 suggests that its goals are in constant flux.

By May 2014, one general strategy crystalized: according to one of the most prominent and well-informed Kremlin advisors, Fyodor Lukyanov, "Russia's aim is not seizing Ukrainian territories, but constructing a kind of Ukrainian state that would not allow it to integrate further with the West or become part of NATO."[11] But this did not seem compatible with a separatist project that Moscow was, for all intents and purposes, supporting: the annexation of Crimea and the war in Donbas did more to push Ukraine away from Russia than anything else. Thanks to Putin, Kyiv was determined to move towards both the European Union and NATO, for understandable reasons.

Kremlin officials claimed, time and again, that they supported reintegrating the self-proclaimed republics back into Ukraine. Given how events played out in 2014 and 2015, this may well have been true, even though Russian policy in the early years often seemed confused, convoluted, unformed. In the early months of 2014, the Kremlin was shopping around for a policy and trying to see what works but not confident enough of any plan to back it overtly and wholeheartedly. Once the line of contact had been established in late 2014, though, the Minsk Package of Measures was indeed necessary in Putin's eyes to push the statelets back into Ukraine, seemingly with two goals: to retain influence over Kyiv (because these territories could be used to further the Kremlin's interests), and to clean up the separatist mess.

* * *

For seven years, until the war began in earnest in 2022, the final text of the Minsk Package of Measures, as it came to be known, would be the only existing peace plan for the war in Donbas. In substance, it differed little from the previous Minsk peace plan signed in 2014, but it offered a few specifics that its brokers thought would make it easier to implement, such as the kinds of measures needed to make the rebel-held areas autonomous territories within Ukraine. While all sides remained officially committed to it in word, right up to the February 2022 invasion, Minsk was in effect like a Rorschach inkblot test of the sort used generations ago to diagnose insanity: each of its points can be—and is—interpreted in different ways depending on the perspective, the desires and, indeed, the repressed anger of the signatory.

To this day, it remains impossible to ascertain what, if any, of the provisions had been fully implemented. While fighting immediately began to die down in February 2015, ceasefire violations by both sides continued. And while efforts were made to follow through on the first two provisions stipulating ceasefire and the withdrawal of weapons, each violation would be used as an excuse by the other side not to comply. Who started what was impossible to ascertain, nor did it really matter, because the real heart of the problems with the peace plan were the fourth and ninth provisions: the commitment to starting dialogue on granting the rebel-held areas autonomy within Ukraine, and passing legislation enshrining that autonomy in Ukrainian law.

After all, autonomy had been the key issue that triggered grassroots protests in Ukraine and Crimea the year before. Many Russian-speakers, whether they were backed by Moscow or not, saw the new government in Kyiv as incompatible with their interests. Though they did not necessarily want to secede, they did want more freedom to enact their own regional laws. For a large country with a growing sense of national identity, but with a concentration of Russian-speakers in the East, and with serious disputes over economic policy and political culture, decentralization could have been a legitimate response. Initiated and implemented through domestic dialogue, it could arguably have helped bolster Ukrainian unity. But the moment the Kremlin

became a self-proclaimed champion of Ukrainian decentralization, the moment it began to co-opt and arm the Russian-
speakers that protested against Kyiv, then decentralization,
however worthy in and of itself, curdled into a direct threat to
Ukrainian integrity. Besides, after annexing Crimea and lying
about it, the Kremlin could insist that the earth revolved around
the sun—only to have critics insist on the opposite and accuse
Russia of weaponizing physics.

The contentious provisions called for the launch of dialogue
on how to conduct elections in the so-called "non-government-
controlled areas" (NGCAs) in accordance with the Ukrainian law
"On Interim Local Self-Government Order in Certain Areas of
the Donetsk and Luhansk Regions." They specified that talks
would be needed to determine the future administration of these
areas so that it did not contradict this law. Next in the provision
was the adoption of a parliamentary resolution defining the area
that was to enjoy "special status" under that law.

There were a lot of problems with this provision, not least the
emotional dimension. Ukrainians understandably felt they were
being forced to legislate under the barrel of a foreign gun. There
were key legal impediments, too: Minsk required, in essence, a
democratically elected, multi-party parliament to vote on a law
that neither they, nor their representatives, had discussed or
agreed. Had the Minsk Package of Measures stipulated that the
law be enacted by presidential decree or executive order—and,
most importantly, had the Ukrainian president signed the document—then it would have at least been possible for the provision
to be legally binding. But in that case, Poroshenko would have
risked either another Maidan or possibly even impeachment on
charges of treason the moment he walked out of the Palace of
Independence in Minsk. He saved his political skin—at least
until he lost to Volodymyr Zelensky in 2019—but at the price of
delegitimizing the Minsk deal from the outset.

In addition to Ukraine's fundamental resistance to imposed decentralization, the question of the sequence of moves was a crucial one that ensured no progress would or could be made. Point 9 of the Package of Measures stipulated that the day after local elections were held, Ukraine would regain full control of its border with Russia. However, this was contingent on the passage of constitutional reform enshrining decentralization. What this all meant was that the document's very sequencing, if Ukraine was to follow it to the letter, was circular. Moscow viewed this as straightforward: elections and constitutional change first, control of the border—which essentially meant the government regaining control of the statelets—to follow. However, the package stipulated that the local elections had to be held under Ukrainian law, and Kyiv argued that this was impossible as long as the government was unable to ensure that Ukrainian laws were being followed in the rebel-held areas where elections were to take place.[12] In other words, control first, elections second.

As Moscow and the separatists refused to give up the border, the Ukrainians had arguably caved to European and Russian pressure and agreed with what Moscow was trying to impose on them but had then drafted the agreement in such a way that it was unimplementable from the start. Both sides got to blame the other for the failure of the peace process.

Perhaps most of these disagreements could have been ironed out, had there been a clearer definition of the actual belligerents. For this was at the heart of the problem: who were the parties to the peace plan? Who negotiated with whom? Who was accountable for his or her words? No one. Moscow insisted it was merely a mediator and that any agreement must be made directly with the separatist leaders. Kyiv refused to dignify a bunch of thugs and rebels by treating them as peers and instead insisted on framing them as no more than Moscow's lackeys. In reality, both of these positions were wrong: Moscow was no mere mediator, but nor did its proxies lack agency and their own agendas that oftentimes contradicted Moscow's. The refusal of both Moscow and Kyiv to recognize this reality entrenched them in a vicious circle, neither willing to implement Minsk, neither able openly to denounce it, both blaming the other for its failure.

III

Two days after the summit, a somewhat dejected and browbeaten Zakharchenko appeared before television cameras to give his thoughts on what had just happened in Minsk.

"Actually, it's a big victory," said the man who just months earlier had called it a betrayal, looking down at his hands and rushing through his words. It was as though the sentence had been placed in his mouth by someone else. But as he went on, he livened up, almost talking himself into looking on the bright side: "The victory, no matter how paradoxical it may sound, is that we can change Ukraine as such: its constitution, the opinion of the people. And in general, as it turns out, its political processes will now be under our control."[13]

That last part didn't sound like it had been agreed and coordinated in advance with his Moscow handlers. But further on, Zakharchenko contradicted not just Minsk, but himself. "Unfortunately, if you carefully read all the clauses of the agreement, these are again vague words that can be interpreted in any way you like. And I am convinced that until there are clear definitions, nothing good will happen."

He went on:

> I said in Minsk, and I repeat again, that the entire territory of the Donetsk region, including the temporarily occupied territories, is part of the Donetsk Republic. It does not matter which way we will take them—by military or political means. Politically, of course, is better ... [but] if that does not work, we have already shown the whole world that we are able to resolve issues by military means.

Zakharchenko had swallowed his pride and stopped calling Minsk a betrayal, but he remained adamant that the line of contact Moscow had taken such pains to entrench should extend all the way to the administrative borders of the Donetsk region.

Zakharchenko had much to lose: displease his curators in Moscow, and he could be shipped back to Russia like Girkin, or worse; but if he gave off even a hint of weakness and defeatism before his peers in Donbas—the warlords and battle-hardened militiamen—well, there were much more dramatic ways of disappearing.

It was for this reason that he seemed to adopt a strategy of acquiescing to the Kremlin publicly but never abandoning hope that by deed or word he could one day convince them of the "right" thing to do. He showed no resistance to the Russian generals who came in to Donbas and took command of militia units that had once answered to him, but he welcomed with open arms new volunteer battalions from Russia like those of Prilepin, who were driven by ideas and not by the vague bureaucratese of Minsk or by even vaguer directives from Moscow. Maybe the gains of his Republican Guard—an elite corps he had stood up in January of 2015 from his most loyal fighters—would sway the minds of the generals commanding the rest of the rebel militias and, little by little, of their bosses in Moscow.

In Moscow, the men who were not fighting in the trenches and who had little to lose were having different conversations.

IV

"Putin," the sign read. "Their lives are more important than your wallet." The woman stood in a crowd of a few hundred people, protesting against what they saw as the Kremlin's inaction in Ukraine, where they feared for their Russian relatives. "My sister lives there," the woman explained, "and I'm afraid for her life.

Someone is dragging us all into a war." And because she felt the government was doing little to help protect them from Ukrainian forces, she and others were scraping together whatever they could muster to send across the border.

It was a small rally, but its size indicated it was genuine, rather than artificially manufactured by the government. That said, the speakers on the stage were very much that part of the establishment that favored a more aggressive policy in Ukraine. There was the lawmaker Yevgeny Fyodorov, one of the most outspoken nationalists in parliament, who lamented that a "Western-backed fifth column" in Russia had infiltrated the Kremlin and prevented it from doing right by its Russian-speaking brothers across the border. In a number of such rallies, often held on Moscow's Suvorov Square, Girkin himself would take the stage to wild cheers, urging for more aid to a Novorossiya that the Kremlin had abandoned.

Soon after the signing of Minsk, grumbles intensified in Moscow about this "betrayal." In June 2015, Girkin held a conference attended by a growing body of Kremlin critics, not from the pro-Western liberal camp but from those who had felt, even long before 2014, that Putin's Kremlin was selling out to the United States.

"Unfortunately, Russia has completely lost the initiative in the Ukrainian direction," Girkin observed sadly. "It obediently follows in the footsteps of development schemes adopted in the United States, which in the end will inevitably lead to defeat." The only way to change this was to launch a full-fledged military operation against the Ukrainian "junta."[14]

In the hybrid authoritarianism that had developed under Putin, public debate within the elite was rare: acting officials of any influence weren't prone to voicing their disagreements with the Kremlin in public. But that didn't mean that privately they didn't harbor resentment over Putin's decisions. Public criticism from figures like Girkin, who maintained deep connections to an FSB that was angling for a more robust foreign agenda, was an indicator that beneath a calm surface, there was still tension and disappointment over the Novorossiya question in the government. Even as Putin approved Minsk, the FSB and the wider security and intelligence community had wanted more.[15]

Caught between the threat of sanctions from the West and pressure from this contingent back home, the Kremlin found itself in a sort of zugzwang, as a number of political scientists would lament—a chess position in which any move can only hasten negative consequences. "It's a dead end—both from the point of view of the continuation of the war, and from the point of view of the Minsk process," according to Alexander Zhuchkovsky, a Russian nationalist who organized humanitarian aid to rebel-held areas:

> Russia has been in a losing situation from the very beginning, so it is trying to pacify it, but I believe that Ukraine is not capable of negotiating in this sense. And the Donbas will now hang like a weight around Russia's neck, and Russia does not want to accept it.[16]

Far from a cunning plan to further Russian influence over Ukraine as it is often depicted, Minsk began to seem more of an afterthought, a clumsy compromise between two equally unappealing options. Officials seemed to be scrambling to find something they could present to the public as a win, while also concocting excuses as to why it was going to fail, publicly blaming Ukraine, and privately, in a number of conversations I witnessed, blaming the separatists.

The parliamentarian Sergei Zheleznyak, for instance, had once called on Russia to conquer all of Ukraine's eastern regions but now scaled back his rhetoric in line with the Kremlin's commitment to Minsk. "We need the issue of the future of Ukraine and Ukrainian regions to be resolved peacefully, in a civilized way," he said on Russian television. "We need, of course, all of Ukraine, but as a partner, as a comrade, a country that, together with us, defeated Nazism within itself. Therefore, there was no betrayal of Novorossiya—our task is not to get involved in the war, but to stop it."[17]

Meanwhile, the closer a policymaker was to the halls of power, the more he spoke of a unified consensus on Minsk and the more he tried to claim that it benefited Russia geopolitically. "[Minsk] means that all levers of influence on the situation in Ukraine are preserved, there are guarantees for the protection of the Russian-speaking population in the east of the country, and the political settlement leads to federalization of [Ukraine]," Alexei Chesnakov, an advisor to Surkov, said at the time.[18]

The problem was that by seeking to take itself out of the equation, official Moscow in effect made itself dependent upon a Ukraine that lacked any incentive to implement the agreement. In Kyiv, each attempt to move forward on Minsk's political provisions was met by fierce resistance from an active minority that called such moves "capitulation" and effectively stymied them. While Kyiv passed a framework bill "on the special terms of local self-governance in certain districts of Donetsk and Luhansk" in September 2014, it was destined to be interim legislation that had to be extended every couple of years and functioned more like an outline for what needed to be done rather than a legally binding law. Even some of the lawmakers who voted for its extension never expected it to actually be implemented.[19]

For Moscow, meanwhile, doing anything to comply with the peace plan meant moving its military out of Donbas and giving up control of the border, which it was not going to do, except on its own terms. The Minsk Package of Measures was written in such a way that it was not required to do these things until Ukraine had implemented its side of the deal. This sequencing loophole allowed Moscow to claim it was off the hook but in reality merely guaranteed its dependence on outside factors beyond its control. And so, for the time being, the Kremlin kept telling itself it was for the best, that a frozen conflict was better for Russia than a hot one, and certainly better than a capitulation that could cost Putin his throne.

9

THE CURATORS

Separatist. The very word had acquired such an allure in some circles that a Donetsk restaurant branded itself under the slang for the term, "Separ." The haunt, with its military paraphernalia, had a special corner for Zakharchenko and his men, with a tea kettle always ready on a wood-burning stove. A sign on the table indicated it was reserved—except instead of the word reserved, *zabronirovano*, the sign read *zaminirovano*—mined. As if, from the start, the whole endeavor—with the guns and tanks stolen from local depots to the intoxicating euphoria of watching world leaders gather to talk about what *you* had started—was a game.

On a warm afternoon on 31 August 2018, four black SUVs pull up to the restaurant. Zakharchenko, accompanied by about five bodyguards wielding Kalashnikovs, walks out of the car towards the entrance. One of the bodyguards goes inside, gives the premises a quick glance and then holds the door open for Zakharchenko to enter. As the DPR leader walks into the closeted anteroom, a massive blast rips through it, sending bodyguards running and one of the SUVs rolling off into the street. By nightfall, Zakharchenko was dead, Kyiv and Moscow were trading accusations of who was behind the assassination, and the Novorossiya project was no more—at least for the time being.

I

To this day, there is no agreement on whose orders Zakharchenko was assassinated. But then again, nor is there clarity on who was behind the killing of Arsen Pavlov, the leader of Sparta militia who went under the nom de guerre Motorola, in October 2016. Nor the death of the leader of the Somali militia, Mikhail Tolstykh (aka Givi), blown up in his office in February 2017. Nor that of Alexei Mozgovoi, the leader of Luhansk's Prizrak Brigade, shot dead in a car ambush in May 2015. Nor that of Alexander Bednov (aka Batman) on 1 January 2015. The list went on. One by one, starting in 2015, the most headstrong commanders of the Russian Spring started getting blown up, shot in their offices and even allegedly poisoned.

There is nothing surprising about the murders of warlords mixed up in vicious power struggles between business, criminal and political clans in an unrecognized state with little to no law and order. In the aftermath of many of these assassinations, it would emerge that each had fallen foul of another powerful separatist official, even Plotnitsky or Zakharchenko himself. Many of these men cultivated flamboyant personas unbeholden to any rules but their own, which, combined with the increasingly criminalized environment they operated in, was sure to make them a lot of enemies. Arsen Pavlov, Motorola, a Russian drifter who worked at a car wash and engaged in drunken auto theft before joining Russian volunteer fighters in Ukraine and rising through the ranks as Girkin's protégé, invited journalists to a flashy wedding with his Kalashnikov-toting bride in June 2014 and liked to boast of his war crimes, telling a reporter once that he "shot fifteen prisoners and I don't give a fuck. I'll kill if I want to."[1] Mozgovoi's Prizrak, or Ghost battalion, meanwhile, once released a video of their leader presiding over a show trial in an auditorium sentencing rapists to death with a show of hands from the audience.[2]

There is also nothing surprising that officials in Kyiv, when blamed for these murders by Russia-backed separatists who had been fighting against Ukraine for years, would in turn point the finger at Moscow or the criminal milieu in which these warlords ran.

Even as Moscow and the "official" separatist leadership blamed Kyiv, Ukraine's Security Service, the SBU, claimed that murders like Motorola's were part of a Russian operation to purge the rebel ranks.[3] According to Ukrainian parliamentarian Dmytro Tymchuk, Givi was killed because he was ignoring orders— presumably to adhere to the Minsk ceasefire.[4] The outspoken advisor to Ukraine's Interior Ministry, Zoryan Shkiryak, saw the murders of Givi and Motorola as part of a "targeted sweep" of warlords who had grown unmanageable and inconvenient from the standpoint of Moscow and the separatist leadership. Zakharchenko and Plotnitsky, he said in 2017, were next.[5]

All these alleged culprits had a potential motive, and all the accusers had a bias. But it was the Ukrainian version of events that found unlikely support in the unofficial accounts and theories of separatist movements and their supporters in Moscow. While Girkin's explanations for the murders were so cautious as to veer on the convoluted, and while he still generally adhered to Moscow's official line in blaming Givi's and Motorola's assassinations on Ukrainian radical groups or special forces, in one interview he directly named Surkov. "I won't assert whether it was Ukrainians ... or not. But I can say with certainty that 'our own' people were involved. And since Surkov curated the Ukrainian line, it couldn't have happened without him. Just as in the murder of Mozgovoi and all the others."[6] The seeming contradiction in his logic can be explained by Girkin's view of the Minsk Agreement as a "conspiracy" between Moscow and Kyiv that included unspoken agreements on what territories and people were fair game.[7] In other words, his view was that Moscow was deliberately "letting" these inconvenient commanders get killed off.

While Girkin is prone to conspiratorial thinking and dramatization, on one level this view made sense—especially as it almost directly corroborated the theories of Ukrainian officials. As Moscow sought more control over the militias but without a clear sense of what, exactly, it wanted to do with them, first it removed Girkin and backed what it thought would be a more manageable Zakharchenko. But when Moscow's strategy finally crystalized into the Minsk Accords, the ideologically driven contingent of the Russian Spring made it clear that they were not on board. Both Givi and Motorola were driving many of the battles that took place after the signing of the first Minsk Protocol in September 2014 and were the chief commanders in the second battle for Donetsk Airport. They were, in other words, starting fights that Moscow then had to send troops to finish for them. Under the circumstances, it was safer for Moscow to impose direct control through serving generals—even if this undermined the narrative of a grassroots civil war that Moscow was still trying to hold on to—than put their trust in unruly warlords who started battles that didn't suit Moscow's needs. According to Russian reports, it was a matter of time before most of the original commanders who rose through local grassroots movements or came into Ukraine out of their own volition were replaced by Russian officers.[8]

And it was a matter of time until Zakharchenko would meet the same fate.

After his death, Girkin called Zakharchenko a "political prostitute who tried to please everyone" and said the reason he was killed was because "everyone got sick of him."[9] A Russian political activist and volunteer close to Zakharchenko and Girkin put it differently: "He had to find compromises because he desperately needed support from Russia. He was ready to say a lot of things out loud—but one thing he would never give up on was joining Russia." And if that was a problem for anyone, it was first and foremost a problem for Zakharchenko's handlers in Moscow, he said.[10]

Zakharchenko was replaced by Denis Pushilin—one of the original leaders of the movement, a local businessman, but one who seemed content to follow Moscow's lead in word and deed if it meant holding on to his position.

Little by little, the rest of the volunteer militias were purged of ideologically driven fighters and replaced with more or less "professional" soldiers recruited from among locals for a salary of a few hundred dollars a month—a fortune compared to the $50 a month that many civilians had to make do on in the statelets.[11] If Minsk was to be implemented, the separatist militias had to follow Moscow's orders.

But years passed—and Minsk wasn't being implemented.

II

The Russian diplomat was clearly frustrated. Sitting across from me in his cozy office in the towering skyscraper that houses the Ministry of Foreign Affairs, piles of folders and books in every corner, was an intellectual forced to parse through the arcane and contradictory minutiae of the Minsk Accords, defend decisions Moscow had officially disavowed making, and find solutions that he had no power to implement (for the Ministry of Foreign Affairs had long been sidelined when it came to Russia's policy in Ukraine). Simultaneously, he bore the brunt of Western animosity towards Moscow and domestic grumbles about betrayals of the Russian cause. In a war that did not exist, in a peace process that Russia was not party to, with the pressures of needing to maintain plausible deniability, it was no surprise that he looked for scapegoats, blaming, by turns, Ukraine and the West for the stalemate. The CIA, he said, was directly dictating to Kyiv whether to implement the Minsk provisions or not and even had a special office in the SBU building for the purpose.

He was not the only diplomat saying such things. It was the spring of 2019, and I was having a number of conversations like this one: that time and again, Kyiv was about to do the "right" thing and make concessions that Russia wanted, only to be talked out of it at the last minute by their handlers in Washington; that Ukraine was a proxy in a coordinated campaign by Washington and London to attack Russian statehood; or that the European Union was merely an American satellite without much agency of its own.[12]

The idea of Washington signing off on every major decision by the Ukrainian president and that Ukraine and other former Soviet republics were not fully sovereign had been a staple among the security services, nationalists and supporters of pro-Russian separatists. It was unusual to hear this line of thinking coming from diplomats and Western-oriented policymakers, whose role had been to gloss over the harder edges of Russian foreign policy in order to maintain constructive relations with Western partners. But it seemed that the statelets had become such a problem for Moscow that even its more moderate voices found it easier to believe the angry fabrications of the hawks: that it was everyone's fault but Russia's.

Suddenly, the official revealed an unexpected source of his frustration. "It's time for the [separatists] to stop being charity cases," he said, "and start trying to break even."

In a way, the separatist pseudo-republics were already trying to do just that. The Lugansk and Donetsk People's Republics didn't really have a choice but to reorient their economies around the black and gray markets generated by Moscow's refusal to formally recognize them. No longer rebels, insurgents or separatists—because officially, as per the Minsk Agreement, separatism was no longer part of their agenda—the leaders of these breakaways were now given the meaningless name of "de facto authorities," while the territories they controlled became "non-government-controlled areas" or NGCAs. In February 2017, after obstruction to the flow of goods and civilians on the line of contact both by de facto authorities and Ukrainian paramilitary battalions backed by local oligarchs, Kyiv imposed a full economic blockade of the NGCAs. This effectively cut off all legal markets—particularly for the coal and steel mined in the Donets Basin, an industry that constituted the bulk of the region's economy. If in the past some of this coal was purchased on the domestic market in Ukraine and some exported to Europe, the entire industry repositioned itself towards Moscow, and its anthracite coal was rerouted eastwards, through Russia, then on to Europe and Turkey, from whence it was often sold back to Ukraine.

For Zakharchenko and his coterie, the blockade was a blessing, as it gave them an excuse to nationalize the region's coal mines and personally profit from them. "We are stopping the shipment of coal to Ukraine," Zakharchenko and Plotnitsky said in an official joint statement on 27 February 2017. "We have neither the means nor the mechanisms of payment for coal shipment. We will re-orient all our production processes towards the Russian market and towards other countries."[13] The following day, he set up a state company, Vneshtorgservis, that in effect took over management of forty coal and steel factories,[14] comprising over 40,000 workers.[15]

The Russian government appeared to encourage this scheme but did very little to actually facilitate it. In fact, it went out of its way to avoid getting mixed up in Zakharchenko's financial shenanigans and wouldn't even allow his company to be registered in Russia, so that banks servicing it wouldn't be affected by Western sanctions. Instead, Vneshtorgservis was registered in South Ossetia, a breakaway republic of Georgia that itself had recognized Lugansk and Donetsk People's Republics and was in turn recognized by Russia.[16] This roundabout allowed Vneshtorgservis to act as an intermediary funneling cash back and forth through its banks and allowing the Russian businesses involved to bypass sanctions.[17]

Instead of the Russian state, it was once again two entrepreneurs who stepped in to facilitate this scheme. The first was Sergei Kurchenko, a Ukrainian energy magnate close to the former president, Viktor Yanukovych. The popular protests of Maidan swept Yanukovych from power, and Kurchenko out of the country, with his Ukrainian assets frozen. A year after fleeing to Russia, Kurchenko was slapped with US sanctions for undermining Ukrainian democracy. As a result, serving Russian interests became his only recourse to maintain a livelihood.[18] Through his company, GazAlliance, he started moving anthracite coal from Donbas into Russia, and then took over Vneshtorgservis outright.[19]

The other entrepreneur was Russian businessman Ruslan Rostovtsev. Through a series of companies he controlled, one of which was registered in Cyprus, he moved anthracite coal from Donbas to Russia's Kemerovo region in Siberia, where it was mixed with local anthracite coal to hide its Donbas origins and thus make it legitimate enough to sell on EU and Turkish markets.[20]

Like Malofeyev, Kurchenko and Rostovtsev found themselves engaged in a public–private partnership: each of them was allowed to make money by technically breaking international law, while Russia benefited from the services they offered, offloading the financial upkeep of territories it had no desire to recognize to private businessmen. It has been alleged that Rostovtsev was encouraged by the Russian government to get involved in the coal trade after he was implicated in a major Moldovan money laundering scheme through which Russian shell companies syphoned off an estimated $20 million between 2010 and 2014.[21] But while Russian authorities investigated the scheme, Rostovtsev did not become a suspect, leading to speculation that he avoided persecution by supporting a "patriotic" project such as helping the mining companies of Donbas.[22]

Such requests by the state towards businessmen, if they took place, cannot be proven. But they fit into an established pattern where self-motivated businessmen engage in facilitating the government's political agendas, either due to genuine ideological support or the promise of Kremlin favor. Such favor in Russia—whether real or perceived—is oftentimes more precious than cash. Indeed, if Western corruption sees money buying power, then in Russia's case power more readily generates wealth. Both sides benefit: "There is ... this hybrid logic that has been a pattern for Putin for a while: if there is a business that can take on part of the government's functions, then it should do it," said a Russian politician with knowledge of the coal export scheme. "They'll earn something for themselves and be more loyal to him as a result."[23]

But while fixing one problem—helping the de facto governments break even, without overt Russian involvement—the scheme created many others.

The strategy was costly enough that the Russian government began to struggle to encourage other businesses to get involved: the new monopoly had become unwanted competition for Russian coal producers, while supplying shady companies in Ukraine wasn't profitable. According to a former Kremlin official, both President Putin and Deputy Prime Minister Dmitry Kozak, who was in charge of Russia's energy sector at the time, tried to find markets for Donbas commodities. They tried to encourage Russian businesses, particularly in the metals sector, to trade with the Lugansk and Donetsk People's Republics, but with little success. According to a press report in March 2017, Kozak met with metals magnates Alisher Usmanov and Alexei Mordashev to lobby them to "help Donbas" by supplying badly needed iron ore to the steel plants under Vneshtorgservis' control, but the Kremlin officially denied the meeting ever took place.[24]

The business trudged on, supplementing unofficial direct financing from the Russian government. While some reports estimated that the latter amounted to about 1 billion euros a year,[25] there is no official or even unofficial information about the figures, given that Russia insists it is not involved. Towards the end of 2014, when it became clear that without recognition Russia was in for a long haul of supporting these statelets, it created a commission on humanitarian aid to "certain territories of Luhansk and Donetsk regions of Ukraine," but little is known about its activities other than that it is curated by Deputy Prime Minister Kozak.[26]

But whatever Russia was sending wasn't enough, and the charity it was offering hardly worked. "They have forgotten about them [people in Eastern Ukraine]," said a Muscovite who regularly traveled to Donetsk to deliver goods and help families buy groceries. After trying to work through established charities operating in Russia, she decided to go solo, citing a lack of transparency and corruption. "The government of L/DPR [Lugansk and Donetsk People's Republics], when it comes to the big convoys going there, they just steal the goods."[27]

It had seemed, for a while, that this could be kept up indefinitely, with Russia and Ukraine insisting by turns that Donbas was the other side's problem. Moscow kept paying the minimum needed to keep the NGCAs on life support while doing little to further the Minsk process but blame Ukraine for non-compliance. Meanwhile, Ukraine continued to call out Russian aggression without doing much else—moving to integrate the territories peacefully or by force was too dangerous, while talking to the separatists directly to move through on Minsk was too politically toxic. Meanwhile, a whole assortment of Russia-friendly entrepreneurs—from billionaires moving coal to the shady entities set up in Donbas to skim money off the mines that produced it, even Ukrainian oligarchs who were in on the action—were enriching themselves.

Even though it looked as if Russia was benefiting from keeping the conflict frozen, in reality the Donbas problem was getting too costly for its comfort and not bringing the kinds of political dividends that the Kremlin had hoped. Ukraine as a state was moving further and further away from Russia's orbit, Moscow was exclusively blamed for the conflict by the West and it was footing the bill for separatist statelets it didn't have the ruthlessness to annex or recognize. Moscow was losing the political war.

III

Some five years after Russian nationalists and Ukrainian separatists first began seizing buildings in Donetsk and Luhansk, a pivotal change occurred to Ukraine that both confounded Moscow and offered some glimmer of hope for the end of the conflict.

In the spring of 2019, Ukraine elected an unlikely new president. Volodymyr Zelensky was a Russian-speaking comedian with no prior political experience, voted into power by a Ukrainian majority that was tired of the war and the politicking that went on in the name of ending it. While a populist, he was also astute and sincere enough to speak to the divides in Ukrainian society and try to mend them. In a campaign speech, he spoke plainly about the fact that Minsk wasn't working, but focused on the need to take concrete actions to first and foremost end the war:

We have to do everything so that our people stop dying ... For a start ... stop shooting there, just stop shooting. [The Minsk agreements] aren't working. We have to broaden the negotiation table ... There's no getting away from it, of course you have to talk to the representatives of the Russian Federation.[28]

Zelensky's wording was extremely cautious—indeed, "representatives" of the Russian Federation were already engaged in talks as part of the Trilateral Contact Group. But his caution reflected the extent to which even mentioning talks with pro-Russian separatists in the East had become taboo in the Ukrainian political establishment. For a war-weary majority in Ukraine, Zelensky's tone was a breath of fresh air. For the many hawks, though, including outgoing President Poroshenko, Zelensky was a potential Russian sellout at best, and a Kremlin agent at worst.

The Russians, meanwhile, were deeply confounded by the election. On the one hand, Zelensky's posture suggested he was genuinely open to moving towards some kind of settlement. But his caution—he did not commit outright to either implementing Minsk or to scrapping it in favor of a new deal—played into deeply held beliefs in Moscow that any government in Kyiv was ultimately a puppet of Washington.

"We don't know who stands behind him," a Russian Foreign Ministry official told me at the time. Washington had stymied every effort by Kyiv to implement Minsk, he said, and it was genuinely hard to tell if anything had changed. "Poroshenko at least was an adversary," another official said, "and at least we knew where we stood with him. With Zelensky, we don't."[29]

At first, there were signs of progress. In the fall of 2019, Zelensky agreed the so-called Steinmeier Formula, a 2016 plan proposed by Germany's then foreign minister, Frank-Walter Steinmeier, that broke down Minsk's political provisions into components that would be more manageable for Ukraine. It stipulated that elections be held in the NGCAs under the

OSCE's supervision, and if they were deemed free and fair, the territories would be granted official self-governing status by Ukraine. Zelensky's move wasn't without its obstacles: hundreds of people, most of them nationalists, protested against the decision, calling it a capitulation. But the president's pledge, for a moment, helped break an impasse. By December, the Normandy format talks, which had been halted for years, resumed, and Russia and Ukraine exchanged all of their prisoners by the end of the year.

Cautious optimism in Moscow about Kyiv's renewed political will to negotiate—coupled with mounting frustration over Surkov's handling of the conflict—fed into a growing sense in the government that it was time for a new approach.

By then, Moscow had been considering replacing Surkov for some time with a new curator. His position had been growing increasingly shaky, and Girkin's public accusations against him were only the tip of the iceberg of criticism from those who had seen him in action. But in terms of the NGCAs, the problems ran far beyond Surkov's particular management style. With a Kremlin unwilling to recognize them nor fully give them up to Ukraine, any official curating of these territories in the name of a government that hadn't fully decided what it wanted to do with them was being set up for failure. Moreover, Surkov's role was alleged by some observers to have exacerbated competition over influence of the Donbas NGCAs between Russia's GRU, which was believed to be backing Surkov (himself a GRU veteran), and the FSB, which some alleged protected Girkin as one of their own.[30] It didn't help matters that while Surkov was charged with handling political matters in Donbas, it was Deputy Prime Minister Kozak who was actually handling the economics of keeping the territories afloat. In the words of a US official involved in talks with Russia, it wasn't clear "what Surkov's mandate is, and whether he has one."[31]

Thus, in late January 2020, Surkov wrote a letter of resignation, and a week later the Kremlin officially announced that Kozak would be handling relations with Ukraine, and the issue of the unrecognized republics in particular. The switch heralded a change in course: Surkov, despite his ambiguity in supporting actual independence for the Lugansk and Donetsk People's Republics, was a hardliner who insisted that Ukraine must accept the territories as de facto under Russian influence and was either unwilling or unable to look for compromises. Kozak, who had experience reaching settlements over Moldova's breakaway Transnistria, was regarded as a tough negotiator but also a pragmatist who represented a growing body of opinion in Moscow that felt the conflict was getting too costly and that it was time to find a compromise.[32]

Indeed, it initially seemed that Russia's new negotiator could move things forward. Kozak and his Ukrainian counterpart, Andriy Yermak, appeared to be making some headway in their talks. In March 2020, the two met and agreed on a special Advisory Council in which Ukrainian officials would discuss the peace process with representatives of the unrecognized territories. The council's statements were not binding but a way to start a conversation about how special status would work and where compromises could be made to avoid this kind of autonomy negatively impacting Ukrainian sovereignty.

But the very idea of discussing anything with representatives of the de facto states went poorly in Ukraine. Zelensky's critics protested fiercely against the Steinmeier Formula and at times even obstructed his efforts—to the point that Yermak himself was slapped with criminal charges of treason by the Ukrainian SBU for trying to start a dialogue.[33] While the charges didn't go anywhere, the damage was done. If Zelensky was to survive politically, he had to walk a fine line of publicly adhering to Minsk while assuring the hardliners in Ukraine that Minsk would never be implemented, that Crimea would be returned to Ukraine and that Russia would never get what it wanted. Control over the Lugansk and Donetsk People's Republics stopped being the point. The undercurrent of these debates in Kyiv was that reintegrating and rebuilding the war-ravaged "republics" would be costly for Ukraine, in addition to undermining its political independence. Russia backed them, so Russia should pay for the reconstruction. But Russia didn't want to bear the costs either—certainly not without some kind of formalized agreement on the statelets' status and, more importantly, on the status of Crimea.

What this came down to was that reintegration under Minsk was becoming more widely interpreted, and not just by the hardliners, to be a capitulation. Besides, finding more creative ways to reintegrate pro-Russian and Russian-speaking communities in Donbas, while avoiding undue Kremlin influence on Ukrainian politics, meant fundamentally revising the Minsk Package of Measures. This was something Moscow was loath to allow, and the EU not keen on undertaking. What it came down to was that even if reintegration was the right thing to do, it could not be done under the barrel of Moscow's gun—not after it had fostered a war there.

Zelensky, initially optimistic about a way out, seemed to exhaust all his options. To survive politically, he had little choice but to focus his energies on drumming up international support against Russian aggression. In 2019, his predecessor, Poroshenko, had signed a constitutional amendment enshrining Ukraine's aspirations to join not just the EU, but NATO. This was intrinsically incompatible with a status quo in which Crimea was de facto Russian, not to mention integrating and enshrining special status for separatist territories controlled by de facto Russian proxies. Zelensky had no alternative but to pursue the same agenda; however unrealistic, it was simply more popular, both domestically and internationally. NATO as an institution had no real intention of accepting Ukraine into its club anytime soon, for all that in 2008, in Bucharest, it had declared that Ukraine (and Georgia) "will become members of NATO" without actually making any concrete moves in that direction.[34] Certain member states in Eastern Europe with their own anti-Kremlin political agendas were happy to offer rhetorical and sometimes material support for Ukraine's cause in resisting Russian aggression, but that support was never going to make a substantive difference and arguably ended up, instead, fueling Russian paranoias.

The idea for an advisory council that would involve people from the "occupied" territories, as the NGCAs became officially known, was scrapped in favor of yet another advisory body, the Crimea Platform. Launched in the summer of 2021, it made its official mission to "peacefully [end] the Russian Federation's temporary occupation of ... Crimea." Given that Russia had made it clear, again and again, that it would fight for Crimea, this was a political nonstarter. But that didn't seem to matter anymore. The platform stated its commitment to "further political, diplomatic and restrictive measures towards the Russian Federation."[35]

After the emergence of the Crimea Platform, Moscow had begun amassing troops around Ukraine's borders. The new threat suggested that maybe the hardliners in Kyiv were right, that maybe the Crimea Platform was the only policy worth pursuing. The only problem, however, was that it wasn't going to work.

* * *

In Kyiv, Moscow, Brussels, London, Istanbul and DC, the meetings dragged on for hours and went nowhere. Human rights workers. Western NGO officials in their swish brick and glass offices with artisanal espresso-makers. Parliamentarians. Former fighters turned politicians meeting furtively in cafés. A Western diplomat who had spent a year living in a hotel in the decrepit Russian mining town of Shakhtinsk, counting muddy trucks that crossed the Russian–Ukrainian border in and out of the territories for the OSCE. Everyone was stuck. For every tentative step forward, there were a million ways someone would sabotage the deal. Hold elections under OSCE oversight? The de facto authorities would never let OSCE monitors do their job. Maybe hold "track two" convenings, where members of Ukraine's Presidential Administration and representatives of civil society groups, rather than "authorities" from the NGCAs, could speak openly in an unofficial capacity? But what real power would such meetings hold, if Kyiv had taken a firm line of not dealing directly with anyone from the "Russian"-occupied territories?

And besides, what constituted "acceptable" civil society anyway? How could you bring humanitarian workers with various points of view in and around the breakaway territories in Donbas—the people who were actually suffering and dying—to the table, and what table would that be? The stigma of being "Russian" was so powerful that every time they crossed the line of contact they risked an ordeal of threats from the de facto authorities on the one hand, and red tape and insults from the Ukrainians on the other. Persecuted at home, they weren't even wanted in the West. When one could access them, which was rare because separatist authorities had imposed draconian restrictions on freedom of speech, while the Ukrainian establishment treated them all like potential Russian agents, their words never fit neatly into policy briefs or tweets, or even into nice, clear talking points that journalists love to quote. Everyone wanted to speak for them, not to them.

"To me being a citizen of Ukraine means freedom of movement," said one humanitarian worker. "And [as I live east of the contact line] I don't have that."

"Farmers can't take their cows out to pasture near the contact line," said another. "Animals are getting sick. To say nothing of the people."

"Children from non-government territories can't cross into government-held territories because they don't have the right documentation," said another.

"People who've seen combat—they fall into the deepest depression, they can't get out of it," said a psychologist.

"Our country is being cut up however they want. We used to be a family and everything worked. And then, someone needed to destroy it all."

All these came from one meeting held to bring together civil society activists from both sides of the line of contact. I opened my mouth to offer another "what if," another attempt to find a solution, another option to try, but suddenly I couldn't utter a word. There could be no diplomacy when neither side was interested in what these people on the ground had to say. Paralyzed by impotence, all I could do was listen, absorb, maybe carry what they were bearing for a little bit, and help tell their story, but nothing more. Across from me in the window of a suburban Kyiv hotel, a janitor swept the autumn leaves off the sidewalk in rhythmic swishes. "We keep talking to the OSCE about dialogue, but ..." One move of the arm, and a meter was cleared, as a cloud of leaves settled on the grass. "Children are being militarized ..." Another step, another swish, another section of the pavement was complete, and order was restored. The sun, its rays diagonally piercing the yellow leaves, was setting; it would be the end of his shift soon, and the job would be done.[36]

"Nobody wants us," someone had said. "Loser gets Donbas," said another.[37]

Because that, at the heart of it, was what it had always been about: no one wanted to deal with these people, their "backwardness," their "victimized harping" about their historic grievances, their constant boring problems, their lack of functioning banks, their subsistence economies, their potato patches, their refusal to just pick a language and stick with it, and their fundamental inability to exist in the right way, in the way that richer, more privileged parts of the society—and the world—expected of them. Neither Russia nor Ukraine: no one truly wanted them.

By the time Russian missiles began hammering Ukrainian cities, by the time air raid sirens wailed in Kyiv in the middle of the night, it was no longer about the people of Donbas, or about Russian-speakers in Ukraine, or even the separatist movement the Kremlin had spearheaded only to destroy.

It was about one man, and his vendetta.

10

THE INVASION

I

In 1994, when Russia was already awash with cash yet still socially and economically broken following the wholesale institutional collapse it had survived just three years earlier, a middle-aged Russian bureaucrat, a *chinovnik*, found himself in Hamburg, attending a lavish dinner for distinguished guests in a beautiful palace.

Like many middling civil servants, the *chinovnik*'s career had been obliterated by the fall of the Soviet Union, so much so that at one point he had found himself scrounging for cash to feed himself, his wife and his two small daughters, and he was impressed by the opulence, and especially by the chance to mingle with such high company. By 1994, he was coming up in the world, but only meagerly—with rampant inflation, there was not much one could afford on a civil servant's salary, even that of a senior city official. Not legally, at least. In St Petersburg and Moscow, whole families were still crammed into decrepit shared apartments with leaky pipes and intermittent hot water and struggled to buy food, while the so-called New Russians—

entrepreneurs who started making fast money in the newly liberalized economy—built themselves McMansions on the outskirts
and drove Mercedes and BMWs to the roaring, flashy clubs that
dotted the two cities. "At one point, I was making so much cash
I was literally stuffing it into bags and didn't know what to do
with it," said one Russian entrepreneur who later emigrated.[1]

The *chinovnik*, too, embezzled when he could. They all did.
He was smart, and while he had always been a patriot and had
been deeply devastated by the collapse of the Soviet Union, he
knew full well, just like many of his rank did, that communism
was a pipe dream that could never work, could never economically sustain the citizens of a great nation with the dignity they
deserved. He welcomed the economic reforms and believed in
the power of money to raise one's station. He also believed in
win-win—it was part of his job, after all, to help the government
and private businesses, especially foreign ones, make as much
money as they could together. As he helped foreign companies
get rich by working in Russia, he too tried to make himself rich.
It was only natural; after all, he was doing his bit to help Russia
transition to the new economy.

The *chinovnik* had had an impoverished childhood, born to
parents who had known real hunger. Not the kind that many
experienced during *perestroika*, when store shelves were bare and
families had to subsist on potatoes and gruel, but the kind of
hunger that sent mothers scavenging for city cats and boiling
leather to feed the remaining child who had *not* starved to
death. During the Soviet period, his station afforded him certain perks, but he never rose far enough to take advantage of the
full privileges enjoyed by the Soviet *nomenklatura*. One official
of the same rank, who had worked in the same offices as the
chinovnik then, described him as an average, amicable guy who
swung his arms in an easy-going manner as he walked. The
official was only entitled to a three-room apartment in an old

building, far from the prestigious accommodation afforded to generals and high-ranking party officials. For all its communism, the Soviet Union remained a society of strict castes, with a class system of its own. It was no wonder, then, that once he could afford to, the *chinovnik* developed a taste for all the attributes of wealth: he affected the oversized maroon jackets that were in vogue among the super-rich, and, when he became much wealthier years later and could afford to refurbish himself a palace, he adorned its interior with artificial blue marble. Why artificial? It was more expensive.[2]

But in 1994, he was still frustrated by the social and infrastructural decrepitude that surrounded him. Having emerged from the grip of the Soviet pipe dream, society was undergoing a deep reckoning with the horrors and crimes of communism, and particularly Stalinism. It was a painful process, not least because the persecuted and the persecutors were often part of the same family: it was not unheard of for the relatives of an NKVD officer to acquire the real estate vacated by the latest purge victim, only for the NKVD officer himself to be purged the same year. The reforms of Mikhail Gorbachev liberalized society from the top: first it was the *nomenklatura* that began speaking of *glasnost*, openness and truth. Then, when the Soviet Union collapsed, it was still the wealthier former Soviet *nomenklatura* and the more privileged, urban intelligentsia who were the most vocal in decrying communism, the old, Soviet way of life and, sometimes with it, Russia itself. Who remembered Russia *before* the Soviet Union, after all? Many of those who were poorer thought differently: they were the ones who had lost more and didn't feel they were gaining much in the new economic turmoil. But general frustration with the poverty, government ineptitude and most of all the seeming historical *inability* of Russians to build a normal, prosperous, European-style life for themselves fed into deep divisions. A vocal

Russophobia emerged among the pro-Western intelligentsia, émigrés and ethnic minorities oppressed under the Soviet Union who had found sovereignty on the one hand, while a simmering, revanchist nationalism and even antisemitism built up among those who believed they had lost from the Soviet collapse, on the other. Both narratives fed each other's in a twisted, toxic dance: the more the one called the other a Sovok (a derogatory term for an uneducated middling beneficiary of the Soviet life-style) and a loser, the more the other camp decried them as traitors, Jews and Americans out to rob the country.

The *chinovnik* was aware of all this but didn't pay it much heed at the time, finding the antisemitism of the nationalists particularly distasteful and, more importantly, not exactly con-ducive if one wanted to be accepted in high society. He was smart and more focused on his career; his visit to Hamburg was a chance to enjoy some of that good German beer, to revel in how he had made it for himself, sitting at a table served by waiters in frock coats, rubbing shoulders with dignitaries in an ancient European city.

The guests were ushered into an ornate conference hall, and the head of state of a European country took the podium. The *chinovnik* heard words about freedom of the mind, freedom of the economy and democracy, about a Europe breaking with its totali-tarian past. But then it became about something else. "What is currently brewing in Russia." "Irrationalism." "Imperialism."

"Why does the new, post-communist Russia," the European president asked, "which claims to have broken with the evil tra-ditions of the USSR, stubbornly refuse to admit that the Baltic nations—Estonians, Latvians and Lithuanians—were occupied and annexed against their will?"

Listening to those words, the *chinovnik* heard them as if they were addressed to him. Not *Soviet* occupation, but *Russian* occu-pation. As if he, personally, was to blame for what had happened in the past. "One unwittingly becomes an accomplice," the president said, "of imperialist forces in Russia who believe that they can solve their country's immense problems by outward expansion and by threatening their neighbors."[3]

Here I am, thought the *chinovnik*, heading a Russian delegation to Europe, demonstrating that our country is opening up to you, that we are changing, that we want to be your partners and equals, and you call us occupiers? Sovoks? Is that what we'll always be to you?

The *chinovnik* suddenly felt that enough was enough. He got up from his seat, walked down the aisle, his heels clacking conspicuously on the parquet, opened the heavy door of the conference hall and left. He didn't mean to slam the door, but it was so heavy that it slammed loudly shut behind him anyway.[4]

II

A dark, surreal quiet had descended on Moscow as the winter months set in late 2021 and the snow began to fall. The coronavirus lockdowns were lifted and life started getting back to normal; the streets buzzed with crowds of people going about their lives, the cafés were full, and it was impossible to get tickets to the Karl Bryullov exhibit at the Tretyakov—everything was booked. In the crisp cold of early winter, Christmas lights lit up the city, a source of warmth made all the more poignant when offset by a such a dark winter. "I don't like the feeling of this," said a Western diplomat based in Kyiv who was on a visit to Moscow, as he ordered another glass of wine.[5] "Every policymaker and official I've talked to here—the mood is different. Their rhetoric is angry and they are afraid of war."

That September, I had spoken to a Russian government advisor who had lobbied the Kremlin heavily since 2014 to take ownership of the pro-Russian separatists and use Russia's full force to back them. "I think something's up," he told me then. "I think people in the government are finally getting ready to recognize the independence of the statelets." At the time, I'd brushed his remarks aside as wishful thinking: after all, he and other advisors like him had been saying much the same thing for nearly eight years.

But the diplomat noticed it too, and it worried him. "They've given up on Zelensky," he said. "They've decided that Zelensky is going to do what [Mikheil] Saakashvili did in Georgia in 2008, and they're preparing to stop him." Saakashvili, counting on help from NATO, responded to Russian and separatist provocations in South Ossetia by attacking its capital, Tskhinvali, and Russian troops invaded Georgia. But how could this happen in Ukraine, given Zelensky had all but ruled out such plans? As we played out the scenarios, none of them made sense: if Russia recognized the pseudo-states, Minsk would be dead and the Kremlin would lose any hope of influencing Ukraine. What it amounted to was something different: fear. The Kremlin, and the officials and policymakers he and I had spoken to, had become convinced that Crimea, and therefore Russia, were about to be attacked by Ukrainian forces backed by NATO.

For the better half of 2021, somewhere between 100 and 120 Russian BTGs and their supporting units and artillery—by various estimates, about 100,000 troops and their tanks and missiles—had been amassing on Ukraine's southern, eastern and northern borders, in Rostov region and Belarus; in the separatist-held areas in Donetsk and Luhansk; and in Crimea. In the beginning, few thought they were there to actually pull the trigger. Troop amassments like this had become a common occurrence since 2014: under the Poroshenko administration in particular, the ebb and flow of Russian muscle around the border would regularly spark cries of imminent invasion that never materialized. The last such scare, in the spring of 2021, ended with a limited withdrawal after President Joe Biden agreed to a summit with Putin.

But this time around, something was different: someone, or something, was growing more desperate, as if tired of the cries about a wolf, it had begun to wish that the real wolf would come and get it over with. In October, US and Ukrainian intelligence officials started warning news media of "irregular" movements and the potential for an invasion. This was not the first time they had done so, but many analysts had always been skeptical of the Kremlin's capability and intent to launch a full-scale invasion and consistently downplayed the fears. But something in the manner that Russia was amassing troops in the fall of 2021 was unsettling. Under the usual pattern, Russia deployed troops to the Ukrainian border under the pretext of exercises. But this time, they weren't being sent home. In October, for instance, Russia's 41st Combined Arms Army, which had been deployed for exercises near Ukraine, joined up with other Russian units on the Ukrainian border in Russia and Belarus, instead of going home to Siberia. "It is not a drill," claimed Michael Kofman, an analyst on Russian military with the DC think tank, Center for Naval Analyses, in October. "It doesn't appear to be a training exercise. Something is happening. What is it?"[6]

* * *

It was June 2000, and less than a month after the *chinovnik* was sworn in as president of Russia in his first inauguration, he invited his American counterpart, Bill Clinton, for a visit to Moscow. He treated him to a lavish informal dinner of boiled boar and goose, proudly gave him a tour of the Kremlin and brought the country's best jazz musicians to play. They talked about many things, from arms control to the situation in the Balkans, both issues on which Moscow had considerable disagreements with the United States.[7] But one thing that the

Russian president remembered, although he didn't mention it at the time, was what happened when he asked Clinton about Russia eventually joining NATO. Though Clinton had just days earlier, while speaking at a European capital, floated the idea of eventual Russian membership in both NATO and the EU, the Russian president was struck by the way Clinton didn't react with any enthusiasm at all, something he would still remember many years later.[8]

But at the time, the Russian president still believed that for his country to be strong, to be the great power that he felt it always was, a "dictatorship of the law" at home, as he called it, wasn't enough—it needed to stand on equal footing with other great powers. The great powers, he assumed, for whom the end justified the means. On 9 September 2001, as his aviation was leveling the Chechen capital of Grozny to the ground to quell an Islamist insurgency there, the Russian president telephoned US President George W. Bush to share intelligence about a planned terrorist attack against the United States. After all, the Russian president felt that they were in this together. And when the terrorist attack happened, he was the first to call Bush with his sincere condolences.

But the United States didn't want to be in this together, whatever "this" was, with anyone, least of all what it thought of as a defeated former superpower that didn't matter anymore. It seemed to have ignored all the issues that were important to Russia on which it had disagreements, whether NATO expansion or missile defense. In June 2002, the United States unilaterally withdrew from the Anti-Ballistic Missile Treaty, under the pretext that it needed to protect itself from Iran, but the Russian president didn't buy those excuses given what came after. In November of that year, NATO held a summit inviting seven new members—three of them former members of the Soviet Union, including Estonia, whose president so infuriated the *chinovnik* in 1994—into the alliance. They would join in 2004.

When the United States decided to invade Iraq in 2003 on the pretext that Saddam Hussein was developing weapons of mass destruction, the Russian president was particularly dismayed. "There was no need for military action to answer the main question that was directly raised by the international community, namely whether or not there are weapons of mass destruction in Iraq," he said at the time. "We must not allow international law to be replaced by the law of the fist, according to which the strong are always right and have the right to everything."[9] It was *wrong*, what the United States was doing. But no one seemed to listen to what the second most powerful man in the world had to say. And underneath it all, that gnawing possibility: if they can do it like that, without pretext or law, just because they don't like him, *then they can do it to me*.

On 10 February 2007, the president made a threatening speech. If they don't listen when we appeal to them in the name of their own values, then we, like them, will appeal to strength. To himself, perhaps he said: *maybe the law of the fist really is how you become a great power, and they were lying to us about it to keep us weak.* At the Munich Security Conference, he denounced the danger of a unipolar world: "Today we are witnessing an almost uncontained hyper use of force—military force—in international relations, force that is plunging the world into an abyss of permanent conflicts."[10] He may have meant it as a warning, he may have wanted to scare them like they were scaring him, or he may have felt he needed to issue a threat: whatever it was, his words were clearly taken to mean the latter. For some Western leaders, and for some in Central Europe in particular, the Munich speech was the best excuse to strengthen and unite NATO against Russia they could have hoped for. And it certainly didn't mean NATO was going to start paying attention to Russian concerns.

On 17 February 2008, Kosovo, then a disputed province of Serbia populated predominantly by Albanians, declared its independence. Despite Serbia's protests that the declaration was illegal and calls on Russia from Kosovar Serbs to send military aid, the following day the United States and most EU member states recognized the declaration. The development opened old wounds for Russia: in 1999, President Yeltsin had vehemently opposed NATO's bombing campaign against Yugoslavia, a Russian ally, but was powerless to do anything as NATO forced Yugoslavia to grant Kosovo autonomy. Russia, after all, was on the wrong side of international opinion: a minority had the right to self-determination, and it was the international community's obligation to protect that right. This impotence, in the eyes of Russian patriots, reached an apotheosis at the end of the war when the Kremlin, opposed to what it saw as an excessive NATO presence in the Kosovo province, deployed about 250 troops to Pristina International Airport. The standoff ended when Russian peacekeeping troops were allowed to be deployed throughout Kosovo, independently of NATO.[11]

Russia felt it had been ignored—until it had forced the West to pay attention. But even then, its interests had still not been recognized, a feeling reinforced eight years later with Kosovo's recognition.

While this was not 1999 and the *chinovnik* was no Boris Yeltsin, still, short of its voice at the UN Security Council and its non-recognition, there was really nothing Russia could do to prevent Kosovo's secession from an ally. Domestically, the Kremlin was gearing up for the election of the *chinovnik*'s anointed presidential successor, Dmitry Medvedev, and all its resources were focused on that transition going smoothly. Power struggles simmered beneath the surface, and the *chinovnik* had to ensure they were contained so that Medvedev could assume the presidency and he himself could seamlessly switch over to the post of prime minister. But of course, on an emotional level, that international slight could not just be brushed away. Just as, in

2007, the Kremlin's then Defense Minister Sergei Ivanov vowed an "asymmetrical response" if the United States ignored its offers of a joint missile defense shield in Europe in favor of a unilateral one,[12] so too it considered nonlinear ways to assert its position. Such strategically ambiguous threats often belied the lack of capabilities to respond symmetrically.

And so, Russia's Foreign Ministry was non-committal on Kosovo's independence: "We will, without doubt, have to take into account a declaration and recognition of Kosovo independence in connection with the situation in Abkhazia and South Ossetia."[13]

Since 2004, when the pro-Western, NATO-oriented Mikheil Saakashvili was elected president of Georgia, there had been saber rattling on the border over the two breakaway states. When he came to power, Saakashvili had reined in Ajaria without firing a shot and had been talking ever since of doing the same with Abkhazia and South Ossetia. Reuniting Georgia was crucial if it was to have a chance at NATO membership, and Saakashvili was so taken with Western promises that he seemed to have come to believe that NATO would back him up in a confrontation with Russia. Moscow, still smarting from losing the Baltics to NATO, had been angry about Georgia's aspirations since 2004 and started bringing increasing military, diplomatic and economic pressure to bear on the country. As a result, for years leading up to 2008 the two had been engaged in military brinkmanship, with Russia building up forces preparing for a Georgian offensive, and Saakashvili waiting for the right moment to seize the breakaway states. After Kosovo, time was running out: Russia felt it had an international precedent, George Bush was pressing Europe to accept Georgia and Ukraine into NATO, and Saakashvili was drawing up military plans.

Russia saw its position as defensive: it was trying to prevent the seizure of the statelets, which would open Georgia's way for NATO membership, but it didn't want to strike without a pretext. It wanted to see if the other side would take the bait, strike first and do, finally, what it had been bragging about. Irregular forces in South Ossetia—themselves eager for Russian protection, money and recognition—sniped at Georgian positions that summer, Georgians fired back; after a bit of this back-and-forth, Tbilisi launched an assault on the South Ossetian capital Tskhinvali on 7 August. Saakashvili had underestimated Moscow's preparedness on the one hand and overestimated Western inclination to back him on the other. Russia countered with an offensive that pushed Georgian forces back from Abkhazia and South Ossetia in eight days and, now that it had a reason, recognized the statelets as independent.

Aside from an increased NATO presence in the Black Sea, there was not much of a response—no sanctions, no NATO membership for Georgia. But the Western condemnation of Russian actions only served to prove to the *chinovnik* what many hawks in his circle, and particularly Patrushev, had already come to be convinced of: *they* get to, *but we don't*. When the *chinovnik* finally caved and pulled the trigger on Crimea in 2014—but not on Donbas, he was too cautious—he became adamant: the condemnation, the isolation, the sanctions, even if they were not deemed nearly enough, *was what they had planned all along*. If *this* is what happens when we do nothing more than international law has allowed others to do, then surely nothing matters; surely Russian actions are merely a pretext to squeeze it into oblivion with sanctions and condemnation, surely *they* would find a pretext no matter what.

III

As the winter of 2021 loomed, Washington was dumbfounded. The Biden administration had no intention of interfering on Ukraine's behalf if it was invaded. But with its departure from

Afghanistan leaving an embarrassing dent in its global reputation, and amid domestic tensions fueled by a possible Trumpist revanche, it found itself in the uncomfortable position of having to demonstrate resolve—both to domestic hawks and to Russia—without the power to actually do much.

In November, US officials started raising the alarm, warning European governments that, based on their intelligence about its troop movements, Russia was planning to invade Ukraine.[14] Anonymous intelligence sources in the US and UK cited data that they wouldn't disclose, to the effect that Putin had made a decision. Some of this was met with due skepticism: given that questionable intelligence had manipulated Western media during the Trump years, it was hard to take such leaks at face value. Some diplomats in Europe came to a different interpretation of Moscow's aims: rather than a full-scale invasion, which would make no sense in terms of Russian objectives, to them it seemed more like a semi-permanent troop presence with the aim of coercing concessions from Ukraine and its European allies.[15] Even the Ukrainians were becoming skeptical and increasingly frustrated that the US was merely warmongering, possibly to pressure Kyiv to implement Minsk and let the West off the hook.[16]

Indeed, from Moscow's perspective, the theory of coercive diplomacy made much more sense—and seemed to have much more promise—than an invasion plan, which, militarily, was doomed to fail. Moscow was frustrated with the lack of progress in Ukraine. Noticing that its troops were indeed scaring the West, it started upping the ante, bringing its NATO concerns into the mix. In December, Russia's Foreign Ministry issued a shopping list of demands that amounted to a new security architecture for Europe, but on Russian terms—with a guarantee, backed up by the United States in writing, that there would be no further NATO expansion.[17] While it did not directly mention Donbas, Crimea or the Minsk plan, it didn't have to: if Russia had guarantees that Ukraine's place in Russia's sphere of influence would not be contested, that there would be no foreign military bases or troops on Ukrainian territory, that it would not join NATO, then the danger that Ukraine would seek to recapture Crimea or Donbas dissipated. The plan had a number of other points, including talks on a new arms treaty; indeed, Moscow seemed to be setting a high bar, seeing what it could get in return for scaling down.

At the same time, what was being openly discussed in Moscow circles was recognizing the "people's republics." First the Communist Party and then the pro-Kremlin United Russia party passed motions petitioning the Kremlin to initiate this recognition, but the Kremlin, for weeks, kept mum. It was assumed, by supporters and detractors alike, and by many officials in the Kremlin itself,[18] that the motion would act as a sort of "stick" in the negotiating process. If Russia got nothing in the negotiations, then it would have no choice but to recognize the statelets and send in troops to defend their newly recognized sovereignty. The problem with this stick, however, was that it gave Moscow nothing but sanctions once it was used. If Ukraine didn't fight for the territories it had already in effect lost, then the conflict would end peacefully. Ukraine would be freed from implementing an unfavorable peace agreement, the separatists would get the independence they had been fighting for, the nationalists in Russia would have been placated, but all Moscow would get were sanctions, and a decision to forgo all that the Kremlin had been fighting for over the last eight years.

Indeed, at first, there were hints that Moscow could get something out of this new initiative. A new round of talks on Minsk was announced, Putin and Biden started talking on the phone regularly, there were a series of high-level security negotiations in Geneva, and Moscow policymakers were hopeful about the renewed contacts. Even the hawks thought Russia might finally be taken seriously and that efforts to build a new security architecture, one that suited Moscow, could begin.[19] On 14 February, just two days after Putin spoke with Biden, Defense Minister Shoigu even announced that military exercises were about to end and troops would be sent home,[20] as good an indication as anything that the buildup was indeed coercive diplomacy as usual, and, more to the point, that it was working.

But in that careful balance Washington tried to strike, teetering between strategic impotence and performative resolve, its messages, by the time they reached Moscow, were jumbled. There was clearly a mismatch between whatever Biden was telling Putin and Zelensky privately, and what he was doing and saying publicly. NATO had no intention of accepting Ukraine anytime soon, but it would never abandon its open-door policy. The United States and NATO would not send troops to Ukraine in case of a Russian invasion,[21] but it was already preemptively sending weapons, and more were to come until Moscow deescalated.[22]

On some level, this was inevitable: there needed to be at least a semblance of deterrence, even when the United States did not fully understand what exactly it was deterring—much as Russia, misconstruing what it was being told, hoped for the best, but was preparing for the worst. While Shoigu might speak of troops going home, there was no evidence on the ground that Russia was actually deescalating. In response, the West, in turn, signaled more resolve: even as the talks continued, so did the intelligence leaks, the warnings about an "imminent" invasion that, it appeared, had become Washington's go-to tactic for deterring Putin. Days after Shoigu's remarks, on 18 February, Biden said he was "convinced" Putin had "made the decision" to launch an invasion in the coming days.[23]

* * *

Was it arrogance for the US president to presume to understand what was going on inside the *chinovnik*'s head, when he himself had so many doubts and fears, doubts that he could not even voice for fear of sounding weak? After all, even as of January, the CIA believed he had still not made up his mind on whether to invade.[24] He felt he was being backed into a corner. "What is it that they don't understand?" the *chinovnik* had retorted to a Western journalist in December. "We want to ensure our security."[25]

Clearly, Russia was *insecure*. Patrushev had once remarked of similar American warnings the previous spring: "If they are predicting, then that means they are planning, and if they are planning, then they can make it happen."[26] In other words, just as Moscow had once needled Saakashvili into taking a self-destructive first step, so too Washington was not just predicting a war— it wanted one. All the US warnings, Ukraine's continued insistence on NATO membership, NATO's refusal to rule it out: to the *chinovnik* and his hawkish confidants, it all sounded like the West wanted to force the issue.

"Imagine that Ukraine is a member of NATO. Article 5 has not been repealed; on the contrary, President Biden recently said that Article 5 is absolutely imperative," the president had said in early February. "This means that there will be a military confrontation between Russia and NATO. I asked at a press conference last time, should we go to war with NATO? But I want to ask you too: do you want to fight with Russia?"[27]

Maybe the president was simply trying to pre-empt what he saw as the West's plans. Maybe he was just looking for confirmation of his own assumptions and fears. Maybe he felt he was too far gone to step back. Either way, on 21 February, he finally did what so many nationalists had been wanting him to do for so long: he officially recognized the Donetsk and Lugansk People's Republics. But even then, it was unclear if he had thought through what this would mean. He was certainly vague on the question of specifically what territories he was recognizing— those currently held by the separatists up to the line of contact, or the administrative borders of the whole Donetsk and Luhansk oblasts, which featured in the statelets' declarations of independence? As he was running out of options, he seemed to be trying to create as many new ones as possible—even as he was feeling the closeness of the wall against his back, and the threats of his enemies, distorted by his own fears, nearing.

Over 100,000 troops amassed at the border, he may have thought, *the full force of our military, backed by our nuclear arsenal, and you still don't understand?*

IV

In 2020, as the new coronavirus swept through the planet killing millions, the president was at a loss. At first, he agreed with the tough measures proposed by his leading regional chief, Moscow Mayor Sergei Sobyanin, and closed the borders. But then he calculated that a stringent lockdown, of the kind imposed in Europe, would place unimaginable costs on the economy. Russia might not survive that double storm. He could not imperil the country's prosperity, the guarantor of its future, and so took a middle path. Regional bosses got to decide the level of quarantine themselves, as long as they adhered to the Kremlin's one unspoken rule: avoid mass protests.

Of course, for Russia to survive, the priority was the survival of its guarantor, the president himself. To keep Russia safe, no precaution was too excessive when it came to his personal health. He already had an army of doctors, including a thyroid cancer surgeon, accompanying him on lengthy trips to Sochi, sparking undying speculation that he is terminally ill.[28] And so, if strict quarantine was excessive for the nation at large, then it was paramount for the protection of its guarantor. The president secluded himself in his leafy residence at Novo-Ogaryovo, and everyone who met him was required to undergo a two-week quarantine and a test.

As the rest of the first world baked and zoomed and virtue-signaled on social media, the president read books. He returned to his love of history, particularly apt given that, whatever the state of his health, he was nearing his eighth decade. But closer to home was the growing realization that having spent twenty years at the helm of the largest country in the world, he himself was part of history's very fabric. And Russian history is strewn with mysticism, for what else can hope to reconcile its darkest pages with its holistic glory? He paged through the works of the early twentieth-century philosopher Nikolai Berdyaev. "Conservatism," he would quote, "is not something preventing upward, forward movement, but something preventing you from sliding back into chaos."[29] But possibly the most compelling narrative came from his rediscovery of Lev Gumilyov, the favorite of Russian nationalists, who viewed anthropology through an esoteric lens and claimed that at certain pivotal moments in time nations acquired a particular energy and destiny. Gumilyov was no ethno-nationalist. He believed it was a mix of ethnicities that gave a nation its particular identity, and an energy—what he termed *passionarity*—that could be empirically measured. The president, who had been perennially in need of a binding national identity to help him govern, was blown away by such pronouncements that traced Russia's historical destiny to the very molecular components of its peoples' blood. "I believe in passionarity," he said in February 2021. "Russia has not reached its peak. We are on the march, on the march of development ... We have an infinite genetic code. It is based on the mixing of blood."[30]

Sitting next to him on those long quarantine evenings and joining him on these excursions into blood, soil, history and Russian Orthodoxy was a man who had become a close confidant, the billionaire and media magnate Yuri Kovalchuk. The two had been close since the 1990s, and now, fed on a similar literary and ideological diet, they reinforced each other's views.[31]

These writings and discussions, and the intelligence from the Fifth Service of the FSB detailing the supposed anti-Russian nationalist plot that the United States was manufacturing in Ukraine, formed the basis of the president's expertise.

Since that summer, the *chinovnik* had taken to publishing lengthy exegeses on the history of Ukraine, trying to hammer home the idea that the two were part of one nation, and that Ukrainian sovereignty was a fiction imposed on it by Western forces seeking to divide Russia. While he had surrounded himself with an increasingly narrowing coterie of advisors and intelligence officials who told him what he wanted to hear (he was finding it increasingly hard to trust the rest), he largely prepared these texts himself, aided with some tweaks from his handpicked experts.[32]

The results were rambling, revisionist historical narratives. But as a policy statement, too, the text made little sense: if Ukraine and Russia are one nation and Ukraine's sovereignty is a fiction, then does that mean Russia should annex it by force? That was the common interpretation in Ukraine and in the West. But it also wasn't exactly what these texts were saying: they were talking, instead, of common economic ties that Ukraine, under the influence of its Western patrons, sought to sever. Furthermore, if full annexation had been the goal from the beginning, then Russia would have had a far better chance of succeeding in the spring of 2014: that summer, it was equally poised for a full-scale invasion and would have faced a still weak and unprepared Ukrainian army, who had over the eight years of the conflict used the Russian threat to strengthen itself and mobilize. That Russia distinctly avoided recognizing or annexing Donbas for eight years was evidence that whatever was going on in the *chinovnik*'s head, it wasn't simply about ownership of Ukraine.

One common strand in all of the writings is that many of the allegations he was leveling against Ukraine were the mirror images of what Ukrainian policymakers and the Russian opposition were saying about him: that his rule was illegitimate and should be destroyed. Domestically, that argument didn't just come from the liberal opposition: up until 2012, it was also a staple of some Russian nationalist thought that Putin was a despot imposed upon Russia by the West, or that he had sold out to Western interests.[33] He seemed to be used to hearing this argument against himself, but it would particularly sting when it came out of the country he was convinced was just as corrupt as Russia, and that, *according to all the intelligence placed on his desk*, itself had capitulated to Western control.

We are not likely to know anytime soon when exactly Putin made the decision that he did. But on 21 February, he once again unleashed all his grievances, all his fury, in a rambling address to the country. Everyone was to blame, everyone who ruined his life also ruined Ukraine and turned it against him: Vladimir Lenin for his utopian revolution that butchered an empire, Ukraine for its nationalists supposedly out for Russian blood, and especially the West and its "empire of lies."

"Are the Ukrainians themselves aware of all these managerial methods?" he railed. "Do they understand that their country is not even under a political and economic protectorate, but reduced to the level of a colony with a puppet regime?"

But what it all came down to for the *chinovnik*, what all the events, all the signals of the last weeks had amounted to, was that *an attack on Russia was imminent*:

> In March 2021, Ukraine adopted a new Military Strategy. It ... spells out the contours of the proposed war, I will quote, "with the assistance of the international community on favorable terms for Ukraine." I also quote, "with military support from the world community in the geopolitical confrontation with the Russian Federation." This is nothing more than preparation for hostilities against our country—against Russia ...

You don't want to see us a friend and ally. But why make an enemy out of us? There is only one answer: it's not about our political regime, it's not about something else, they just don't need such a big independent country like Russia. This is the answer to all questions.[34]

He may have not quite figured out yet what exactly *they* were trying to do, but the documents being placed on his desk, the projections that had crystalized and calcified in his head over the years, convinced him of one thing: Russia was about to be attacked. Whether he believed at this stage that Russia was *literally* about to be invaded by troops, or dragged into a war over Crimea, or the 700 American spies that, according to his intelligence, had infiltrated Moscow alone,[35] were planning to foment a popular revolt or a palace coup to topple him from power—was immaterial. Whatever it was, Russia was not safe, and he had run out of time. This time, he couldn't afford to wait for the other side to make the first move.

IV

In the middle of the night on 24 February 2022, Russian aviation began bombarding military targets around Kyiv, Kharkiv and across central and eastern Ukraine. For the first time since World War II, air raid sirens wailed over Kyiv, civilians huddled in basements and subway tunnels as explosions boomed above, and Muscovites awoke in shock, horror and the sick despair of impotent shame. The propaganda blasted from Russian state television took on a particularly bombastic tone: Russia was conducting a "special military operation" to rid Ukraine of Nazi elements and liberate its civilians from "genocide." It would only take a few days, the generals suddenly ordering their troops to assault had thought, or had made themselves believe (because the alternative was unbearable), before the Ukrainian people would shake off their Western-imposed Nazi yoke and embrace Russia's forces of liberation.

In Russia, it was as if the Iron Curtain had come back down virtually overnight. The Kremlin shut down the last two oppositionist media outlets—Ekho Moskvy radio and *Novaya Gazeta*. It made spreading "fakes" about the "military operation" punishable by up to fifteen years in prison. In effect, this new draconian law equated any statements questioning the official narrative with treason. Saying or printing anything deviating from a fabricated official line—that this was not a war, that Ukrainians had massacred their own civilians and blamed it on Russia—was now a crime. The aim was not mass imprisonments—not yet, at least—but ensuring people were afraid to speak up. Putin's threats about ridding the country of "scum and traitors,"[36] with a criminal case here and there based on denunciations[37]—that feared self-policing tactic of the Soviet Union—were enough to keep hundreds of thousands of civil servants in line. And not just civil servants: opinion polls began to show as many as 74 percent supporting the "military operation."[38] What these numbers masked, however, was that a good deal of Russians were also opposed to the war—but it was impossible to tell how many. A significant number even protested, given that there were tens of thousands of registered detentions for such protests across the country.[39] But a majority was cowed by threat of repressions into silence, some perhaps writing furtive graffiti in Moscow alleys, or writing and talking between the lines. Silver Rain radio, a station that mostly played music, announced that it was taking all news commentary programs off the air, proclaiming defiantly: "We cannot say the truth but we do not want to lie," while in one of its last segments two male presenters wept on air as they talked to listeners calling in about their relatives in Ukraine. Fearing repression, tens, possibly hundreds of thousands of Russians who could leave the country did so in the first weeks. The country they had lived in, some said as they departed, the country that, for all the repressiveness of its regime, they had loved—to them it had become unlivable.

Many others, though—especially those who could not leave or afford to risk their lives and the livelihoods of their families to protest—succumbed to the propaganda in full. Cognitive dissonance took its toll. As images surfaced of Ukrainian civilians executed in the streets of suburban Kyiv by retreating Russian troops, many Russians could simply not fathom Russian soldiers, acting under orders from their own government, being capable of killing civilians in Ukraine—a people with whom Russians still had close familial ties. For them, it was easier to buy into the multitude of fabrications denying Russian actions and blaming everything on a hostile West than live with knowledge, shame and fear that they couldn't even speak openly about. Western sanctions, intended to squeeze the Russian economy and make it more difficult to fund the war, inadvertently only furthered this process of cognitive isolation: it was easier to believe the Kremlin's narratives about a hostile West "cancelling" Russia when Western companies refused to do business with the country, disrupting supply chains and making vital products like medicines suddenly unavailable. "What message are they trying to send? What do they expect us to do? Protest?" one woman, a manager at a dry cleaning chain, scoffed when I asked about the effect of sanctions. "Haven't they been watching? We protest when the government lets us protest. Who wants to go to jail?"

The Kremlin's repression and propaganda campaigns, however, also signaled a confusion and paranoia about what, exactly, it had unleashed.

Far from the easy victory many had been led to believe, within weeks, Kyiv had driven off the Russian attack from the north, Kharkiv lay in ruins, and in Mariupol, that town where eight years earlier Russian-speaking civilians and local police had fought off the Ukrainian National Guard and set their tank on fire, those same Russian-speaking civilians were fiercely fighting Russian soldiers in the streets and defying surrender ultimatums.

Men joined volunteer battalions to fight against better-equipped Russian troops as mothers wandered off in search of water for their children, never to be seen again.

The initial objective of the military campaign appeared to have been the seizure of Kyiv and the replacement of its notionally Washington-backed government with one friendlier to Russia. But if that were the plan, there was no evidence that it had been thought through in any detail and communicated to the policy-making community or even the military.

Within days, it became clear that the Russian military was ill-prepared and seemed to have been ordered to invade at the last minute. While Ukraine understandably launched an informa-tion war seeking to demoralize and shame invading Russian troops, it was still true that equipment was breaking down and being abandoned, and in one instance that quickly became a meme and a trend, a Ukrainian farmer used his tractor to tow away a Russian tank.[40] CIA officials began to reassess their initial claims and decided that Putin's decision was actually made on the fly, that he told few people what he was planning, and that even the generals were confused.[41] When the Kremlin officially recognized the Donetsk and Lugansk People's Republics, Russian policymakers had expected at most a military operation limited to the statelets, not more. A full-scale invasion of Ukraine with an attempt to take Kyiv—and especially the Kremlin's stated goals of "denazification" and "demilitarization"—made no strate-gic sense.[42] Take down Zelensky and impose a puppet regime? Occupy the country indefinitely? The military wasn't prepared for either. "I was shocked because for a long time, I thought that a military operation was not feasible. It was not plausible," said Andrei Kortunov, a leading foreign policy advisor.[43]

The Kremlin was worried, and heads began to roll. In early March, Putin reportedly arrested the head and deputy head of the Fifth Service of the FSB, responsible for political missions abroad, for providing poor intelligence and bungling subversive operations in the run-up to the invasion.[44] This suggested that the center for strategic planning of the war lay not so much with the Ministry of Defense, as logic would dictate, but with the FSB and the security structures, who had focused for years on political war. The whole invasion, it seemed, was planned as a *political* operation. Either Putin was becoming aware that he had based his calculus on false premises, or he simply wanted to punish someone for the mess.

By the end of March, the "military operation" suddenly changed its focus from the northwest to the southeast. Troops began to retreat from Kyiv, and the Defense Ministry announced it was "fundamentally cutting back operations" after "achieving all the main tasks" and moving into a "final phase" to "liberate" Donbas.[45] The Russian propaganda machine, egged on by the Kremlin and by itself into a militaristic frenzy for weeks, was so stupefied that it started talking about "treason." In the beginning, it was not clear whether the Kremlin was simply buying time to regroup, or indeed refocusing on Donbas after understanding that its initial goals didn't make sense. But by April, Russian forces renewed their operations around Donbas, trying to surround Ukrainian troops in Donetsk and Luhansk that were part of the Joint Forces Operation countering Russian and separatist troops in the NGCAs. They seemed to be aiming to capture the entire two oblasts, as well as a land bridge to Crimea that included Mariupol. For the time being, it became a war for territory as the chief point of contention in negotiations became about Ukraine's borders: for Ukraine, the borders under which it agreed to accept neutrality, and for Russia the borders from which it agreed to withdraw its troops.

As for the Russian nationalists, the ones who had gone to Donbas in 2014 and, in the words of one Kremlin advisor, "started this mess in the first place," it was no longer their war.

Many supported it but criticized the Kremlin's methods. Sasha, the Russian volunteer who had joined Girkin's battalion in 2014, tried to sign up to go fight in Ukraine in March but was politely declined the honor: "We don't need bloggers and tourists," he was told. He finally decided that "whether due to stupidity or intentionally, Moscow is ruining the Donbas infantry by sending them into senseless and disorganized attacks. I don't want to go there."[46] Yegor Kholmogorov, the nationalist publicist and policymaker who had coined the term "Russian Spring" back in 2014, tried to organize a rally in support of Putin and the war—but not only was he denied a permit; he also received threats from the Prosecutor General's Office.[47] And Igor Girkin—the self-styled trigger-man of Donbas—was talking of defeat. "After twenty-nine days of the military operation, there are no strategic successes anywhere. My worst forecasts, that we would get dragged into a bloody tug of war, bloody, lengthy, and extraordinarily dangerous for the Russian Federation, came true."[48]

* * *

Dima, the former Ukrainian rebel fighter, had met me in a run-down, industrial district of Moscow, near where he worked and lived, and talked incessantly on the way to the mall food court where he suggested we sit down for tea. He had a lot to say—mostly about his struggles. He went over in detail the bureaucratic obstacles Russian authorities were putting in the way of his efforts to get citizenship, even though he had fought in a partisan war he felt they should have been fighting themselves. His struggles in getting a job somehow wound in and out of a more political narrative, about a corrupt and inefficient Russian government that was abandoning Russians in Ukraine, which itself had sold out to a West bent on punishing Russians for being Russian. I asked him about family; he was single, he said, and didn't have any children.

Dima was exceptionally polite, considerate and even sincere. So it took me a while to decipher a hint of repressed rage in all this, but just a hint: his talkativeness, for one, was a tell-tale sign. But as we sat down in the food court, he reprimanded a group of teenagers at the next table for being loud and disrespectful, even though I'd barely noticed them until he brought it up.

As I talked to him about his reasons for joining the insurgency, it began to make more sense. Growing up poor in Eastern Ukraine, he watched an empire that had taken care of his family crumble and, then a teenager, found himself in an entirely new country virtually overnight. He was badly positioned, like many, to adapt to the new economy, one as corrupt as it was impoverished. Lacking the social skills or education or money, he never managed to rise beyond the status of bored security guard—until he noticed the pro-Russian protests around him and decided to join.

His was the barely repressed rage of someone who couldn't make it and, deep down, feared it was all his fault. All the Russian nationalists who supported the Russian Spring I had spoken to seemed to have that rage, manifested in different ways, but usually channeled into an embittered nationalistic chauvinism. Dima's was the most understated, and hence the most revealing: an underdog eternally looking for someone or something stronger to stand up for him at last and, for a brief moment until the mirage dissipated into yet another betrayal, finding that someone in the Kremlin.

In his own way, Putin seems to have been equally disaffected. The common strand—from Dima, to Sasha, to the protesters in Donbas and, finally, to Putin himself—is fear and the doubt of one's own agency. Explosive, destructive efforts to demonstrate that agency are the tests one undertakes to compensate for the doubt about whether it exists at all. At the heart of this doubt is victimhood: the staple of nationalisms around the world.

"This Russophobia, akin to anti-Semitism of the previous centuries, this demonization of Russia," wrote the prominent policymaker Sergei Karaganov, arguing why Russia must overturn the "illegitimate" security order imposed on it from the West, "would lead us eventually to a worse confrontation than we have now ... Even Russian culture is being erased in Europe by a new cancel culture."[49]

The aggrieved underdog does, in fact, have agency—the pent-up power to move mountains, if it so chooses. When it feels cornered, when it fears an existential threat where none may lie, that is when it musters all its will to prove to the world *I exist and I deserve to*—even if it might destroy itself in the process. But erasing, ignoring and, especially, minimizing the underdog and his ridiculous ramblings—as history has demonstrated from the dawn of time, from the snubbed evil witch in primordial fairytales to Weimar Germany—can be deadly. In the context of the history that Putin so loves and so misunderstands, Russia and Ukraine are in a violent clash of nationalisms—the painful processes in which nationhood is formed. These have rarely been peaceful. While Ukraine's nationalism was merely latently aggressive, Russia's has turned overtly, spectacularly so. But in Russia's case, this war may represent the last, violent throws of a dying empire that will leave something new in its wake. Ukraine will emerge and rebuild as a new nation from the war. For Russia, the process might be harder—and yet, from the devastation that the Kremlin's decisions have wreaked not just on Ukraine but on its own country, a new Russia, with its own, new national identity, will eventually emerge.

NOTES

1. THE ENTHUSIASTS

1. Names have been changed for security.
2. Bērziņš, Jānis, "Russian New Generation Warfare Is Not Hybrid Warfare," in *The War in Ukraine: Lessons for Europe*, ed. Artis Pabriks and Andis Kudors, Riga: University of Latvia Press, 2015, p. 43.
3. Galeotti, Mark, *The Weaponization of Everything: A Field Guide to the New Way of War*, New Haven: Yale University Press, 2022, pp. 9–11.
4. Frye, Timothy, *Weak Strongman: The Limits of Power in Putin's Russia*, Princeton: Princeton University Press, 2021.
5. Kramer, Andrew, "Ukrainian Forces Attack Militant-Held Police Station," *New York Times*, 9 May 2014, https://www.nytimes.com/2014/05/10/world/europe/ukraine-forces-destroy-police-building-in-restive-east.html
6. Conversation, Moscow, fall 2018.
7. See Zygar, Mikhail, *All the Kremlin's Men: Inside the Court of Vladimir Putin*, New York: PublicAffairs, 2016.
8. "Peace in Ukraine (III): The Costs of War in Donbas," International Crisis Group report, 3 Sept. 2020, https://www.crisisgroup.org/europe-central-asia/eastern-europe/ukraine/261-peace-ukraine-iii-costs-war-donbas
9. Conversations with protesters, Odessa, Donetsk, May 2014.
10. "Ukrainian Front to Hold Congress of MPs from Southeastern Regions," Tass, 21 Feb. 2014, http://tass.com/world/720245. See also: Zygar, *All the Kremlin's Men*.

11. Zygar, *All the Kremlin's Men*.

12. Kalyvas, Stathis N., "The Ontology of 'Political Violence': Action and Identity in Civil Wars," *Perspectives on Politics* 1, no. 3 (Sept. 2003), pp. 475–94.

13. Matveeva, Anna, "No Moscow Stooges: Identity Polarization and Guerrilla Movements in Donbass," *Southeast European and Black Sea Studies* 16, no. 1 (2016), pp. 25–50, https://www.tandfonline.com/doi/abs/10.1080/14683857.2016.1148415?journalCode=fbss20

14. Interviews with local residents, Donetsk, Ukraine, May 2014.

15. See poll, Kyiv International Institute of Sociology, Apr. 2014, http://www.kiis.com.ua/?lang=eng&cat=reports&id=302&page=1&y=2014&m=4

2. THE LITTLE GREEN MEN

1. See Kofman, Michael et al., "Lessons from Russia's Operations in Crimea and Eastern Ukraine," Santa Monica, CA: Rand Corporation, 2017.

2. Hiatt, Fred, "As Yeltsin Strengthens, Regions' Hopes for Autonomy Fade," *Washington Post*, 22 Nov. 1993, https://www.washingtonpost.com/archive/politics/1993/11/22/as-yeltsin-strengthens-regions-hopes-for-autonomy-fade/9e6162c5-2900-4c34-862a-c6b90eec13a1

3. Katchanovsky, Ivan, "Crimea: People and Territory before and after Annexation," E-International Relations, 24 Mar. 2015, https://www.e-ir.info/2015/03/24/crimea-people-and-territory-before-and-after-annexation

4. Belitser, Natalya, "The Constitutional Process in the Autonomous Republic of Crimea in the Context of Interethnic Relations and Conflict Settlement," International Committee for Crimea, Mar. 2000, http://www.iccrimea.org/scholarly/nbelitser.html. See also: Coomarasamy, James, "Crimea: Yuri Revels in Reversal of Fortune," BBC, 23 Mar. 2014, https://www.bbc.com/news/world-europe-26681653

5. Polunov, A. Y., "Общественные организации русского Крыма: Политическая деятельность, стратегия взаимоотношений с властью" (Civil organizations in Russian Crimea: Political activity and strategies of government cooperation), Gosudarstvennoye Upravlenie: Elektronny Vestnik, Dec. 2009, http://e-journal.spa.msu.ru/vestnik/item_345

6. "Лужков вновь предлагает Украине исправить ошибки и вернуть России Крым" (Luzhkov again suggests Ukraine correct its mistakes and return Crimea to Russia), RIA Novosti, 11 July 2008, https://ria.ru/20080711/113743396.html

7. "Maverick Writer Freed," Gazeta.ru, 30 June 2003, retrieved from https://web.archive.org/web/20120204033927/http://www.cdi.org/russia/johnson/7245-11.cfm

8. In 2003, this circle of intellectuals published the *Konservator* newspaper (full disclaimer: the author occasionally contributed articles at the time). See also: Lewis, David G., *Russia's New Authoritarianism*, Edinburgh: Edinburgh University Press, 2020, p. 41.

9. Conversation, Moscow, 2004.

10. "Украинских политиков 'заштормило' после заявления Юрия Лужкова" (Ukrainian politicians "bothered" by Yuri Luzhkov's comments), *Rossiiskaya Gazeta*, 16 May 2008, https://rg.ru/2008/05/16/sevastopol-vyzhutivich.html

11. Polunov, "Общественные организации русского Крыма."

12. "Черноморский флот уйдет из Крыма, если Москве к 2017 году не удастся договориться с Киевом о продлении договора—Иванов" (Black Sea Fleet will leave Crimea if Moscow does not manage to extend agreement with Kyiv by 2017), Interfax, 19 Oct. 2008, https://www.interfax.ru/russia/40184

13. See Alexei Venediktov's interview with Ukrainian television, "Венедиктов: Путин мне сказал: 'Твой интернет—сплошная дезинформация. Смотри, там лежат папки, каждая подписана генералом, если меня обманут, могу погоны сорвать!" (Venediktov: Putin said to me, "Your internet is all disinformation. Look, there's folders there, each is signed by a general, if they lie to me, I'll tear their epaulets off."), Gordon, 19 Aug. 2019, https://gordonua.com/publications/venediktov-putin-mne-skazal-tvoj-internet-sploshnaja-dezinformatsija-smotri-tam-lezhat-papki-kazhdaja-podpisana-generalom-esli-menja-obmanut-mogu-pogony-sorvat-1191705.html

14. "Путин: Россия признает границы Украины" (Putin: Russia recognizes the borders of Ukraine), RIA Novosti, 30 Aug. 2008, https://ria.ru/20080830/150807671.html

15. See transcript of Putin's speech on official presidential site, 10 Feb. 2007, http://en.kremlin.ru/events/president/transcripts/24034

16. See Patrushev's 2009 interview, Egorov, Ivan, "Советы по секрету" (Secret counsels), *Rossiiskaya Gazeta*, 30 May 2009, https://rg.ru/2012/05/30/patrushev.html

17. "Медведев раскритиковал слова Путина о резолюции по Ливии" (Medvedev criticized Putin's words about the resolution on Libya), BBC, 21 Mar. 2011, https://www.bbc.com/russian/russia/2011/03/110321_putin_resolution_on_libya

18. "Clinton Cites 'Serious Concerns' about Russian Election," CNN, 6 Dec. 2011, https://www.cnn.com/2011/12/06/world/europe/russia-elections-clinton

19. "Чекисты сканировали мысли Мадлен Олбрайт" (Chekists scanned the thoughts of Madeleine Albright), *Rossiiskaya Gazeta*, 22 Dec. 2006, https://rg.ru/2006/12/22/gosbezopasnostj-podsoznanie.html

20. "За дестабилизацией Украины скрывается попытка радикального ослабления России" (Ukraine stabilization conceals attempts to radically weaken Russia), *Kommersant*, 22 June 2015, https://www.kommersant.ru/doc/2752250

21. "Если люди приходят на митинги, власти нужно думать не о том, кто кого финансирует" (If people are going to protests, the government shouldn't be thinking about who financed what), *Kommersant*, 15 Dec. 2011, https://www.kommersant.ru/doc/1838828

22. Bennetts, Marc, "Russia's Alexei Navalny Arrested as 1,600 Detained Nationwide," *The Guardian*, 5 May 2018, https://www.theguardian.com/world/2018/may/05/russian-police-arrest-more-than-200-anti-putin-protesters-siberia

23. "Leaked Audio Reveals Embarrassing U.S. Exchange on Ukraine, EU," Reuters, 6 Feb. 2014, https://www.reuters.com/article/us-usa-ukraine-tape/leaked-audio-reveals-embarrassing-u-s-exchange-on-ukraine-eu-idUSBREA1601G20140207

24. "Виктория Нуланд возмущена: В СМИ рассказали, что она раздавала в Киеве печенье, а это были сэндвичи" (Victoria Nuland is indignant: The media said she was giving out cookies in Kyiv, but they were sandwiches), RT, 17 Dec. 2014, https://russian.rt.com/article/64997

25. "Как Янукович покинул Украину: Версии из первых уст" (How Yanukovych left Ukraine), BBC, 22 Feb. 2017, https://www.bbc.com/ukrainian/features-russian-39049755

26. "Путин: Вашингтон нас обманул" (Putin: Washington lied to us), Gazeta.ru, 7 Mar. 2018, https://www.gazeta.ru/politics/2018/03/07_a_11674645.shtml

27. This is common knowledge among policymakers and insiders in Moscow, as confirmed to the author. See also Alexei Venediktov's interview with Ukrainian television. "Венедиктов: Путин мне сказал: 'Твой интернет—сплошная дезинформация'" (Venediktov: Putin told me: 'Your internet is all disinformation').

28. Galimova, Natalia, "Мы идем в Россию: Как—не знаю" (We are going into Russia: How—we don't know), Gazeta.ru, 11 Mar. 2015, https://www.gazeta.ru/politics/2015/03/11_a_6503589.shtml?updated

29. See Zygar, *All the Kremlin's Men.*

30. Barantsev, Viktor, *Спецоперация "Крым"* (Special operation: Crimea), Moscow: Komsomolskaya Pravda Publishing House, 2019. See also: Vlasov, Anton, "Военный обозреватель 'КП' Виктор Баранец подарил Шойгу свою книгу о возвращении Крыма" (KP military correspondent Viktor Baranets gave Shoigu his book about the return of Crimea), *Komsomolskaya Pravda*, 27 Mar. 2019, https://www.kp.ru/daily/26959.4/4012882

31. Shoigu recounted these and other instances in his book. See Elkov, Igor, "'Про вчера' и сегодня," (*About Yesterday* and today), *Rossiiskaya Gazeta*, 20 Oct. 2020. https://rg.ru/2020/10/20/sergej-shojgu-napisal-knigu-o-svetlyh-i-tenevyh-storonah-epohalnyh-sobytij.html

32. "Псковских десантников наградили за возвращение Крыма и другие заслуги" (Pskov paratroopers awarded for the return of Crimea and other accomplishments), RBC, 22 Aug. 2008, https://www.rbc.ru/society/22/08/2014/5704210a9a794760d3d40e38

33. See Lavrov, Anton, "Russian Again: The Military Operation for Crimea," in *Brothers Armed: Military Aspects of the Crisis in Ukraine*, ed. Colby Howard and Ruslan Pukhov, Minneapolis: East View Press, 2015, pp. 157–84.

34. See Galeotti, Mark, *Russian Political War: Moving beyond the Hybrid*, London: Routledge, 2018.

35. Gerasimov, Valery, "The Value of Science in Prediction," *Military-Industrial Kurier*, 27 Feb. 2013, http://cs.brown.edu/people/jsavage/VotingProject/2017_03_09_MoscowsShadow_GerasimovDoctrineAndRussianNon-LinearWar.pdf

36. See interview with Grach, "Если бы нас не поддержал Патрушев, в Крыму стоял бы американский флот" (If Patrushev hadn't supported us, the American fleet would be stationed in Crimea), Meduza, 21 Mar. 2017, https://meduza.io/feature/2017/03/21/esli-by-nas-ne-podder-zhal-patrushev-v-krymu-stoyal-by-amerikanskiy-flot

37. See Zygar, *All the Kremlin's Men*.

3. THE HYBRID WARRIORS

1. Name changed for security.

2. The Kremlin-funded RIA Novosti news agency, which published *The Moscow News*, of which I was political editor, underwent an overhaul in Dec.–Jan. 2013–14, coinciding with the events in Kyiv. Until then, we had had relative freedom to publish articles critical of the Kremlin, including about corruption and the abuse of power. But in Dec. 2013, the chief of RIA, Svetlana Mironyuk, was replaced by a pro-Kremlin propagandist, Dmitry Kiselyov, whom Putin, explaining the decision for the replacement, described as a "patriot." When Kiselyov made it clear that objective reporting would no longer be possible at our paper, I and the rest of the staff of *The Moscow News* resigned, and the paper was closed down.

3. Galimova, "Мы идем в Россию."

4. See interview with Temirgaliev: Kozlov, Pyotr, "Если это имело определенную режиссуру, режиссеру нужно поставить пять с плюсом" (If this was orchestrated, then the orchestration gets an A+), *Vedomosti*, 16 Mar. 2015, https://www.vedomosti.ru/politics/characters/2015/03/16/esli-eto-imelo-opredelennuyu-rezhissuru—rezhisseru-nuzhno-posta-vit-pyat-s-plyusom

5. Galimova, "Мы идем в Россию."

6. See interview with Temirgaliev: Kozlov, "Если это имело определенную режиссуру, режиссеру нужно поставить пять с плюсом."

7. Zygar, *All the Kremlin's Men*.

8. Galimova, "Мы идем в Россию."

9. Ibid.

10. See Kofman et al., "Lessons from Russia's Operations in Crimea and Eastern Ukraine."

11. See interview with Temirgaliev: Kozlov, "Если это имело определенную режиссуру, режиссеру нужно поставить пять с плюсом."

12. Although Aksyonov has denied them, these allegations rumble on. In May 2021, the government in Kyiv included him on a list of sanctioned criminal kingpins. Decree of the president of Ukraine no. 203/2021, "Про рішення Ради національної безпеки і оборони України від 14 травня 2021 року, 'Про застосування персональних спеціальних економічних та інших обмежувальних заходів (санкцій)" (On the decision of the National Security and Defense Council of Ukraine of 14 May 2021, "On the application of personal special economic and other restrictive measures (sanctions)"), 21 May 2021, https://www.president.gov.ua/documents/2032021-38949

13. For this quote, and the following ones, see: Galimova, "Мы идем в Россию."

14. Official transcript, presidential website, Kremlin.ru, 4 Mar. 2014, http://kremlin.ru/events/president/news/20366

15. Galimova, "Мы идем в Россию."

16. "Бюджетные гранты для НКО получат православные следопыты и казаки" (Orthodox investigators and Cossacks will get budget grants for NGOs), Lenta.ru, 24 Oct. 2012, https://lenta.ru/news/2012/10/24/nko

17. Turovsky, Daniil, "Овечкам от волков совсем житья не стало" (The sheep can't escape the wolves), Lenta.ru, 23 Aug. 2013, https://lenta.ru/articles/2013/08/23/bike

18. Ibid.

19. Bryanski, Gleb, "Black-Clad Putin Roars into Ukraine Biker Fest," Reuters, 24 July 2010, https://www.reuters.com/article/oukoe-uk-putin-bikers/black-clad-putin-roars-into-ukraine-biker-fest-idUK-TRE66N1D120100724

20. See fragment of Putin's televised press conference from 16 Dec. 2010, https://www.youtube.com/watch?v=26dcHyMASYs

21. McNeal, Robert, *Tsar and Cossack: 1855–1914*, Houndmills, Basingstoke: Palgrave, 1987, pp. 37–8.

22. See Arutunyan, Anna, *The Putin Mystique*, Newbold on Stour: Skyscraper, 2014, pp. 245–62.

23. Zygar, *All the Kremlin's Men*.

24. "Спецтуристы" (Special tourists), *Novaya Gazeta*, 2 July 2014, https://nn.by/?c=ar&i=131165&lang=ru

25. "В Думе предложили создать фонд помощи российским добровольцам в Донбассе" (State Duma members suggest the creation of a foundation to aid Russian volunteers in Donbas), RBC, 19 Dec. 2014, https://www.rbc.ru/politics/19/12/2014/5493fc369a794787cda02d9d

26. Shiryayev, Valery, "Крым: Год спустя; Что мы знаем теперь" (Crimea: One year later; What we know now), *Novaya Gazeta*, 20 Feb. 2015, https://novayagazeta.ru/articles/2015/02/20/63128-krym-god-spustya-chto-my-znaem-teper

27. Conversations, current and former FSB special forces officers, Moscow, summer 2014.

28. For interviews with Russian-speakers in Eastern Ukraine on this abandonment, see Katharine Quinn Judge's reporting in "'Nobody Wants Us': The Alienated Civilians of Eastern Ukraine," International Crisis Group, 1 Oct. 2018, https://www.crisisgroup.org/europe-central-asia/eastern-europe/ukraine/252-nobody-wants-us-alienated-civilians-eastern-ukraine

29. For a qualitative analysis of the mechanisms of motivation of separatist militants in Ukraine, see Kudelia, Serhiy, "How They Joined? Militants and Informers in the Armed Conflict in Donbas," *Small Wars and Insurgencies* 30, no. 2 (2019), pp. 279–306.

30. "Тысячи одесситов собрались на народное собрание" (Thousands of Odessites hold a public gathering), Timer-Odesa.net, 1 Mar. 2014, https://timer-odessa.net/news/odessiti_sobralis_na_narodnoe_sobranie_pryamaya_translyatsiya_489.html

31. "В Донецке задержан 'народный губернатор' Павел Губарев" ("People's

Governor" Pavel Gubarev detained in Donetsk), RBC, 6 Mar. 2014, https://www.rbc.ru/politics/06/03/2014/570418e99a794761c0ce78ee

32. Roth, Andrew, "From Russia, 'Tourists' Stir the Protests," *New York Times*, 3 Mar. 2014, https://www.nytimes.com/2014/03/04/world/europe/russias-hand-can-be-seen-in-the-protests.html

33. See Kofman et al., "Lessons from Russia's Operations in Crimea and Eastern Ukraine."

34. Prentice, Alessandra, "Criticism of Ukraine's Language Law Justified: Rights Body," Reuters, 8 Dec. 2017, https://www.reuters.com/article/us-ukraine-language/criticism-of-ukraines-language-law-justified-rights-body-idUSKBN1E227K

35. See Kofman et al., "Lessons from Russia's Operations in Crimea and Eastern Ukraine."

36. Luhn, Alec, "Pro-Russian Occupiers of Ukrainian Security Service Building Voice Defiance," *The Guardian*, 9 Apr. 2014, https://www.theguardian.com/world/2014/apr/10/luhansk-protesters-occupy-security-headquarters

37. "Длинные выходные: захват Луганской ОГА, арест Клинчаева, 'дружеский визит' на телеканал ИРТА, Болотских снова губернатор" (Long weekend: Seizure of the Luhansk regional administration building, Klinchayev's arrest, "friendly visit" to the IRTA television station, Bolotskikh is governor again), Parallel Media, 11 Mar. 2014, http://paralel-media.com.ua/p62966.html

38. Conversations intercepted by Ukraine's Prosecutor General's Office and alleged to be between Glazyev and Zatulin, https://www.youtube.com/watch?v=l6K1_vHrJPU. The specific role of these two officials in supporting separatist movements and rallies in Ukraine will be discussed in detail in the next chapter; while they did support some groups in Odessa, their backing was far more substantial in Donetsk and Luhansk regions.

39. Coynash, Halya, "Odesa Smoking Gun Leads Directly to Moscow," Kharkiv Human Rights Protection Group, 20 Sept. 2016, https://khpg.org/en/1473972066

40. "Report on the Human Rights Situation in Ukraine, 15 June 2014," Office of the United Nations High Commissioner for Human Rights,

15 June 2014, https://www.ohchr.org/Documents/Countries/UA/HRMMUReport15June2014.pdf

41. Ibid.

42. The question of where Ukrainian separatists got their weapons has been a controversial issue, given that Russia has indeed armed them at different times during the conflict but has consistently denied doing so, claiming that the separatists armed themselves by buying weapons or taking them from depots. However, most of the heavy caliber arms supplied by Russia began arriving later in the conflict, in late May and June. In March and April, a small number of weapons were supplied by Sergei Aksyonov's government in Crimea, while most tanks, guns and some heavy artillery were seized from local depots. This was corroborated to me by local militants in Simferopol, Sevastopol, and Donetsk, who described the origins of their weapons. For a more systemic analysis of the Ukrainian origins of a lot of these weapons in the early months of the conflict, see Kofman et al., "Lessons from Russia's Operations in Crimea and Eastern Ukraine."

4. FRIENDS OF THE KREMLIN

1. See interview with Temirgaliev: Kozlov, "Если это имело определенную режиссуру, режиссеру нужно поставить пять с плюсом."

2. "Как фонд Константина Малофеева помогает Новороссии" (How Konstantin Malofeyev's foundation helps Novorossiya), RBC, 8 Sept. 2014, https://www.rbc.ru/politics/08/09/2014/5424884bcbb20f18b6e4b903

3. See Malofeyev's interview in *Vedomosti*, 13 Nov. 2014, https://www.pressreader.com/russia/vedomosti/20141113/281487864641481

4. Seregina, Yelizaveta, Kozlov, Petr, "Интервью—Константин Малофеев, основатель «Маршал капитала»" (Interview—Konstantin Malofeyev, founder of Marshal Capital), Vedomosti, 13 Nov. 2014. https://www.vedomosti.ru/newspaper/articles/2014/11/13/v-sankcionnye-spiski-vklyuchali-posovokupnosti-zaslug

5. "Как фонд Константина Малофеева помогает Новороссии."

6. Ibid. In the copy of the agreement dated 17 July 2014 and published by RBC, one of the sides is specifically referred to as the Donetsk People's Republic and its prime minister, Alexander Borodai.

7. See Muratov's interview on Ekho Moskvy, https://echo.msk.ru/programs/personalno/1494328-echo

8. "Представляется правильным инициировать присоединение восточных областей Украины к России" (It seems right to initiate the reunification of eastern regions of Ukraine to Russia), *Novaya Gazeta*, 25 Feb. 2015, https://novayagazeta.ru/articles/2015/02/24/63168-171-predstavlyaetsya-pravilnym-initsiirovat-prisoedinenie-vostochnyh-oblastey-ukrainy-k-rossii-187

9. Dugin, Alexander, "Tvorit istoriyu slovom i delom: Russkaya Vesna Konstantina Malofeyeva" (Makes history in word and deed: The Russian Spring of Konstantin Malofeyev), Tsargrad TV, 3 July 2021, https://tsargrad.tv/articles/tvorit-istoriju-slovom-i-delom-russkaja-vesna-konstantina-malofeeva_377034

10. Conversation, Moscow, 2021. See also: Kholmogorov, Yegor, *Karat karatelei: Khroniki russkoi vesny* (To punish the punishers: Chronicles of the Russian Spring), Moscow: Knizhny Mir, 2015.

11. Telegina, Natalia, "Путь Малофеева: От детского питания к спонсорству Донбасса и прощенным $500 млн" (Malofeyev's path: From baby formula to sponsoring Donbas and $500 million written off), Republic.ru, 12 May 2015, https://republic.ru/posts/50662

12. See Malofeyev's interview on Tsargrad TV, 9 Sept. 2017, https://tsargrad.tv/shows/krasnyj-ugol-s-elenoj-sharojkinoj-v-gostjah-konstantin-malofeev_84563

13. Weaver, Courtney, "Konstantin Malofeev, Marshall Capital Partners," *Financial Times*, 8 Sept. 2013, https://www.ft.com/content/569e533e-051c-11e3-9e71-00144feab7de

14. Clover, Charles, "Putin and the Monk," *Financial Times*, 25 Jan. 2013, https://www.ft.com/content/f2fcba3e-65be-11e2-a3db-00144feab49a

15. Weaver, "Konstantin Malofeev, Marshall Capital Partners."

16. "Миноритарий от Бога: Путь Константина Малофеева от богатства до обыска" (Minority holder from God: Malofeyev's path from riches to search), *Forbes*, 21 Nov. 2012, https://www.forbes.ru/sobytiya/lyudi/215436-minoritarii-ot-boga-put-konstantina-malofeeva-ot-bogatstva-do-obyska

17. "Епископ Тихон Шевкунов—РБК: 'Есть команда репрессировать

церковь? Нет'" (Bishop Tikhon Shevkunov—RBC: "Is there an order to repress the Church? No"), RBC, 24 Feb. 2016, https://www.rbc.ru/interview/society/24/02/2016/56c482da9a7947a6a062c297

18. "Moscow: Third Rome" conference, video, summary and participants published on Pravoslavie.ru, https://www.pravoslavie.ru/75070.html

19. Telegina, "Путь Малофеева."

20. "Как строится бизнес человека, 'фактически управляющего российским рынком связи'" (How a man's business running the Russian telecoms industry was built), *Vedomosti*, 11 Oct. 2010, https://www.vedomosti.ru/library/articles/2010/10/11/ne_zamministra_a_drug_ministra

21. Telegina, "Путь Малофеева."

22. Ibid.

23. "Иванов: Государство использует 'всю силу закона' для защиты религиозных чувств граждан" (Ivanov: The government is using "the full force of the law" to protect citizens' religious feelings), *Vedomosti*, 1 Oct. 2012, https://www.vedomosti.ru/politics/news/2012/10/01/ivanov_gosudarstvo_ispolzuet_vsyu_silu_zakona_dlya_zaschity

24. "Сергей Иванов отмечает роль Православной церкви в развитии русской культуры" (Sergei Ivanov marks the role of the Orthodox Church in the development of Russian culture), Interfax, 16 June 2016, http://www.interfax-religion.ru/cis.php?act=news&div=63429

25. Conversation, Washington, DC, 2020.

26. Shleinov, Roman, "Высокие отношение" (High relations), *Vedomosti*, 18 Mar. 2013, https://www.vedomosti.ru/politics/articles/2013/03/18/vysokie_otnosheniya

27. "Marshall Малофеев: Как российский рейдер захватил Юго-Восток Украины" (Marshall Malofeyev: How a Russian raider took over Southeastern Ukraine), *The Insider*, 27 May 2014, https://theins.ru/politika/796

28. See Ivanov's interview in *Komsomolskaya Pravda*, 14 Oct. 2014, https://www.kp.ru/daily/26294/3172985

29. Rubin, Mikhail, "Сергей Иванов выступил на 'Валдае' с необычно жесткой речью" (Sergei Ivanov presents unusually harsh speech at Valdai), RBC, 23 Oct. 2014, https://www.rbc.ru/politics/23/10/2014/54493c71cbb20fc237f7cdab

30. Butrin, Dmitry, "Какие российские благотворительные фонды спонсируют Крым" (Which Russian charities sponsor Crimea), *Kommersant*, 12 Mar. 2014, https://www.kommersant.ru/doc/2427276

31. "Малофеев: Обыски по делу о кредите ВТБ—часть давления на руководство 'Ростелекома'" (Malofeyev: Searches in VTB loan case are part of pressure on Rostelecom management), *Vedomosti*, 20 Nov. 2012, https://www.vedomosti.ru/technology/articles/2012/11/20/k_provotorovu_i_malofeevu_prishli_s_obyskami

32. Conversation, Washington, DC, 2020.

33. "Беседы 'Сергея Глазьева' о Крыме и беспорядках на востоке Украины: Расшифровка" (Sergei Glazyev's conversation about Crimea and unrest in Eastern Ukraine: Transcript), Meduza, 22 Aug. 2016, https://meduza.io/feature/2016/08/22/besedy-sergeya-glazieva-o-kryme-i-besporyadkah-na-vostoke-ukrainy-rasshifrovka

34. Conversation, Tallinn, Estonia, May 2018.

36. "Вступая в последнюю полосу испытаний: Председатель думского комитета Константин Затулин в интерьере Конгресса русских общин" (Entering the final phase of struggle: Duma committee chairman Konstantin Zatulin at the Congress of Russian Communities), *Russian Federation Magazine*, no. 21, 1995. Published on Zatulin's official State Duma page: https://zatulin.ru/vstupaya-v-poslednyuyu-polosu-ispytanij-predsedatel-dumskogo-komiteta-konstantin-zatulin-v-interere-kongressa-russkix-obshhin

37. See Reshetnikov's interview, "Цивилизация России" (Russian civilization), *Argumenty Nedeli*, 1 Apr. 2015, https://argumenti.ru/toptheme/n481/394395

38. Sytin, A., "Анатомия провала: О механизме принятия внешнеполитических решений Кремля" (The anatomy of failure: On the mechanisms of the Kremlin's foreign policy decision-making), Censor.net, https://censor.net/ru/resonance/320398/anatomiya_provala_o_mehanizme_prinyatiya_vneshnepoliticheskih_resheniyi_kremlya

39. See RISI's official site: https://en.riss.ru/about-us

40. See text of the petition, published on a site devoted to Cossack issues, Летка.рф: http://xn—80ajpc0b.xn—p1ai/obrascheniya/obraschenie-o-priznanii-v-konstitucii-osoboy-roli-pravoslaviya

41. Sytin, "Анатомия провала."

42. See Zygar, *All the Kremlin's Men*.

43. Conversation, Moscow, Mar. 2018.

5. THE TRIGGER-MAN OF THE RUSSIAN SPRING

1. Loiko, Sergei, "The Unraveling of Moscow's 'Novorossia' Dream," RFE/RL, 1 June 2016, https://www.rferl.org/a/unraveling-moscow-novorossia-dream/27772641.html

2. Kashin, Oleg, "Oleg Kashin: Vtoroi reportazh iz Kryma" (Oleg Kashin: Second report from Crimea), Sputnik and Pogrom, 2 Mar. 2014, https://sputnikipogrom.com/politics/9614/kashin-crimea-second-report

3. Zhuchkovsky, Alexander, *85 Dnei Slavyanska* (85 days of Slovyansk), Nizhny Novgorod: Chyornaya Sotnya Press, 2018, pp. 43–4.

4. Ibid., p. 21.

5. Prokhanov, Alexander, "Kto ty, Strelok?" (Who are you, Sharpshooter?), *Zavtra*, 20 Nov. 2014. Archived: https://web.archive.org/web/20151022094126/http://zavtra.ru/content/view/kto-tyi-strelok. Original: http://zavtra.ru/content/view/kto-tyi-strelok

6. Ibid.

7. Loiko, "Unraveling of Moscow's 'Novorossia' Dream."

8. "Экс-начальник Генштаба Замана: Янукович не отдавал приказ стрелять по Майдану; Зачистить его приказали Лебедев, Якименко и Пшонка" (Former Chief of Staff Zamana: Yanukovych did not order to open fire on Maidan; Orders were given by Lebedev, Yakimenko and Pshonka), Gordon, 31 July 2014, https://gordonua.com/publications/eks-nachalnik-genshtaba-zamana-yanukovich-ne-otdaval-prikaz-strelyat-po-maydanu-zachistit-ego-prikazali-lebedev-yakimenko-i-pshonka-33981.html

9. Interviews given to the author, Simferopol, Sevastopol, Mar. 2014. See also: Arutunyan, Anna, "Russia's Possible Undercover Military Intervention," *USA Today*, 15 Mar. 2014, https://www.usatoday.com/story/news/world/2014/03/15/russias-possible-undercover-military-intervention/6464433

10. For more explanation of Girkin's role vis-à-vis regular troops, see Zhuchkovsky, *85 Dnei Slavyanska*, p. 89.

11. Gubarev, Pavel, *Fakel Novorossii* (The torch of Novorossiya), St Petersburg: Piter, 2016.

12. Interviews with two pro-Russian militiamen given to the author, Donetsk, May 2014.

13. Gubarev, *Fakel Novorossii*.

14. Zhuchkovsky, *85 Dnei Slavyanska*, p. 22.

15. Ibid., p. 23. This ratio has apparently remained consistent throughout the conflict and has been corroborated to the author by several sources in the militia: in each unit, about eight out of ten people were local Ukrainian citizens, two were Russian. Interviews given to the author, Moscow, Mar. 2018, Apr. 2019; Kyiv, Sept. 2019.

16. Gubarev, Pavel, Fakel Novorossii (The Torch of Novorossia), St. Petersburg: Piter, 2016.

17. Zhuchkovsky, *85 Dnei Slavyanska*, p. 44.

18. Ibid., p. 44.

19. Shargunov, Sergei, "Семнадцать километров мы шли маршем через границу" (We marched 17 kilometers across the border), *Svobodnaya Pressa*, 11 Nov. 2014, https://svpressa.ru/war21/article/103643

20. Kashin, Oleg, "Из Крыма в Донбасс: Приключения Игоря Стрелкова и Александра Бородая" (From Crimea to Donbas: The adventures of Igor Strelkov and Alexander Borodai), Republic.ru, 19 May 2014, https://republic.ru/posts/l/1099696

21. Ibid., pp. 44–5.

22. Kashin, "Из Крыма в Донбасс."

23. Zhuchkovsky, *85 Dnei Slavyanska*, p. 45.

24. Interview with Vyacheslav Ponomaryov, "Народный мэр Славянска: 'Мы не думали, что дойдёт до войны, так как надеялись на помощь России'" (People's Mayor of Slavyansk: "We didn't think it would lead to war, we were counting on Russia"), Regnum Information Agency, 20 Oct. 2014, https://regnum.ru/news/polit/1858546.html

25. Interview with Ponomaryov, "Народный мэр Славянска."

26. "Протестующие в Донецке требуют провести референдум о вхождении в РФ" (Protesters in Donetsk demand referendum on joining Russia), RIA Novosti, 6 Apr. 2014, https://ria.ru/20140406/1002757450.html

27. "Ukraine: Pro-Russians Storm Offices in Donetsk, Luhansk, Kharkiv," BBC, 7 Apr. 2014, https://www.bbc.co.uk/news/world-europe-26910 210

28. "Донецк подал заявку на республику" (Donetsk applied to be a republic), *Kommersant*, 8 Apr. 2014, https://www.kommersant.ru/doc/ 2447641?from=doc_vrez

29. "Глава Донецкой области объявил о режиме спецоперации в регионе" (Head of the Donetsk oblast declares special operation regime in the region), RBC, 14 Apr. 2014, https://www.rbc.ru/society/14/04/2014 /57041b219a794761c0ce8e69

30. See text of declaration posted on so-called Committee of Donetsk Voters site: http://komitet.net.ua/article/120042

31. "Pro-Moscow Protesters Seize Arms, Declare Republic; Kiev Fears Invasion," Reuters, 7 Apr. 2014, https://www.reuters.com/article/us-ukraine-crisis-protesters-idUSBREA360TI20140407

33. See Pushilin's profile on "official" site of the DPR: https://dnronline. su/en/head-of-the-dpr

34. ""'Донецкая народная республика' начала формировать ЦИК для референдума" (Donetsk People's Republic began creating central election committee for the referendum), Gazeta.ru, 10 Apr. 2014, https:// www.gazeta.ru/politics/news/2014/04/10/n_6074869.shtml?updated

35. "Донецк подал заявку на республику" (Donetsk applied to be a republic), *Kommersant*, 8 Apr. 2014, https://www.kommersant.ru/ doc/2447641?from=doc_vrez

36. See audio of telephone conversation, claimed to have been intercepted by the Ukrainian Security Service: https://www.youtube.com/ watch?v=xVDx-TqeWj4

37. Conversation, London, Aug. 2021.

38. Kramer, Andrew, "Ukraine Turns to Its Oligarchs for Political Help," *New York Times*, 3 Mar. 2014, https://www.nytimes.com/2014/03/03/ world/europe/ukraine-turns-to-its-oligarchs-for-political-help.html

39. Conversation, Moscow, Aug. 2014.

30. Conversation, Donetsk, May 2014.

40. Kanygin, Pavel, "Все подступы к Мариуполю защищены: Будем давать по зубам" (All paths to Mariupol are defended: We will hit them in

the teeth), *Novaya Gazeta*, 15 Apr. 2014, https://novayagazeta.ru/articles/2015/04/15/63813-171-vse-podstupy-k-mariupolyu-zaschischeny-budem-davat-po-zubam-187

41. "Захватчики здания СБУ в Луганске выдвинули требования" (Militants who seized SBU building in Luhansk issued demands), Fraza, 8 Apr. 2014, https://fraza.com/news/192963-zahvatchiki_zdanija_sbu_v_luganske_vydvinuli_trebovanija

42. "В Луганске выбрали 'народного губернатора'" ("People's governor" elected in Luhansk), Vesti.ua, 21 Apr. 2014, https://vesti.ua/donbass/48519-v-lugansve-vybrali-narodnogo-gubernatora

43. "Турчинов спростував описані сепаратистами чудеса явки на 'референдум'" (Turchynov denied miracles described by separatists at the "referendum"), *Ukrainska Pravda*, 12 May 2014, https://www.pravda.com.ua/news/2014/05/12/7025064

44. Arutunyan, Anna, "Pro-Russians Finding Less Support for Vote in East Ukraine," *USA Today*, 8 May 2014, https://eu.usatoday.com/story/news/world/2014/05/08/ukraine/8864473

45. See poll conducted by Kyiv International Institute of Sociology, Apr. 2014, http://kiis.com.ua/?lang=eng&cat=news&id=258. See also Luhn, Alec, "Ukraine Crisis Strains Family Ties in Divided Donetsk," *The Guardian*, 22 Apr. 2014, https://www.theguardian.com/world/2014/apr/22/ukraine-families-divided-donetsk-russia

46. Interviews, Donetsk, May 2014.

47. "Уважаем, но не признаем" (We respect but don't recognize), Gazeta.ru, 5 Nov. 2014, https://www.gazeta.ru/politics/2014/11/05_a_6290025.shtml

48. Girkin's interview with *Komsomolskaya Pravda*, 26 Apr. 2014, https://www.youtube.com/watch?v=8mGXDcO9ugw

49. Interview with Igor Girkin, "Игорь Стрелков: 'Рано или поздно эта война перейдет в горячую стадию'" (Igor Strelkov: "Sooner or later this war will enter a hot phase"), *Moskovsky Komsomolets*, 15 Aug. 2019, https://www.mk.ru/politics/2019/08/15/igor-strelkov-rano-ili-pozdno-eta-voyna-pereydet-v-goryachuyu-stadiyu.html

50. Zhuchkovsky, *85 Dnei Slavyanska*.

51. Konstantin Krylov, interview with the author, Moscow, Apr. 2016.

6. THE BETRAYAL

1. Audio of intercepted phone call published by JIT: https://www.youtube.com/watch?v=eahMvdRoC-g&t=352s

2. "Премьером Донецкой республики избран Александр Бородай, бывший консультант 'Маршал капитала'" (Alexander Borodai, former consultant for Marshall Capital, elected premier of Donetsk Republic), *Vedomosti*, 16 May 2014, https://www.vedomosti.ru/politics/articles/2014/05/16/premerom-doneckoj-respubliki-izbran-aleksandr-borodaj

3. Alexander Borodai, in an interview with Zakhar Prilepin, on Malofeyev's television channel, Tsar-Grad, 27 Feb. 2017, https://www.youtube.com/watch?v=x3Hp0sL0JpI

4. Zhuchkovsky, Alexander, *85 Dnei Slavyanska (85 Days of Slovyansk)*, Nizhny Novgorod: Chyornaya Sotnya Press, 2018, pp. 44-45.

5. Alexander Borodai, in an interview with Zakhar Prilepin, on Malofeyev's television channel, Tsar-Grad, 27 Feb. 2017, https://www.youtube.com/ watch?v=x3Hp0sL0JpI.

6. Strelkov, Igor, "Kadarskaya zone," *Zavtra*, 27 Sept. 1999, https://zavtra.ru/blogs/1999-09-2821

7. "На Лубянку приходит новое руководство" (New leadership comes to Lubyanka), APN, 25 July 2002, https://www.apn.ru/news/article13719.htm

8. Alexander Borodai, interview with Zakhar Prilepin on Tsar-Grad, 27 Feb. 2017, https://www.youtube.com/watch?v=x3Hp0sL0JpI

9. Ibid.

10. Conversations with two former rebel fighters and one Russian separatist supporter, Moscow, 2018–19.

11. See Girkin's interview, "Стрелков: Малофеев отказался помогать Донбассу, выручил Аксёнов" (Strelkov: Malofeyev refused to help Donbas, Aksyonov saved the day), Politnavigator.ru, 5 July 2020, https://m.politnavigator.news/strelkov-malofeev-otkazalsya-pomogat-donbassu-vyruchil-aksjonov.html/amp?imnu=61399219ecec7cb4ce1782681d1f4aaa

12. Conversation, Moscow, Mar. 2018.

13. Conversation, Moscow, Mar. 2018.

14. "Satellite Images Reveal Russian Military Buildup on Ukraine's Border," *The Guardian*, 10 Apr. 2014, https://www.theguardian.com/world/2014/apr/10/satellite-images-russian-military-ukraine-border

15. Alexander Borodai, interview with Zakhar Prilepin on Tsar-Grad, 27 Feb. 2017, https://www.youtube.com/watch?v=x3Hp0sL0JpI

16. See Girkin's interview: "Стрелков: Малофеев отказался помогать Донбассу, выручил Аксёнов."

17. Ibid.

18. Conversation, Moscow, Sept. 2021

19. Conversation, former Kremlin official, Moscow, spring 2018.

20. "Joint Geneva Statement on Ukraine from April 17: The Full Text," *Washington Post*, 17 Apr. 2014, https://www.washingtonpost.com/world/joint-geneva-statement-on-ukraine-from-april-17-the-full-text/2014/04/17/89bd0ac2-c654-11e3-9f37-7ce307c56815_story.html

21. See press conference transcript on the presidential site, 7 May 2014, http://en.kremlin.ru/events/president/transcripts/20973?

22. "Владимир Путин отодвигает войска и пододвигает выборы" (Vladimir Putin withdraws troops and moves elections), *Kommersant*, 8 May 2014, https://www.kommersant.ru/doc/2467504

23. Ibid.

24. "'Позорная капитуляция' или 'все по-прежнему'?" ("Shameful capitulation" or "business as usual"?), *Golos Ameriki* (VOA), 8 May 2014, https://www.golosameriki.com/a/putin-statements-experts/1910008.html

25. Conversations, policymaker close to the Defense Ministry, Moscow, Apr. 2020, Kremlin-linked policymaker with ties to Malofeyev, Moscow, Sept. 2021. See also: Zygar, *All the Kremlin's Men*.

26. Soldatov, Andrei, "The True Role of the FSB in the Ukrainian Crisis," *The Moscow Times*, 15 Apr. 2014, https://www.themoscowtimes.com/2014/04/15/the-true-role-of-the-fsb-in-the-ukrainian-crisis-a33985

27. See audios of intercepted phone calls released by the Joint Investigation Team investigating the downing of Flight MH-17, 19 Nov. 2019, https://www.politie.nl/en/information/witness-appeal-crash-mh17-nov-19.html

28. Galeotti, Mark, "Putin's Hydra: Inside Russia's Intelligence Service," European Council on Foreign Relations, 11 May 2016, https://ecfr.eu/publication/putins_hydra_inside_russias_intelligence_services

29. Interview, Moscow, June 2014.

30. Ivshina, Olga, "Чеченцы на востоке Украины: Расследование Би-би-си" (Chechens in Eastern Ukraine: BBC investigation), BBC, 29 May 2014, https://www.bbc.com/russian/international/2014/05/140529_donetsk_chechens_ivshina

31. "Vostok Battalion Raids, Empties Headquarters of Donetsk People's Republic in Ukraine," Breitbart, 29 May 2014, https://www.breitbart.com/national-security/2014/05/29/Vostok-Battalion-Raids-Empties-Headquarters-of-Donetsk-People-s-Republic-in-Ukraine

32. "Секретарь Совбеза ДНР: 'Стрелков решал задачу по втягиванию России в войну'" (DNR Security Council secretary: "Strelkov was trying to draw Russia into a war"), Forbes, https://www.forbes.ru/sobytiya/vlast/284617-sekretar-sovbeza-dnr-strelkov-reshal-zadachu-po-vtyagivaniyu-rossii-v-voinu

33. Galeotti, Mark, Armies of Russia's War in Ukraine, London: Osprey, 2019.

34. See audio of intercepted call released by the JIT, 13 Nov. 2019, https://www.youtube.com/watch?v=n6MZxSLsUM4&t=26s

35. Audio of intercepted phone call published by JIT: https://www.youtube.com/watch?v=w6oG5BzxQkY

36. Audio of intercepted phone call published by JIT: https://www.youtube.com/watch?v=w4pG3vXFBYg

37. Interview with Borodai, "Бородай: Сурков—наш человек в Кремле" (Borodai: Surkov is our man in the Kremlin), Aktualnye Kommentarii, 16 June 2014, https://actualcomment.ru/boroday_surkov_nash_chelovek_v_kremle.html

38. Interviews with a businessman, a former official and a former Kremlin advisor, Moscow, 2011–19.

39. "Произведение Пелевина в авторской трактовке Суркова Владислав Сурков уходит из политики: Почему его работа в Донбассе провалилась?" (Pelevin's novels as told by Surkov: Vladislav Surkov is leaving politics; Why did his work in Donbas fail?) Meduza, 25 Jan.

2020, https://meduza.io/feature/2020/01/25/proizvedenie-pelevina-v-avtorskoy-traktovke-surkova

40. "В. Сурков: Лучшая часть нашего общества требует уважения к себе" (V. Surkov: The best part of our society is demanding respect), *RBC*, 23 Dec. 2011, https://www.rbc.ru/politics/23/12/2011/5703f1189a79 47ac81a6350c

41. Interview, "Сурков: Мне интересно действовать против реальности" (Surkov: I am interested in acting against reality), *Aktualnye Kommentarii*, 26 Feb. 2020, https://actualcomment.ru/surkov-mne-interesno-deystvovat-protiv-realnosti-2002260855.html

42. Krutov, Mark, "Тайны серого кардинала" (Secrets of the gray cardinal), *Radio Svoboda*, 26 Oct. 2016, https://www.svoboda.org/a/280 76558.html

43. Conversation, Moscow, Sept. 2021.

44. Conversation with Kremlin advisor, Moscow, Sept. 2021. Alexander Khodakovsky, the leader of the Vostok Battalion and DPR's security chief, also mentioned Sablin's name as a potential replacement for Borodai in the fall of 2014. "Ходаковский: 'ДНР' мог возглавить депутат из 'Единой России'" (Khodakovsky: "DNR" could be headed by United Russia deputy), *Novosti.dn*, 17 July 2021, https://novosti.dn.ua/news/313932-hodakovskij-dnr-mog-vozglavit-deputat-iz-edi-noj-rossii

45. Conversation with Kremlin advisor, Moscow, Sept. 2021.

46. Conversation, Moscow, Mar. 2018.

47. Conversation with Kremlin advisor, Moscow, Sept. 2021.

48. Conversation with a consultant to Malofeyev, Moscow, Sept. 2021.

49. Audio of intercepted phone call published by JIT: https://www.youtube.com/watch?v=rkApToeoPgI

50. Zhuchkovsky, *85 Dnei Slavyanska*, p. 216.

51. Ibid., p. 218.

52. See Kofman et al., "Lessons from Russia's Operations in Crimea and Eastern Ukraine."

53. Zhuchkovsky, *85 Dnei Slavyanska*, p. 258.

54. "Стрелков предостерег Путина от 'пути Милошевича'" (Strelkov warns Putin against "Milošević's path"), Republic, 17 June 2014, https://republic.ru/posts/l/1114514

55. "Без Стрелкова и Болотова" (Without Strelkov and Bolotov), RBC, 15 Aug. 2014, https://www.rbc.ru/society/15/08/2014/56bdf75b9a79 47299f72cb33

56. Conversation, former rebel fighter, Moscow, Apr. 2018. Conversation, pro-Novorossiya policymaker, Moscow, Sept. 2021.

57. Conversation with Kremlin advisor, Moscow, Sept. 2021.

7. THE NORTHERN WIND

1. "СНБО: Украинские военные захватили две машины десанта ВДВ России" (National Security and Defense Council: Ukrainian troops captured two vehicles of Russian airborne forces), Ukraine Crisis Media Center, 21 Aug. 2014, https://uacrisis.org/ru/8163-nsdc-7

2. Ponomaryov, Alexei, "Опубликованы косвенные доказательства присутствия российских десантников на Украине" (Indirect evidence of the presence of Russian paratroopers in Ukraine has been published), Republic, 21 Aug. 2008, https://republic.ru/posts/l/1146062

3. "В Пскове прошли закрытые похороны местных десантников" (Closed funeral for local paratroopers held in Pskov), Republic, 25 Aug. 2014, https://republic.ru/posts/l/1147710

4. "Журналисту Дождя в Пскове пригрозили расправой" (TV Rain journalist threatened with reprisals), TV Rain, 26 Aug. 2014, https://tvrain.ru/news/zhurnalistu_dozhdja_v_pskove_prigrozili_raspravoj-374570

5. Telephone conversation, Moscow, Aug. 2014.

6. Conversation, retired officer of the signal troops of the Russian airborne forces, Murmansk, 2015.

7. Sutyagin, Igor, "Russian Forces in Ukraine," Briefing paper, Royal United Services Institute (RUSI.org), March 2015, https://rusi.org/explore-our-research/publications/briefing-papers/russian-forces-ukraine

8. See Zakharchenko's video briefing, https://echo.msk.ru/blog/echomsk/1380942-echo

9. "СБУ заявила о задержании 10 десантников из России" (SBU claims it detained ten paratroopers from Russia), Forbes, 25 Aug. 2014, https://www.forbes.ru/news/266215-sbu-zayavila-o-zaderzhanii-10-desant-nikov-iz-rossii

10. "С места приземления скрылись" (Disappeared from the place of dis-

location), *Kommersant*, 28 Aug. 2014, https://www.kommersant.ru/doc/2553898

11. "Немощь обратилась за помощью" (The helpless ask for help), *Kommersant*, 28 Aug. 2014, https://www.kommersant.ru/doc/2554704

12. Sutyagin, "Russian Forces in Ukraine."

13. "Ukraine Reinstates Conscription as Crisis Deepens," BBC, 2 May 2014, https://www.bbc.com/news/world-europe-27247428

14. "Число батальонных групп, состоящих из контрактников, в российской армии через два года достигнет 125—начальник Генштаба ВС РФ" (The number of battalion groups in the Russian army consisting of contract soldiers will reach 125 in two years—chief of the General Staff of the Russian armed forces), Interfax AVN, 14 Sept. 2016, https://www.militarynews.ru/story.asp?rid=1&nid=425709&lang=RU

15. Maiorova, Alina, ed., "Donbas in Flames: Guide to the Conflict Zone," Prometheus Security Environment Research Center, Lviv, 2017, https://prometheus.ngo/wp-content/uploads/2017/04/Donbas_v_Ogni_ENG_web_1-4.pdf

16. Ibid., see map, p. 6.

17. "Силы ДНР взяли Новоазовск" (DPR forces take Novoazovsk), *Kommersant*, 27 Aug. 2014, https://www.kommersant.ru/doc/2554000

18. Shramovich, Vyacheslav, "Ukraine's Deadliest Day: The Battle of Ilovaisk, August 2014," BBC, 29 Aug. 2014, https://www.bbc.com/news/world-europe-49426724

19. Figures cited by the UN Office for the Coordination of Humanitarian Affairs, Situation Report no. 29, 27 Feb. 2015, https://reliefweb.int/sites/reliefweb.int/files/resources/Sitrep%20%2329%20FINAL_1.pdf

20. Prilepin, Zakhar, *Некоторые не попадут в ад* (Some will not go to hell), Moscow: Ast Press, 2021, p. 14.

21. Interview with Prilepin, "Есть чувство ответственности перед русской историей" (There is a sense of responsibility before Russian history), *Kommersant*, 13 Feb. 2017, https://www.kommersant.ru/doc/3218149

22. Prilepin, *Некоторые не попадут в ад*, pp. 32–5.

23. "Ветеран ДНР рассказал о плохом оснащении и выучке ополченцев Донбасса" (DNR veteran talks about bad equipment and preparedness of Donbas militiamen), *Moskovsky Komsomolets*, 15 July 2021, https://

www.mk.ru/politics/2021/07/15/veteran-dnr-rasskazal-o-nishhete-armii-donbassa.html

24. "Аваков назвал численность войск ДНР и ЛНР в Донбассе" (Avakov gave numbers for DNR and LNR forces in Donbas), RIA Novosti Ukraine, 28 Nov. 2017, https://rian.com.ua/politics/20171128/10298 52333/Avakov-nazval-chislennost-voysk-DNR-LNR-Donbass.html

25. "Ветеран ДНР рассказал о плохом оснащении и выучке ополченцев Донбасса."

26. Conversations, former separatist fighters, Moscow, Kyiv, 2018–19.

27. Coalson, Robert, "Who Are the Russian Generals that Ukraine Says Are Fighting in the Donbas?," RFE/RL, 28 Aug. 2015, https://www.rferl.org/a/russian-generals-fighting-in-ukraine/27108296.html

28. "Спецоперация России на Украине: Онлайн-трансляция 9 апреля" (Russian special operation in Ukraine: Live updates, 9 April), *MK*, 9 Apr. 2022, https://www.mk.ru/politics/2022/04/09/specoperaciya-ros-sii-na-ukraine-onlayntranslyaciya-9-aprelya.html

29. Prilepin, *Некоторые не попадут в ад*, pp. 32–5.

30. Ibid.

31. Conversations, former separatist fighters, Istanbul, July, Kyiv, October 2019.

32. "'Я вас победю и передам милиции': Об украинских контрреволюционерах: репортаж 'Ленты.ру'" ("I'll defeat you and hand you over to the police": Ukrainian counterrevolutionaries; Lenta.ru report), Lenta.ru, 3 Feb. 2014, https://lenta.ru/articles/2014/02/03/vostok

33. See audio of telephone conversation intercepted and leaked by the Ukrainian SBU: https://storage2.censor.net/video/3/211217_rom.mp4

34. Akhmedova, Marina, "Начальник Донбасса" (The boss of Donbas), Ekspert, 9 Oct. 2014, https://expert.ru/russian_reporter/2014/39/nachalnik-donbassa

35. Conversation, Russian volunteer, Moscow, Sept. 2018.

36. Prilepin, *Некоторые не попадут в ад*, p. 17.

37. "Здание Донецкого горсовета захватили активисты харьковской организации 'Оплот'" (Oplot activists seize city council building in Donetsk), TASS, https://tass.ru/mezhdunarodnaya-panorama/1125050

38. Akhmedova, "Начальник Донбасса."

39. "Ex-Rebel Leaders Detail Role Played by Putin Aide in East Ukraine," Reuters, 11 May 2017, https://www.reuters.com/article/us-ukraine-crisis-russia-surkov-insight/ex-rebel-leaders-detail-role-played-by-putin-aide-in-east-ukraine-idUSKBN1870TJ

40. "Стрелков о Захарченко: 'Тупой вор и жулик'" (Strelkov on Zakharchenko: "A dumb thief and crook"), Infox, 1 Sept. 2018, https://www.infox.ru/news/278/208387-strelkov-o-zaharcenko-tupoj-vor-i-zulik

41. Akhmedova, "Начальник Донбасса."

42. "Власти ДНР опровергли информацию об отставке Захарченко с поста премьера" (DNR authorities denied reports about Zakharchenko's resignation), RBC, 8 Oct. 2014, https://www.rbc.ru/politics/08/10/2014/54351f90cbb20fccd907d106

43. "Map of the Demarcation Line between the Forces in Donbass Based on the Minsk Agreement," Inform Napalm, 1 Nov. 2015, https://informnapalm.org/en/map-demarcation-line-forces-donbass-based-minsk-agreement

44. "Кроме Захарченко: Кто стоял у истоков 'русской весны' в Донбассе" (Besides Zakharchenko: Who stood at the foundation of the "Russian Spring" in Donbas), RTVI, 7 Sept. 2018, https://rtvi.com/stories/kto-stoyal-u-istokov-russkoy-vesny-v-donbasse

45. See Avidzba's interview, https://www.youtube.com/watch?v=8wiTAMpctJQ&t=578s

46. "Для прекращения огня в Донецкий аэропорт выехали украинский и российский генералы—АТО," Unian, 1 Dec. 2014, https://www.unian.net/politics/1016128-dlya-prekrascheniya-ognya-v-donetskiy-aeroport-vyiehali-ukrainskiy-i-rossiyskiy-generalyi-ato.html

47. See 30 Dec. Facebook post by one of OUN's commanders, Borys Humeniuk: https://www.facebook.com/borys.humenyuk/posts/1529156464016361?pnref=story

48. Loiko, Sergei, *Airport*, Kyiv: Bright Star Publishing, 2016, p. 12.

49. "Spot Report by the OSCE Special Monitoring Mission to Ukraine (SMM), 16 Dec. 2014: OSCE SMM Patrol Caught Up in Small Arms Crossfire," OSCE, 12. Dec. 2014, https://www.osce.org/ukraine-smm/132096

50. Kramer, Andrew, "Chaotic Retreat Follows Ukrainians' Withdrawal from Donetsk Airport," *New York Times*, 22 Jan. 2015, https://www.nytimes.com/2015/01/23/world/europe/ukraine-cedes-donetsk-airport-to-rebels-as-fighting-continues.html?_r=0

51. Charap, Samuel and Colton, Timothy, *Everyone Loses: The Ukraine Crisis and the Ruinous Contest for Post-Soviet Eurasia*, London: Routledge, 2018.

52. "Глава ДНР пообещал взять Краматорск, Славянск и Мариуполь" (The head of the DNR vows to take Kramatorsk, Slovyansk, and Mariupol), Interfax, 23 Oct. 2014, https://www.interfax.ru/world/403434

53. "Ополченцы заявили о скором взятии Мариуполя" (Militants claim they will take Mariupol soon), Interfax, 18 Aug. 2014, https://www.interfax.ru/world/393667

54. Maiorova, "Donbas in Flames."

55. Blair, David, "Russia Sends 9,000 Troops into Ukraine, Says Petro Poroshenko," *The Telegraph*, 21 Jan. 2015, https://www.telegraph.co.uk/news/worldnews/europe/ukraine/11361286/Russia-sends-9000-troops-into-Ukraine-says-Petro-Poroshenko.html

56. Statement on official site of the Russian embassy in the UK, 21 Jan. 2015, https://www.rus.rusemb.org.uk/foreignpolicy/2884

57. "Ukraine Crisis: Army Retreats at Donetsk Airport," BBC, 22 Jan. 2015, https://www.bbc.com/news/world-europe-30929344

58. "Захарченко опроверг намерение ополченцев штурмовать Мариуполь" (Zakharchenko denied reports of militias' plans to storm Mariupol), RBC, 24 Jan. 2015, https://www.rbc.ru/politics/24/01/2015/54c3d7799a7947f29e76b775

8. THE NEGOTIATORS

1. "Ukraine Vote Could Push the Country into Chaos," BBC, 24 Oct. 2014, https://www.bbc.com/news/world-europe-29755967

2. "Ukraine Rebel Zakharchenko 'Rejects Truce Talks,'" BBC, 23 Jan. 2015, https://www.bbc.com/news/world-europe-30949527

3. "Минский формат: Как проходили переговоры по решению кризиса на Украине в 2014–2015 годах" (Minsk format: How the negotiations

on resolving the crisis in Ukraine in 2014–15 were held), TASS, 12 Feb. 2015, https://tass.ru/politika/1762508?page=3

4. See "Can Merkel's Diplomacy Save Europe?," *Der Spiegel*, 14 Feb. 2015, https://www.spiegel.de/international/europe/minsk-deal-represents-and-fragile-opportunity-for-peace-in-ukraine-a-1018326.html. See also: Kolesnikov, Andrei, "С чувством выполненного: Долго" (With a long sense of accomplishment), *Kommersant*, 12 Feb. 2015, https://www.kommersant.ru/doc/2666248

5. See text of the Minsk Package of Measures: https://peacemaker.un.org/sites/peacemaker.un.org/files/UA_150212_MinskAgreement_en.pdf

6. "Минский мир: О чем за 16 часов договорились лидеры 'нормандской четверки'" (Minsk Peace: What the Normandy Four agreed on in sixteen hours), RBC, 12 Feb. 2015, https://www.rbc.ru/politics/12/02/2015/54dc807d9a79477315ee3703

7. "Can Merkel's Diplomacy Save Europe?"

8. Kolesnikov, "С чувством выполненного."

9. "Can Merkel's Diplomacy Save Europe?"

10. Ibid. See also Kolesnikov, "С чувством выполненного."

11. "Владимир Путин отодвигает войска и пододвигает выборы" (Vladimir Putin is moving troops and moving elections), *Kommersant*, 8 May 2014, https://www.kommersant.ru/doc/2467504

12. See text of the Minsk Package of Measures: https://peacemaker.un.org/sites/peacemaker.un.org/files/UA_150212_MinskAgreement_en.pdf

13. See Zakharchenko's address, 14 Feb. 2015: https://www.youtube.com/watch?v=5y3p7q1hkZM

14. "В Москве хоронили 'Новороссию'" (Moscow held a funeral for Novorossiya), BBC, 4 June 2015, https://www.bbc.com/russian/russia/2015/06/150603_novorossia_round_table

15. Soldatov, Andrei, "The True Role of the FSB in the Ukrainian Crisis," *The Moscow Times*, 15 Apr. 2014, https://www.themoscowtimes.com/2014/04/15/the-true-role-of-the-fsb-in-the-ukrainian-crisis-a33985

16. "'Слив Донбасса': Конец необъявленной войны" (Throwing out Donbas: The end of the undeclared war), BBC, 12 Oct. 2015, https://www.bbc.com/russian/international/2015/10/151009_donbass_russia_latest_comments

17. "Игра в 'перемирие' и 'слив Новороссии'" (The game of "truce" and "giving up Novorossiya"), 19 May 2015, *Segodnia*, https://www.segodnia.ru/content/160678

18. "'Слив Донбасса.'"

19. Stanko, Nastya and Kamenev, Maksim, "Под прикрытием деоккупации: Как Порошенко и Турчинов добились продления закона об особом статусе Донбасса" (Under cover of deoccupation: How Poroshenko and Turchynov got the law on special status for Donbas extended), Hromadske, 6 Oct. 2017, https://hromadske.ua/ru/posts/pod-pokrovom-deokkupatsyy-kak-poroshenko-y-turchynov-dobylys-prodlenyia-deistvyia-zakona-ob-osobom-statuse-donbassa

9. THE CURATORS

1. Audio of comments given to *Kyiv Post*, 6 Apr. 2015, https://www.youtube.com/watch?v=yXSctfYItaM

2. Video of trial, 19 Oct. 2014, https://www.youtube.com/watch?v=l8UQ76dSLuI

3. "Separatist Commander 'Givi' Killed in Eastern Ukraine," RFE/RL, 8 Feb. 2017, https://www.refworld.org/docid/5975a500c.html

4. "Ukraine Conflict: Rebel Leader Givi Dies in Rocket Attack," BBC, 8 Feb. 2016, https://www.bbc.com/news/world-europe-38905110

5. "Убийство Гиви: Как погиб один из лидеров ДНР" (The murder of Givi: How one of the leaders of the DPR died), RBC, 8 Feb. 2017, https://www.rbc.ru/politics/08/02/2017/589ac2229a7947bada2e35d2

6. Igor Girkin, TV interview fragment and transcript: https://ru-polit.livejournal.com/21425649.html?utm_source=3userpost

7. Igor Girkin interview, Roi TV, 17 Oct. 2016, https://www.youtube.com/watch?v=aEuvPGXuJW4

8. "Моторола. Последняя серия" (Motorola: Latest series), *Novaya Gazeta*, 17 Oct. 2016, https://novayagazeta.ru/articles/2016/10/17/70209-motorola-poslednyaya-seriya

9. "'Он всем надоел': Игорь Стрелков и другие о гибели Александра Захарченко" ("Everyone got sick of him": Igor Strelkov and others about Alexander Zakharchenko's death), Snob, 31 Aug. 2018, https://snob.ru/entry/165173

10. Conversation, Moscow, Sept. 2018.

11. Conversations, humanitarian workers from non-government-controlled areas of Ukraine, Rostov-on-Don, 2019, Kyiv, 2019.

12. Conversation, Russian diplomatic officials and policymakers, spring 2019.

13. "Совместное заявление Глав ДНР и ЛНР Александра Захарченко и Игоря Плотницкого" (Joint statement of the heads of DNR and LNR Alexander Zakharchenko and Igor Plotnitsky), Donetsk News Agency, 27 Feb. 2017, https://dan-news.info/official/sovmestnoe-zayavlenie-glav-dnr-i-lnr-aleksandra-zaxarchenko-i-igorya-plotnickogo-2/

14. "Под внешнее управление в ДНР перешли порядка 40 предприятий украинской юрисдикции—Захарченко" (About forty enterprises under Ukrainian jurisdiction subject to external management of the DNR), Donetsk News Agency, 1 Mar. 2017, https://dan-news.info/ukraine/pod-vneshnee-upravlenie-v-dnr-pereshli-poryadka-40-predpriyatij-ukrainskoj-yurisdikcii-zaxarchenko.html

15. "Во главе угля: Кто помогает восстанавливать экономику Донбасса" (Cornerstone of coal: Who is helping restore the Donbas economy), *Izvestia*, 24 Dec. 2018, https://iz.ru/827269/elena-poltavskaia/vo-glave-uglia-kto-pomogaet-vosstanavlivat-ekonomiku-donbassa. See also Zakharchenko's decree: "Указ Главы Донецкой Народной Республики № 77 от 04.04.2017 г.," https://gb-dnr.com/normativno-pravovye-akty/4435

16. "Компания Курченко стала единственным поставщиком угля из Донбасса" (Kurchenko's company has become the only supplier of Donbas coal), RBC, 22 Mar. 2018, https://www.rbc.ru/business/22/03/2018/5ab240569a7947e39a8159bc

17. Troianovsky, Anton, "To Avoid Sanctions, Kremlin Goes Off the Grid," *Washington Post*, 21 Nov. 2018, https://www.washingtonpost.com/news/world/wp/2018/11/21/feature/how-russia-avoids-sanctions-and-supports-rebels-in-eastern-ukraine-using-a-financial-system/?noredirect=on

18. "Treasury Sanctions Individuals and Entities Involved in Sanctions Evasion Related to Russia and Ukraine," US Treasury Press Release, 30 July 2015, https://www.treasury.gov/press-center/press-releases/Pages/jl0133.aspx

19. "Компания Курченко стала единственным поставщиком угля из Донбасса."

20. Interview, private sector source, London, Aug. 2019. See also: Rapoza, Kenneth, "Who Profits from the Broken Russia–Ukraine Peace Deal?," *Forbes*, 26 Jan. 2018, https://www.forbes.com/sites/kenrapoza/2018/01/26/who-profits-from-the-broken-russia-ukraine-peace-deal/#46c2860c37d4

21. See "Laundromats: Responding to New Challenges in the International Fight against Organised Crime, Corruption and Money-Laundering," Parliamentary Assembly of the Council of Europe report, 4 Mar. 2019, http://website-pace.net/documents/19838/5636250/20190304-MoneyLaundering-EN.pdf/c69d9ea9-e583-4fd2-9cb2-65ed360a4b3e. See also: "Dirty Money Laundered to Reinvest in Moldovan Banks," OCCRP, 1 Aug. 2016, https://www.occrp.org/en/thebankingwars/dirty-money-laundered-to-reinvest-in-moldovan-banks

22. Conversations, Russian politician, Kyiv, Aug. 2019. See also: "Угольный магнат Руслан Ростовцев и его любимая финансовая прачечная" (Coal magnate Ruslan Rostovtsev and his favorite money laundromat), Compromat.ru, 7 July 2019, http://rucompromat.com/articles/ugol-nyiy_magnat_ruslan_rostovtsev_i_ego_lyubimaya_finansovaya_prachechnaya

23. Conversation, former Russian politician, Kyiv, Aug. 2019.

24. "Правительство попросило Усманова и Мордашова помочь Донбассу" (Government asks Usmanov and Mordashev to help Donbas), RBC, 15 Mar. 2017, https://www.rbc.ru/politics/15/03/2017/58c7f8c69a79 47312027714e

25. Ropke, Julian, "Milliarden aus Moskau," *Bild*, 16 Jan. 2016, https://www.bild.de/politik/ausland/ukraine-konflikt/donbas-finanzierung-44031556.bild.html###wt_ref=https%3A%2F%2Fm.bild.de%2Fpolitik%2Fausland%2Fukraine-konflikt%2Fdonbas-finanzierung-44031556.bildMobile.html&wt_t=1650326399178

26. "Новые старые кураторы: Почему Москва не оставит Донбасс без помощи" (New old curators: Why Moscow will not leave Donbas without aid), *RBC*, 15 June 2018, https://www.rbc.ru/politics/15/06/201 8/5b2281fa9a794763ff30234f

27. Arutunyan, Anna, "Getting Aid to Separatist-Held Ukraine," *International Crisis Group*, 13 May 2019, https://www.crisisgroup. org/europe-central-asia/eastern-europe/ukraine/getting-aid-separatist-held-ukraine

28. See interview with Western press: https://www.youtube.com/ watch?v=Ls0tv5M6fMs

29. Conversations, Moscow, 2019. See also Arutunyan, Anna, "Is Russia Changing Its Calculus in Eastern Ukraine?," *International Crisis Group* commentary, 11 June 2019, https://www.crisisgroup.org/europe-central-asia/eastern-europe/ukraine/russia-changing-its-calculus-eastern-ukraine

30. Conversation, Kremlin advisor, Sept. 2021. See also Tymchuk, Dmitry, "С ликвидацией Захарченко Сурков и ГРУ проигрывают ФСБ очередную партию по Донбассу" (With Zakharchenko's liquidation Surkov and the GRU are losing another Donbas gambit to the FSB), Gordonua.com, 4 Sept. 2018, https://gordonua.com/blogs/tymchuk/s-likvidaciey-zaharchenko-surkov-i-gru-proigryvayut-fsb-ocherednuyu-partiyu-po-donbassu-335162.html

31. Conversation, Western capital, 2018.

32. Conversations with Russian official and government-linked Russian policymakers, Moscow, 2019–20, see also Soloviev, Vladimir, "Дмитрий Козак собирается в новый подход на Украину" (Dmitry Kozak is going to take a new approach to Ukraine), *Kommersant*, 25 Jan. 2020, https:// www.kommersant.ru/doc/4233004

33. Korniienko, Artur, "SBU Investigates Yermak, Kuchma for High Treason on Lawmaker's Appeal," *Kyiv Post*, 19 May 2020, https://www. kyivpost.com/ukraine-politics/sbu-investigates-yermak-kuchma-for-high-treason-on-lawmakers-appeal.html

34. "Bucharest Summit Declaration," NATO, 3 Apr. 2008, https://www. nato.int/cps/en/natolive/official_texts_8443.htm

35. Declaration statement published on official site: https://crimea-platform.org/en/samit/deklaraciya

36. Conversations, humanitarian workers from Donetsk and Luhansk regions, Kyiv, Oct. 2019.

37. Based on quotes widely overheard in Eastern Ukraine. See "'Nobody

Wants Us': The Alienated Civilians of Eastern Ukraine." See also: Brunson, Jonathan, "Implementing the Minsk Agreements Might Drive Ukraine to Civil War: That's Been Russia's Plan All Along," War on the Rocks, 1 Feb. 2019, https://warontherocks.com/2019/02/implementing-the-minsk-agreements-might-drive-ukraine-to-civil-war-thats-been-russias-plan-all-along

10. THE INVASION

1. Conversation, Russian émigré, Washington, DC, 2020.
2. According to a guided tour of Konstantinov Palace, attended by the author in 2004.
3. Goble, Paul, "When Putin Couldn't Take the Truth Spoken by Lennart Meri," *Estonian World*, 30 Jan. 2022, https://vp1992-2001.president.ee/eng/k6ned/K6ne.asp?ID=9401
4. "Путин рассказал о 'захваченном самолете' во время Олимпиады в Сочи" (Putin talked about "seized airplane" during the Sochi Olympics), КР, 11 Mar. 2018, https://www.kp.ru/daily/26804.5/3839535. See also televised documentary, https://www.youtube.com/watch?v=0a9UvJxxRog
5. Conversation, Moscow, Dec. 2021; name has been changed to protect the source.
6. "Russian Troop Movements Near Ukraine Border Prompt Concern in U.S., Europe," *Washington Post*, 30 Oct. 2021, https://www.washingtonpost.com/world/russian-troop-movements-near-ukraine-border-prompt-concern-in-us-europe/2021/10/30/c122e57c-3983-11ec-9662-399cfa75efee_story.html
7. "Vladimir Putin and Bill Clinton Had Their First Meeting as the US President Visited Moscow," Official Site of the President of Russia, 3 June 2000, http://en.kremlin.ru/events/president/news/38511. See also Tyler, Patrick, "Clinton and Putin Meet at Kremlin with Wide Agenda," *New York Times*, 4 June 2000, https://www.nytimes.com/2000/06/04/world/clinton-and-putin-meet-at-kremlin-with-wide-agenda.html
8. "Путин рассказал, как спросил Клинтона о возможности РФ вступить в НАТО" (Putin described how he asked Clinton about the possibility of Russia joining NATO), Interfax, 21 Feb. 2022, https://www.interfax.ru/russia/823529

9. "В. Путин: Война в Ираке грозит катастрофой всему региону" (V. Putin: War in Iraq threatens catastrophe in the whole region), RBC, 20 Mar. 2003, https://www.rbc.ru/politics/20/03/2003/5703b5 509a7947783a5a45bb

10. See transcript of speech, official presidential website, 10 Feb. 2007, http://en.kremlin.ru/events/president/transcripts/24034

11. "How James Blunt Saved Us from World War 3," *Independent*, 15 Nov. 2010, https://www.independent.co.uk/news/people/news/how-james-blunt-saved-us-from-world-war-3-2134203.html

12. "Россия ставит ракетный ультиматум" (Russia makes a missile ultimatum), Deutsche Welle, 4 July 2007, https://www.dw.com/ru/%D 1%80%D0%BE%D1%81%D1%81%D0%B8%D1%8F-%D1%81%D1%82%D0%B0%D0%B2%D0%B8%D1%82-%D1%80%D0%B0%D0%BA%D0%B5%D1%82%D0%BD%D1%8B%D0%B9-%D1%83%D0%BB%D1%8C%D1%82%D0%B8%D0%BC%D0%B0%D1%82%D1%83%D0%BC/a-2670411

13. Lowe, Christian, "Russia Warns of Kosovo Repercussions," Reuters, 15 Feb. 2008, https://www.reuters.com/article/uk-serbia-kosovo-russia-idUKL1558219520080215

14. "U.S. Warns Europe That Russia May Be Planning Ukraine Invasion," Bloomberg, 11 Nov. 2021, https://www.bloomberg.com/news/articles/2021-11-11/u-s-warns-europe-that-russian-troops-may-plan-ukraine-invasion

15. Conversation, EU diplomat, Moscow, Dec. 2021.

16. "Why 'Imminent' Pisses Zelenskyy Off," *Politico*, 28 Jan. 2022, https://www.politico.com/newsletters/national-security-daily/2022/01/28/why-imminent-pisses-zelensky-off-00003339

17. Facebook post of the Russian Foreign Ministry, 17 Dec. 2021: https://www.facebook.com/264205757012206/posts/4042412449191499/?d=n

18. "'Будет трудно—но напряжение будет спадать': Как Совбез полтора часа уговаривал Путина признать ЛНР и ДНР" ("It will be difficult, but the tensions will decrease": How the Kremlin spent an hour and a half convincing Putin to recognize LNR and DNR), BBC, 21 Feb. 2022, https://www.bbc.com/russian/features-60472017

19. "Biden Warns Putin of 'Severe Costs' of Ukraine Invasion in Phone

Call," *The Guardian*, 12 Feb. 2022, https://www.theguardian.com/world/2022/feb/12/biden-putin-ukraine-phone-call-us-russia

20. "Russia's Shoigu Says Some Military Drills Have Ended, Others Close to Completion," Reuters, 14 Feb. 2022, https://www.reuters.com/world/europe/russias-shoigu-says-some-military-drills-have-ended-others-close-completion-2022-02-14

21. "Russia Ukraine: Sending US Troops Not on Table—Biden," BBC, 8 Dec. 2021, https://www.bbc.com/news/world-europe-59582013

22. Mitchell, Ellen, "US Considering Sending Military Advisers, Weaponry to Ukraine: Report," *The Hill*, 23 Nov. 2021, https://thehill.com/policy/defense/582823-us-considering-sending-military-advisers-weaponry-to-ukraine-report

23. "U.S. Warns of Imminent Russian Invasion of Ukraine with Tanks, Jet Fighters, Cyberattacks," *Wall Street Journal*, 18 Feb. 2022, https://www.wsj.com/articles/ukraine-troops-told-to-exercise-restraint-to-avoid-provoking-russian-invasion-11645185631

24. Risen, James, "U.S. Intelligence Says Putin Made a Last-Minute Decision to Invade Ukraine," *The Intercept*, 11 Mar. 2022, https://theintercept.com/2022/03/11/russia-putin-ukraine-invasion-us-intelligence

25. Transcript of Putin's annual news conference, official presidential site, 23 Dec. 2021, http://en.kremlin.ru/events/president/news/67438

26. See interview with Nikolai Patrushev, Mar. 2021: https://www.youtube.com/watch?v=WfNvJcu7jDY

27. "Путин ожидает войну НАТО с Россией в случае вступления Украины в альянс" (Putin expects a NATO war with Russia if Ukraine joins the alliance), *Kommersant*, 8 Feb. 2022, https://www.kommersant.ru/doc/5205675

28. "Meminit Mori: Investigation for Vladimir Putin's 70th Birthday," Proekt.media, 1 Apr. 2022, https://www.proekt.media/en/investigation-en/putin-health

29. Valdai Discussion Meeting, transcript published on official presidential site, 21 Oct. 2021, http://en.kremlin.ru/events/president/news/66975

30. Laruelle, Marlène, "The Intellectual Origins of Putin's Invasion,"

Unherd.com, 16 Mar. 2022, https://unherd.com/2022/03/the-brains-behind-the-russian-invasion

31. Zygar, Mikhail, "How Vladimir Putin Lost Interest in the Present," *New York Times*, 10 Mar. 2022, https://www.nytimes.com/2022/03/10/opinion/putin-russia-ukraine.html

32. Conversation, Kremlin advisor, Moscow, 2021.

33. Conversation, former Russian GRU officer, Moscow, 2011.

34. Presidential Address, official presidential site, 21 Feb. 2022, http://kremlin.ru/events/president/news/67828

35. Conversation, Russian senator.

36. "Putin Calls Opponents 'Scum and Traitors' as Moscow Announces New Crackdown on 'False Information,'" CBS News, 18 Mar. 2022, https://www.cbsnews.com/news/putin-opponents-scum-traitors-repression

37. "Арестованный сотрудник ГУВД Москвы распространял фейки про армию по телефону" (Arrested Moscow police officer spread fakes about the army in telephone conversations), *Kommersant*, 24 Mar. 2022, https://www.kommersant.ru/doc/5272277

38. See VTsIOM opinion poll, 23 Mar. 2022: https://wciom.ru/analytical-reviews/analiticheskii-obzor/specialnaja-voennaja-operacija-monitoring

39. See statistics by OVD.info, a media project tracking political arrests and offering legal aid to prisoners: https://ovdinfo.org

40. Footage of Ukrainian farmer towing Russian tank with his tractor: https://www.youtube.com/watch?v=RGrwSb2J_qo

41. Risen, "U.S. Intelligence Says Putin Made a Last-Minute Decision to Invade Ukraine," *The Intercept*, 11 Mar. 2022.

42. Conversations, policymakers, Moscow, Feb. 2022.

43. Waghorn, Dominic, "Ukraine Invasion: Kremlin Policy Adviser Reveals His Shock over Vladimir Putin's Decision to Invade," Sky News, 2 Mar. 2022, https://news.sky.com/story/ukraine-invasion-kremlin-policy-adviser-reveals-his-shock-over-vladimir-putins-decision-to-invade-12555163

44. Borogan, Irina and Soldatov, Andrei, "Putin Places Spies under House Arrest," CEPA, 11 Mar. 2022, https://cepa.org/putin-places-spies-under-house-arrest

45. "Ukraine War: Russia to 'Fundamentally Cut Back' Military Activity Near Kyiv and Chernihiv—But West Says They're Just Playing for Time," Sky News, 29 Mar. 2022, https://news.sky.com/story/ukraine-war-russia-says-it-will-fundamentally-cut-back-military-activity-near-kyiv-and-chernihiv-to-increase-trust-in-peace-talks-12577452. See also "US Casts Doubt on New Kremlin Claims of Curtailed Kyiv Offensive," *Financial Times*, 30 Mar. 2022, https://www.ft.com/content/6afc2715-3f4e-48fc-bbb6-5a50b54f7e4b

46. Electronic correspondence, Mar. 2022.

47. Screenshot of correspondence between Kholmogorov and authorities: https://twitter.com/litavrinm/status/1503290205289295872

48. Video of Girkin's comments, OSN.ru, 10 Mar. 2022: https://www.youtube.com/watch?v=0qJujhoiros

49. Karaganov, Sergei, "We Are at War with the West: The European Security Order Is Illegitimate," Russian International Affairs Council, 15 Apr. 2022.

INDEX

INDEX

INDEX

INDEX

INDEX

INDEX

INDEX

INDEX

INDEX

INDEX

INDEX